Human-Computer Interaction

Human-Computer Interaction

Edited by
Marley Harding

Larsen & Keller
www.larsen-keller.com

Human-Computer Interaction
Edited by Marley Harding
ISBN: 978-1-63549-145-6 (Hardback)

© 2017 Larsen & Keller

 Larsen & Keller

Published by Larsen and Keller Education,
5 Penn Plaza,
19th Floor,
New York, NY 10001, USA

Cataloging-in-Publication Data

Human-computer interaction / edited by Marley Harding.
   p. cm.
Includes bibliographical references and index.
ISBN 978-1-63549-145-6
1. Human-computer interaction. 2. Human engineering. I. Harding, Marley.
QA76.9.H85 H85 2017
004.019--dc23

The publisher's policy is to use permanent paper from mills that operate a sustainable forestry policy. Furthermore, the publisher ensures that the text paper and cover boards used have met acceptable environmental accreditation standards.

Printed and bound in the United States of America.

For more information regarding Larsen and Keller Education and its products, please visit the publisher's website www.larsen-keller.com

Table of Contents

Preface

Human-computer interaction refers to the science of developing better interfaces for users (humans) and computers. It includes the elements of multimedia studies, computer sciences, design and behavioral sciences, etc. This area of study is growing at a rapid pace and is re-designing technology as we know it. This book aims to provide deep knowledge about this subject. It makes constant efforts to make the understanding of the difficult concepts as easy and informative as possible, for the readers. This text is an essential guide for both academicians and those who wish to pursue this discipline further. Topics included in this textbook discusses the fundamental concepts of human behavior and machine language.

Given below is the chapter wise description of the book:

Chapter 1- Human-computer interaction studies the use of computer technology. It majorly focuses on the interaction between the users and computers. This section will provide an integrated understanding of human computer interaction.

Chapter 2- Computer accessibility, usability, computer user satisfaction, gender HCI, interaction technique and mode are some of the significant concepts of human-computer interaction included in this chapter. The accessibility of a computer system for everyone is known computer accessibility whereas usability is the ease at which a user can use software. This chapter is a compilation of the various branches of human-computer interaction that form an integral part of the broader subject matter.

Chapter 3- The practices of human-computer interaction are user experience, first-time user experience, 3D interaction and 3D user interaction. User experience is the experience of users when they are using particular products or systems whereas first time user experience is the initial stage of using a particular software. The major practices of human-computer interactions are discussed in this chapter.

Chapter 4- Methods and techniques are important components of any field of study. Some of the techniques discussed within this text are usability testing, heuristic evaluation, card sorting, drag and drop and point and click. Usability testing is the method that is used to evaluate a product by testing it on users. The following section elucidates the various techniques that are related to human-computer interaction.

Chapter 5- The study of the time it takes for a professional to complete a task without errors using a computer system is known as the keystroke level model. Human processor models are used to calculate the time it takes to perform a particular task. This chapter helps the reader in understanding all the models and laws related to human-computer interactions.

Chapter 6- The following text briefly explains the concept of user interface. User interface is the design of the human – machine interaction. The aim of this is to achieve an efficient interaction between machines and humans. This section is an overview of the subject matter incorporating all the major aspects of user interface.

Chapter 7- Electronic devices interact with users with the help of a graphical user interface. Multiple document interface is a user interface which allows windows to reside under a single window. The chapter also focuses on object-action interfaces, pointers and widgets.

Chapter 8- User interface has a number of designs. Some of these are user interface design, user-centered design, usage-centered design, contextual design, user experience design etc. The interface of machines, such as computers, mobiles and electronic devices is known as the user interface design. The topics discussed in the text are of great importance to broaden the existing knowledge on user interface.

Chapter 9- The branch of human computer interaction that focuses on the response of computer interface to human touch is known as hands-on computing. This chapter is a compilation of the allied fields related to human-computer interaction. Some of the fields explained are hands-on computing, human-centered computing, interactive computing, mobile interaction and mobile computing.

At the end, I would like to thank all those who dedicated their time and efforts for the successful completion of this book. I also wish to convey my gratitude towards my friends and family who supported me at every step.

Editor

Introduction to Human–computer Interaction

Human-computer interaction studies the use of computer technology. It majorly focuses on the interaction between the users and computers. This section will provide an integrated understanding of human computer interaction.

Human–computer interaction (commonly referred to as HCI) researches the design and use of computer technology, focused on the interfaces between people (users) and computers. Researchers in the field of HCI both *observe* the ways in which humans interact with computers and *design* technologies that let humans interact with computers in novel ways.

As a field of research, human-computer interaction is situated at the intersection of computer science, behavioral sciences, design, media studies, and several other fields of study. The term was popularized by Stuart K. Card, Allen Newell, and Thomas P. Moran in their seminal 1983 book, *The Psychology of Human-Computer Interaction*, although the authors first used the term in 1980 and the first known use was in 1975. The term connotes that, unlike other tools with only limited uses (such as a hammer, useful for driving nails but not much else), a computer has many uses and this takes place as an open-ended dialog between the user and the computer. The notion of dialog likens human-computer interaction to human-to-human interaction, an analogy which is crucial to theoretical considerations in the field.

Introduction

Humans interact with computers in many ways; and the interface between humans and the computers they use is crucial to facilitating this interaction. Desktop applications, internet browsers, handheld computers, and computer kiosks make use of the prevalent graphical user interfaces (GUI) of today. Voice user interfaces (VUI) are used for speech recognition and synthesising systems, and the emerging multi-modal and gestalt User Interfaces (GUI) allow humans to engage with embodied character agents in a way that cannot be achieved with other interface paradigms. The growth in human-computer interaction field has been in quality of interaction, and in different branching in its history. Instead of designing regular interfaces, the different research branches have had different focus on the concepts of multimodality rather than uni-modality, intelligent adaptive interfaces rather than command/action based ones, and finally active rather than passive interfaces

The Association for Computing Machinery (ACM) defines human-computer interaction as "a discipline concerned with the design, evaluation and implementation of interactive computing systems for human use and with the study of major phenomena surrounding them". An important facet of HCI is the securing of user satisfaction (or simply End User Computing Satisfaction). "Because human–computer interaction studies a human and a machine in communication, it draws from supporting knowledge on both the machine and the human side. On the machine side, techniques in computer graphics, operating systems, programming languages, and development environments are relevant. On the human side, communication theory, graphic and industrial design disciplines, linguistics, social sciences, cognitive psychology, social psychology, and human factors such as computer user satisfaction are relevant. And, of course, engineering and design methods are relevant." Due to the multidisciplinary nature of HCI, people with different backgrounds contribute to its success. HCI is also sometimes termed *human–machine interaction* (HMI), *man–machine interaction* (MMI) or *computer–human interaction* (CHI).

Poorly designed human-machine interfaces can lead to many unexpected problems. A classic example of this is the Three Mile Island accident, a nuclear meltdown accident, where investigations concluded that the design of the human–machine interface was at least partly responsible for the disaster. Similarly, accidents in aviation have resulted from manufacturers' decisions to use non-standard flight instrument or throttle quadrant layouts: even though the new designs were proposed to be superior in basic human–machine interaction, pilots had already ingrained the "standard" layout and thus the conceptually good idea actually had undesirable results.

Leading academic research centers include CMU's Human-Computer Interaction Institute, GVU Center at Georgia Tech, and the University of Maryland Human–Computer Interaction Lab.

Goals

Human–computer interaction studies the ways in which humans make, or don't make, use of computational artifacts, systems and infrastructures. In doing so, much of the research in the field seeks to *improve* human-computer interaction by improving the *usability* of computer interfaces. How usability is to be precisely understood, how it relates to other social and cultural values and when it is, and when it may not be a desirable property of computer interfaces is increasingly debated.

Much of the research in the field of human-computer interaction takes an interest in:

- Methods for designing novel computer interfaces, thereby optimizing a design for a desired property such as, e.g., learnability or efficiency of use.

- Methods for implementing interfaces, e.g., by means of software libraries.

- Methods for evaluating and comparing interfaces with respect to their usability and other desirable properties.

- Methods for studying human computer use and its sociocultural implications more broadly.

- Models and theories of human computer use as well as conceptual frameworks for the design of computer interfaces, such as, e.g., cognitivist user models, Activity Theory or ethnomethodological accounts of human computer use.

- Perspectives that critically reflect upon the values that underlie computational design, computer use and HCI research practice.

Visions of what researchers in the field seek to achieve vary. When pursuing a cognitivist perspective, researchers of HCI may seek to align computer interfaces with the mental model that humans have of their activities. When pursuing a post-cognitivist perspective, researchers of HCI may seek to align computer interfaces with existing social practices or existing sociocultural values.

Researchers in HCI are interested in developing new design methodologies, experimenting with new devices, prototyping new software and hardware systems, exploring new interaction paradigms, and developing models and theories of interaction.

Differences with Related Fields

HCI differs from human factors and ergonomics as HCI focuses more on users working specifically with computers, rather than other kinds of machines or designed artifacts. There is also a focus in HCI on how to implement the computer software and hardware mechanisms to support human–computer interaction. Thus, *human factors* is a broader term; HCI could be described as the human factors of computers – although some experts try to differentiate these areas.

HCI also differs from human factors in that there is less of a focus on repetitive work-oriented tasks and procedures, and much less emphasis on physical stress and the physical form or industrial design of the user interface, such as keyboards and mouse devices.

Three areas of study have substantial overlap with HCI even as the focus of inquiry shifts. In the study of personal information management (PIM), human interactions with the computer are placed in a larger informational context – people may work with many forms of information, some computer-based, many not (e.g., whiteboards, notebooks, sticky notes, refrigerator magnets) in order to understand and effect desired changes in their world. In computer-supported cooperative work (CSCW), emphasis is placed on the use of computing systems in support of the collaborative work of a group of people. The principles of human interaction management (HIM) extend the scope of CSCW to an organizational level and can be implemented without use of computers.

Design
Principles

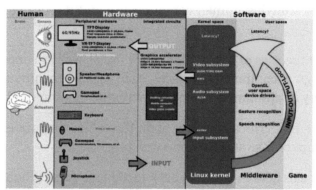

The user interacts directly with hardware for the human *input* and *output* such as displays, e.g. through a graphical user interface. The user interacts with the computer over this software interface using the given input and output (*I/O*) hardware. Software and hardware must be matched, so that the processing of the user input is fast enough, the latency of the computer output is not disruptive to the workflow.

When evaluating a current user interface, or designing a new user interface, it is important to keep in mind the following experimental design principles:

- Early focus on user(s) and task(s): Establish how many users are needed to perform the task(s) and determine who the appropriate users should be; someone who has never used the interface, and will not use the interface in the future, is most likely not a valid user. In addition, define the task(s) the users will be performing and how often the task(s) need to be performed.

- Empirical measurement: Test the interface early on with real users who come in contact with the interface on a daily basis. Keep in mind that results may vary with the performance level of the user and may not be an accurate depiction of the typical human-computer interaction. Establish quantitative usability specifics such as: the number of users performing the task(s), the time to complete the task(s), and the number of errors made during the task(s).

- Iterative design: After determining the users, tasks, and empirical measurements to include, perform the following iterative design steps:

  1. Design the user interface

  2. Test

  3. Analyze results

  4. Repeat

Repeat the iterative design process until a sensible, user-friendly interface is created.

Methodologies

A number of diverse methodologies outlining techniques for human–computer interaction design have emerged since the rise of the field in the 1980s. Most design methodologies stem from a model for how users, designers, and technical systems interact. Early methodologies, for example, treated users' cognitive processes as predictable and quantifiable and encouraged design practitioners to look to cognitive science results in areas such as memory and attention when designing user interfaces. Modern models tend to focus on a constant feedback and conversation between users, designers, and engineers and push for technical systems to be wrapped around the types of experiences users want to have, rather than wrapping user experience around a completed system.

- Activity theory: used in HCI to define and study the context in which human interactions with computers take place. Activity theory provides a framework to reason about actions in these contexts, analytical tools with the format of checklists of items that researchers should consider, and informs design of interactions from an activity-centric perspective.

- User-centered design: user-centered design (UCD) is a modern, widely practiced design philosophy rooted in the idea that users must take center-stage in the design of any computer system. Users, designers and technical practitioners work together to articulate the wants, needs and limitations of the user and create a system that addresses these elements. Often, user-centered design projects are informed by ethnographic studies of the environments in which users will be interacting with the system. This practice is similar but not identical to participatory design, which emphasizes the possibility for end-users to contribute actively through shared design sessions and workshops.

- Principles of user interface design: these are seven principles of user interface design that may be considered at any time during the design of a user interface in any order: tolerance, simplicity, visibility, affordance, consistency, structure and feedback.

- Value sensitive design: Value Sensitive Design (VSD) is a method for building technology that account for the values of the people who use the technology directly, as well as those who the technology affects, either directly or indirectly. VSD uses an iterative design process that involves three types of investigations: conceptual, empirical and technical. Conceptual investigations aim at understanding and articulating the various stakeholders of the technology, as well as their values and any values conflicts that might arise for these stakeholders through the use of the technology. Empirical investigations are qualitative or quantitative design research studies used to inform the designers' understanding of the users' values, needs, and practices. Technical investigations can involve either analysis of how people use related technologies, or the design of systems to support values identified in the conceptual and empirical investigations.

Display Designs

Displays are human-made artifacts designed to support the perception of relevant system variables and to facilitate further processing of that information. Before a display is designed, the task that the display is intended to support must be defined (e.g. navigating, controlling, decision making, learning, entertaining, etc.). A user or operator must be able to process whatever information that a system generates and displays; therefore, the information must be displayed according to principles in a manner that will support perception, situation awareness, and understanding.

Thirteen Principles of Display Design

Christopher Wickens et al. defined 13 principles of display design in their book *An Introduction to Human Factors Engineering*.

These principles of human perception and information processing can be utilized to create an effective display design. A reduction in errors, a reduction in required training time, an increase in efficiency, and an increase in user satisfaction are a few of the many potential benefits that can be achieved through utilization of these principles.

Certain principles may not be applicable to different displays or situations. Some principles may seem to be conflicting, and there is no simple solution to say that one principle is more important than another. The principles may be tailored to a specific design or situation. Striking a functional balance among the principles is critical for an effective design.

Perceptual Principles

1. *Make displays legible (or audible).* A display's legibility is critical and necessary for designing a usable display. If the characters or objects being displayed cannot be discernible, then the operator cannot effectively make use of them.

2. *Avoid absolute judgment limits.* Do not ask the user to determine the level of a variable on the basis of a single sensory variable (e.g. color, size, loudness). These sensory variables can contain many possible levels.

3. *Top-down processing.* Signals are likely perceived and interpreted in accordance with what is expected based on a user's experience. If a signal is presented contrary to the user's expectation, more physical evidence of that signal may need to be presented to assure that it is understood correctly.

4. *Redundancy gain.* If a signal is presented more than once, it is more likely that it will be understood correctly. This can be done by presenting the signal in alterna-

tive physical forms (e.g. color and shape, voice and print, etc.), as redundancy does not imply repetition. A traffic light is a good example of redundancy, as color and position are redundant.

5. *Similarity causes confusion: Use discriminable elements.* Signals that appear to be similar will likely be confused. The ratio of similar features to different features causes signals to be similar. For example, A423B9 is more similar to A423B8 than 92 is to 93. Unnecessary similar features should be removed and dissimilar features should be highlighted.

Mental Model Principles

6. *Principle of pictorial realism.* A display should look like the variable that it represents (e.g. high temperature on a thermometer shown as a higher vertical level). If there are multiple elements, they can be configured in a manner that looks like it would in the represented environment.

7. *Principle of the moving part.* Moving elements should move in a pattern and direction compatible with the user's mental model of how it actually moves in the system. For example, the moving element on an altimeter should move upward with increasing altitude.

Principles Based on Attention

8. *Minimizing information access cost.* When the user's attention is diverted from one location to another to access necessary information, there is an associated cost in time or effort. A display design should minimize this cost by allowing for frequently accessed sources to be located at the nearest possible position. However, adequate legibility should not be sacrificed to reduce this cost.

9. *Proximity compatibility principle.* Divided attention between two information sources may be necessary for the completion of one task. These sources must be mentally integrated and are defined to have close mental proximity. Information access costs should be low, which can be achieved in many ways (e.g. proximity, linkage by common colors, patterns, shapes, etc.). However, close display proximity can be harmful by causing too much clutter.

10. *Principle of multiple resources.* A user can more easily process information across different resources. For example, visual and auditory information can be presented simultaneously rather than presenting all visual or all auditory information.

Memory Principles

11. *Replace memory with visual information: knowledge in the world.* A user should not need to retain important information solely in working memory or retrieve it from long-term memory. A menu, checklist, or another display can aid the user

by easing the use of their memory. However, the use of memory may sometimes benefit the user by eliminating the need to reference some type of knowledge in the world (e.g., an expert computer operator would rather use direct commands from memory than refer to a manual). The use of knowledge in a user's head and knowledge in the world must be balanced for an effective design.

12. *Principle of predictive aiding*. Proactive actions are usually more effective than reactive actions. A display should attempt to eliminate resource-demanding cognitive tasks and replace them with simpler perceptual tasks to reduce the use of the user's mental resources. This will allow the user to focus on current conditions, and to consider possible future conditions. An example of a predictive aid is a road sign displaying the distance to a certain destination.

13. *Principle of consistency*. Old habits from other displays will easily transfer to support processing of new displays if they are designed consistently. A user's long-term memory will trigger actions that are expected to be appropriate. A design must accept this fact and utilize consistency among different displays.

Human–computer Interface

The human–computer interface can be described as the point of communication between the human user and the computer. The flow of information between the human and computer is defined as the *loop of interaction*. The loop of interaction has several aspects to it, including:

- Visual Based :The visual based human computer inter-action is probably the most widespread area in HCI research.

- Audio Based : The audio based interaction between a computer and a human is another important area of in HCI systems. This area deals with information acquired by different audio signals.

- *Task environment*: The conditions and goals set upon the user.

- *Machine environment*: The environment that the computer is connected to, e.g. a laptop in a college student's dorm room.

- *Areas of the interface*: Non-overlapping areas involve processes of the human and computer not pertaining to their interaction. Meanwhile, the overlapping areas only concern themselves with the processes pertaining to their interaction.

- *Input flow*: The flow of information that begins in the task environment, when the user has some task that requires using their computer.

- *Output*: The flow of information that originates in the machine environment.

- *Feedback*: Loops through the interface that evaluate, moderate, and confirm processes as they pass from the human through the interface to the computer and back.

- *Fit*: This is the match between the computer design, the user and the task to optimize the human resources needed to accomplish the task.

Current Research

Topics in HCI include:

User Customization

End-user development studies how ordinary users could routinely tailor applications to their own needs and use this power to invent new applications based on their understanding of their own domains. With their deeper knowledge of their own knowledge domains, users could increasingly be important sources of new applications at the expense of generic systems programmers (with systems expertise but low domain expertise).

Embedded Computation

Computation is passing beyond computers into every object for which uses can be found. Embedded systems make the environment alive with little computations and automated processes, from computerized cooking appliances to lighting and plumbing fixtures to window blinds to automobile braking systems to greeting cards. To some extent, this development is already taking place. The expected difference in the future is the addition of networked communications that will allow many of these embedded computations to coordinate with each other and with the user. Human interfaces to these embedded devices will in many cases be very different from those appropriate to workstations.

Augmented Reality

A common staple of science fiction, augmented reality refers to the notion of layering relevant information into our vision of the world. Existing projects show real-time statistics to users performing difficult tasks, such as manufacturing. Future work might include augmenting our social interactions by providing additional information about those we converse with.

Social Computing

In recent years, there has been an explosion of social science research focusing on interactions as the unit of analysis. Much of this research draws from psychology, social psychology, and sociology. For example, one study found out that people expected a computer with a man's name to cost more than a machine with a woman's name. Other research finds that individuals perceive their interactions with computers more positively than humans, despite behaving the same way towards these machines.

Knowledge-driven Human-computer Interaction

In human and computer interactions, there usually exists a semantic gap between human and computer's understandings towards mutual behaviors. Ontology (information science), as a formal representation of domain-specific knowledge, can be used to address this problem, through solving the semantic ambiguities between the two parties.

Factors of Change

Traditionally, as explained in a journal article discussing user modeling and user-adapted interaction, computer use was modeled as a human-computer dyad in which the two were connected by a narrow explicit communication channel, such as text-based terminals. Much work has been done to make the interaction between a computing system and a human. However, as stated in the introduction, there is much room for mishaps and failure. Because of this, human-computer interaction shifted focus beyond the interface (to respond to observations as articulated by D. Engelbart: "If ease of use was the only valid criterion, people would stick to tricycles and never try bicycles."

The means by which humans interact with computers continues to evolve rapidly. Human–computer interaction is affected by the forces shaping the nature of future computing. These forces include:

- Decreasing hardware costs leading to larger memory and faster systems

- Miniaturization of hardware leading to portability

- Reduction in power requirements leading to portability

- New display technologies leading to the packaging of computational devices in new forms

- Specialized hardware leading to new functions

- Increased development of network communication and distributed computing

- Increasingly widespread use of computers, especially by people who are outside of the computing profession

- Increasing innovation in input techniques (e.g., voice, gesture, pen), combined with lowering cost, leading to rapid computerization by people formerly left out of the *computer revolution.*

- Wider social concerns leading to improved access to computers by currently disadvantaged groups

The future for HCI, based on current promising research, is expected to include the following characteristics:

- *Ubiquitous computing and communication.* Computers are expected to communicate through high speed local networks, nationally over wide-area networks, and portably via infrared, ultrasonic, cellular, and other technologies. Data and computational services will be portably accessible from many if not most locations to which a user travels.

- *High-functionality systems.* Systems can have large numbers of functions associated with them. There are so many systems that most users, technical or non-technical, do not have time to learn them in the traditional way (e.g., through thick manuals).

- *Mass availability of computer graphics.* Computer graphics capabilities such as image processing, graphics transformations, rendering, and interactive animation are becoming widespread as inexpensive chips become available for inclusion in general workstations and mobile devices.

- *Mixed media.* Commercial systems can handle images, voice, sounds, video, text, formatted data. These are exchangeable over communication links among users. The separate fields of consumer electronics (e.g., stereo sets, VCRs, televisions) and computers are merging partly. Computer and print fields are expected to cross-assimilate.

- *High-bandwidth interaction.* The rate at which humans and machines interact is expected to increase substantially due to the changes in speed, computer graphics, new media, and new input/output devices. This can lead to some qualitatively different interfaces, such as virtual reality or computational video.

- *Large and thin displays.* New display technologies are finally maturing, enabling very large displays and displays that are thin, lightweight, and low in power use. This is having large effects on portability and will likely enable developing paper-like, pen-based computer interaction systems very different in feel from desktop workstations of the present.

- *Information utilities.* Public information utilities (such as home banking and shopping) and specialized industry services (e.g., weather for pilots) are expected to proliferate. The rate of proliferation can accelerate with the introduction of high-bandwidth interaction and the improvement in quality of interfaces.

Scientific Conferences

One of the main conferences for new research in human-computer interaction is the annually held Association for Computing Machinery's (ACM) *Conference on Human Factors in Computing Systems*, usually referred to by its short name CHI (pronounced *kai*, or *khai*). CHI is organized by ACM Special Interest Group on Computer–Human Interaction (SIGCHI). CHI is a large conference, with thousands of attendants, and is quite broad in scope. It is attended by academics, practitioners and industry people, with company sponsors such as Google, Microsoft, and PayPal.

There are also dozens of other smaller, regional or specialized HCI-related conferences held around the world each year, including:

- ASSETS: ACM International Conference on Computers and Accessibility

- CSCW: ACM conference on Computer Supported Cooperative Work

- CC: Aarhus decennial conference on Critical Computing

- DIS: ACM conference on Designing Interactive Systems

- ECSCW: European Conference on Computer-Supported Cooperative Work

- GROUP: ACM conference on supporting group work

- HRI: ACM/IEEE International Conference on Human–robot interaction

- ICMI: International Conference on Multimodal Interfaces

- ITS: ACM conference on Interactive Tabletops and Surfaces

- MobileHCI: International Conference on Human–Computer Interaction with Mobile Devices and Services

- NIME: International Conference on New Interfaces for Musical Expression

- OzCHI: Australian Conference on Human-Computer Interaction

- TEI: International Conference on Tangible, Embedded and Embodied Interaction

- Ubicomp: International Conference on Ubiquitous computing

- UIST: ACM Symposium on User Interface Software and Technology

- i-USEr: International Conference on User Science and Engineering

- INTERACT: IFIP TC13 Conference on Human-Computer Interaction

2

Concepts of Human–computer Interaction

Computer accessibility, usability, computer user satisfaction, gender HCI, interaction technique and mode are some of the significant concepts of human-computer interaction included in this chapter. The accessibility of a computer system for everyone is known computer accessibility whereas usability is the ease at which a user can use software. This chapter is a compilation of the various branches of human-computer interaction that form an integral part of the broader subject matter.

Computer Accessibility

In human–computer interaction, computer accessibility (also known as accessible computing) refers to the accessibility of a computer system to all people, regardless of disability type or severity of impairment. The term "accessibility" is most often used in reference to specialized hardware or software, or a combination of both, designed to enable use of a computer by a person with a disability or impairment. Specific technologies may be referred to as assistive technology.

There are many disabilities or impairments that can be a barrier to effective computer use. These impairments, which can be acquired from disease, trauma, or may be congenital, include but are not limited to:

- Cognitive impairments (head injury, autism, developmental disabilities), and learning disabilities, such as dyslexia, dyscalculia or ADHD.

- Visual impairment such as low-vision, complete or partial blindness, and color blindness.

- Hearing-related disabilities including deafness, being hard of hearing, or hyperacusis.

- Motor or dexterity impairment such as paralysis, cerebral palsy, dyspraxia, carpal tunnel syndrome and repetitive strain injury.

Accessibility is often abbreviated as the numeronym a11y, where the number 11 refers to the number of letters omitted. This parallels the abbreviations of internationalization and localization as i18n and l10n respectively.

Special-needs Assessment

People wishing to overcome an impairment in order to use a computer comfortably and productively may require a "special needs assessment" by an assistive technology consultant (such as an occupational therapist, a rehabilitation engineering technologist, or an educational technologist) to help them identify and configure appropriate assistive technologies to meet individual needs. Even those who are unable to leave their own home or who live far from assessment providers may be assessed (and assisted) remotely using remote desktop software and a web cam. For example, the assessor logs on to the client's computer via a broadband Internet connection, observes the users computer skills, and then remotely makes accessibility adjustments to the client's computer where necessary.

Considerations for Specific Impairments

BBC News shown in 'desktop mode,' with Accessibility links at the top. The screenshot is taken from Windows Mobile.

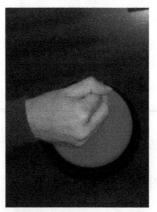

A single switch assistive device that enables the user to access an on-screen computer keyboard.

Cognitive Impairments and Illiteracy

The biggest challenge in computer accessibility is to make resources accessible to people with cognitive disabilities - particularly those with poor communication and reading skills. As an example, people with learning disabilities may rely on proprietary symbols and thus identify particular products via the product's symbols or icons. Unfortunately copyright laws can limit icon or symbol release to web-based programs and websites by owners who are unwilling to release them to the public.

In these situations, an alternative approach for users who want to access public computer based terminals in libraries, ATMs, and information kiosks is for the user to present a token to the computer terminal, such as a smart card, that has configuration information to adjust the computer speed, text size, etcetera to their particular needs. The concept is encompassed by the CEN EN 1332-4 Identification Card Systems - Man-Machine Interface. This development of this standard has been supported in Europe by SNAPI and has been successfully incorporated into the Local Authority Smartcards Standards e-Organisation (LASSeO) specifications.

Visual Impairment

Since computer interfaces often solicit visual input and provide visual feedback, another significant challenge in computer accessibility involves making software usable by people with visual impairments. For individuals with mild to medium vision impairment, it is helpful to use large fonts, high DPI displays, high-contrast themes and icons supplemented with auditory feedback, and screen magnifying software. In the case of severe vision impairment such as blindness, screen reader software that provides feedback via text to speech or a refreshable braille display is a necessary accommodation for interaction with a computer.

About 8% of people suffer from some form of color-blindness. The main color combinations that might be confused by people with visual deficiency include red/green and blue/green. However, in a well-designed user interface, color will not be the primary way to distinguish between different pieces of information.

Motor and Dexterity Impairments

Some people may not be able to use a conventional input device, such as the mouse or the keyboard, therefore, it is important for software functions to be accessible using both devices. Ideally, software will use a generic input API that permits the use even of highly specialized devices unheard of at the time of software's initial development. Keyboard shortcuts and mouse gestures are ways to achieve this access, as are more specialized solutions, including on-screen software keyboards and alternate input devices (switches, joysticks and trackballs). Speech recognition technology is also a compelling and suitable alternative to conventional keyboard and mouse input as it simply requires a commonly available audio headset.

The astrophysicist Stephen Hawking's use of assistive technology is an example of a person with severe motor and physical limitations who uses technology to support activities of daily living. He uses a switch, combined with special software, that allows him to control his wheelchair-mounted computer using his limited and small movement ability. This personalized system allows him to remain mobile, do research, produce his written work. Mr. Hawking also uses augmentative and alternative communication technology to speak and an environmental control device to access equipment independently.

A small amount of modern research indicates that utilizing a standard computer mouse device improves fine-motor skills.

Hearing Impairment

While sound user interfaces have a secondary role in common desktop computing, these interfaces are usually limited to using system sounds such as feedback. Some software producers take into account people who can't hear due to hearing impairments, silence requirements or lack of sound producing software. System sounds like beeps can be substituted or supplemented with visual notifications and captioned text (akin to closed captioning). Closed captions are a very popular means of relaying information for the Deaf and hearing impaired communities.

Software Accessibility

Accessibility Application Programming Interfaces (APIs)

Software APIs exist to allow assistive technology products such as screen readers and screen magnifiers to work with mainstream software. The current or past APIs include:

- Java Accessibility and the Java Access Bridge for Java software (being standardized as ISO/IEC TR 13066-6);

- Assistive Technology Service Provider Interface (AT-SPI) on UNIX and Linux (being standardized as ISO/IEC PDTR 13066-4);

- Microsoft Active Accessibility (MSAA) on Microsoft Windows;

- IAccessible2 on Microsoft Windows, a competitor of Microsoft UI Automation also replacing MSAA by Free Standards Group (standardized as ISO/IEC 13066-3:2012);

- Mac OS X Accessibility;

- Microsoft UI Automation on Microsoft Windows, replacing MSAA.

Some of these APIs are being standardized in the ISO/IEC 13066 series of standards.

Accessibility Features in Mainstream Software

Accessibility software can also make input devices easier to access at the user level:

- Keyboard shortcuts and MouseKeys allow the user to substitute keyboarding for mouse actions. Macro recorders can greatly extend the range and sophistication of keyboard shortcuts.

- Sticky keys allows characters or commands to be typed without having to hold down a modifier key (Shift, Ctrl, Alt) while pressing a second key. Similarly, ClickLock is a Microsoft Windows feature that remembers a mouse button is down so that items can be highlighted or dragged without holding the mouse button down while scrolling.

- Customization of mouse or mouse alternatives' responsiveness to movement, double-clicking, and so forth.

- ToggleKeys is a feature of Microsoft Windows 95 onwards. A high sound is heard when the CAPS LOCK, SCROLL LOCK, or NUMBER LOCK key is switched on while a low sound is heard when any of those keys is switched off.

- Customization of pointer appearance, such as size, color and shape.

- Predictive text

- Spell checkers and grammar checkers

Support for Learning Disabilities

Other approaches that may be particularly relevant to users with a learning disability include:

- Cause and effect software

- Switch accessible software

- Hand–eye coordination skills software

- Diagnostic assessment software

- Mind mapping software

- Study skills software

- Symbol-based software

- Text-to-speech

- Touch typing software

Web Accessibility

Enabling access to Web content for all users is the concern of the Web accessibility movement, which strives to create accessible websites via conformance to certain design principles. For example, screen readers are of limited use when reading text from websites designed without consideration to accessibility. Sometimes these limitations are due to the differences between spoken and written language and the complexity of text, but it is often caused by poor page design practices. The tendency to indicate semantic meaning using methods that are purely presentational (e.g. larger or smaller font sizes, using different font colors, embedded images, or multimedia to provide information) restricts meaningful access to some users. Therefore, designing sites in accordance with Web accessibility principles helps enable meaningful access for all users.

Open Accessibility Framework

The Open Accessibility Framework (OAF) provides an outline of the steps that must be in place in order for any computing platform to be considered accessible. These steps are analogous to those necessary to make a physical or built environment accessible. The OAF divides the required steps into two categories: creation and use.

The "creation" steps describe the precursors and building blocks required for technology developers to create accessible applications and products. They are as follows:

1. Define what "accessible" means for the identified use of the platform. It must be clear what is meant by "accessible" as this will differ according to the modality and capabilities of each platform. Accessibility features may include tabbing navigation, theming, and an accessibility API.

2. Provide accessible stock user interface elements. Pre-built "stock" user interface elements, used by application developers and authoring tools, must be implemented to make use of the accessibility features of a platform.

3. Provide authoring tools that support accessibility. Application developers and content authors should be encouraged to implement tools that will improve the accessibility features of a platform. Using these tools can support accessible stock user interface elements, prompt for information required to properly implement an accessibility API, and identify accessibility evaluation and repair tools.

The "use" steps describe what is necessary in the computing environment in which these accessible applications will run. They are as follows:

1. Provide platform supports. Computing platforms must properly implement the accessibility features that are specified in their accessibility definition. For example, the accessibility API definitions must be implemented correctly in the program code.

2. Provide accessible application software. Accessible applications must be available for the platform and they must support the accessibility features of the platform. This may be achieved by simply engaging the accessible stock elements and authoring tools that support accessibility.

3. Provide assistive technologies. Assistive technologies (e.g. screen readers, screen magnifiers, voice input, adapted keyboards) must actually be available for the platform so that the users can effectively interface with the technology.

The following examples show that the OAF can be applied to different types of platforms: desktop operating systems, web applications and the mobile platform. A more complete list can be found in the Open Source Accessibility Repository by the Open Accessibility Everywhere Group (OAEG).

1. Accessibility APIs include the Assistive Technology Service Provider Interface and UI Automation on the desktop, WAI-ARIA in web applications, and the Blackberry Accessibility API on the Blackberry operating system.

2. Other APIs are keyboard access and theming in widget libraries like Java Swing for desktop applications, the jQuery UI and Fluid Infusion for Web applications, and the Lightweight User Interface Toolkit (LWUIT) for mobile applications.

3. Support for accessible development can be effective by using Glade (for the GTK+ toolkit), the DIAS plugin for NetBeans IDE, Xcode IDE for iOS applications. Accessibility inspection tools like Accerciser (for AT-SPI) and support for accessible authoring with the AccessODF plugin for LibreOffice and Apache OpenOffice also fit into this step.

4. Support for UI Automation on Microsoft Windows, support for ATK and AT-SPI in Linux GNOME, WAI-ARIA support in Firefox, and the MIDP LWUIT mobile runtime (or the MIDP LCDUI mobile runtime) that is available on mobile phones with Java are examples of APIs.

5. The DAISY player AMIS on the Microsoft Windows desktop and the AEGIS Contact Manager for phones with Java ME are designed for accessibility.

6. The GNOME Shell Magnifier and Orca on the GNOME desktop, GNOME's ATK (Accessibility Toolkit), the web-based screen reader WebAnywhere, and the alternative text-entry system Dasher for Linux, iOS and Android are examples of assistive technologies.

The goal of the listed tools is to embed accessibility into various mainstream technologies.

Standards and Regulations

ISO 9241-171

ISO 9241-171: Ergonomics of human-system interaction - Guidance on software accessibility

Compiled from independent standards experts, this document is the most comprehensive and technical standard for designing accessible features for software, covering all disabilities and all aspects of software. It provides examples of two priority levels ('Required' and 'Recommended') and offers a handy checklist designed to help with recording software testing results.

The only trouble is that because of its complexity and technical nature, and with upwards of 150 individual statements, ISO 9241-172 is difficult to interpret and apply. Luckily, not every statement is relevant to every situation, therefore it may be advisable to identify a subset of statements that are tailored to the particular software environment, making the use of this document much more achievable.

Usability

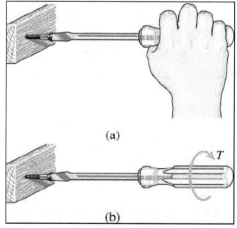

Many tools are designed to be easy to hold and use for their intended purpose. For example, a screwdriver typically has a handle with rounded edges and a grippable surface, to make it easier for the user to hold the handle and twist it to drive a screw.

Usability is the ease of use and learnability of a human-made object such as a tool or device. In software engineering, usability is the degree to which a software can be used by specified consumers to achieve quantified objectives with effectiveness, efficiency, and satisfaction in a quantified context of use.

The object of use can be a software application, website, book, tool, machine, process, vehicle, or anything a human interacts with. A usability study may be conducted as a primary job function by a *usability analyst* or as a secondary job function by designers, technical writers, marketing personnel, and others. It is widely used in consumer electronics, communication, and knowledge transfer objects (such as a cookbook, a document or online help) and mechanical objects such as a door handle or a hammer.

Usability includes methods of measuring usability, such as needs analysis and the study of the principles behind an object's perceived efficiency or elegance. In human-computer interaction and computer science, usability studies the elegance and clarity with which the interaction with a computer program or a web site (web usability) is designed. Usability differs from user satisfaction and user experience because usability does not directly consider usefulness or utility.

Introduction

The primary notion of usability is that an object designed with a generalized users' psychology and physiology in mind is, for example:

- More efficient to use—takes less time to accomplish a particular task

- Easier to learn—operation can be learned by observing the object

- More satisfying to use

Complex computer systems find their way into everyday life, and at the same time the market is saturated with competing brands. This has made usability more popular and widely recognized in recent years, as companies see the benefits of researching and developing their products with user-oriented methods instead of technology-oriented methods. By understanding and researching the interaction between product and user, the *usability expert* can also provide insight that is unattainable by traditional company-oriented market research. For example, after observing and interviewing users, the usability expert may identify needed functionality or design flaws that were not anticipated. A method called *contextual inquiry* does this in the naturally occurring context of the users own environment. In the user-centered design paradigm, the product is designed with its intended users in mind at all times. In the user-driven or participatory design paradigm, some of the users become actual or de facto members of the design team.

The term *user friendly* is often used as a synonym for *usable*, though it may also refer to accessibility. Usability describes the quality of user experience across websites, software, products, and environments. There is no consensus about the relation of the terms ergonomics (or human factors) and usability. Some think of usability as the software specialization of the larger topic of ergonomics. Others view these topics as tangential, with ergonomics focusing on physiological matters (e.g., turning a door handle) and usability focusing on psychological matters (e.g., recognizing that a door can be opened by turning its handle). Usability is also important in website development (web usability). According to Jakob Nielsen, "Studies of user behavior on the Web find a low tolerance for difficult designs or slow sites. People don't want to wait. And they don't want to learn how to use a home page. There's no such thing as a training class or a manual for a Web site. People have to be able to grasp the functioning of the site immediately after scanning the home page—for a few seconds at most." Otherwise, most casual users simply leave the site and browse or shop elsewhere.

Definition

ISO defines usability as "The extent to which a product can be used by specified users to achieve specified goals with effectiveness, efficiency, and satisfaction in a specified context of use." The word "usability" also refers to methods for improving ease-of-use during the design process. Usability consultant Jakob Nielsen and computer science professor Ben Shneiderman have written (separately) about a framework of system acceptability, where usability is a part of "usefulness" and is composed of:

- Learnability: How easy is it for users to accomplish basic tasks the first time they encounter the design?

- Efficiency: Once users have learned the design, how quickly can they perform tasks?

- Memorability: When users return to the design after a period of not using it, how easily can they re-establish proficiency?

- Errors: How many errors do users make, how severe are these errors, and how easily can they recover from the errors?

- Satisfaction: How pleasant is it to use the design?

Usability is often associated with the functionalities of the product (cf. ISO definition, below), in addition to being solely a characteristic of the user interface (cf. framework of system acceptability, also below, which separates *usefulness* into *usability* and *utility*). For example, in the context of mainstream consumer products, an automobile lacking a reverse gear could be considered *unusable* according to the former view, and *lacking in utility* according to the latter view. When evaluating user interfaces for usability, the definition can be as simple as "the perception of a target user of the effectiveness (fit for purpose) and efficiency (work or time required to use) of the Interface". Each component may be measured subjectively against criteria, e.g., Principles of User Interface Design, to provide a metric, often expressed as a percentage. It is important to distinguish between usability testing and usability engineering. Usability testing is the measurement of ease of use of a product or piece of software. In contrast, usability engineering (UE) is the research and design process that ensures a product with good usability. Usability is a non-functional requirement. As with other non-functional requirements, usability cannot be directly measured but must be quantified by means of indirect measures or attributes such as, for example, the number of reported problems with ease-of-use of a system.

Intuitive Interfaces

The term intuitive is often listed as a desirable trait in usable interfaces, often used as a synonym for learnable. Some experts such as Jef Raskin have discouraged using this term in user interface design, claiming that easy to use interfaces are often easy because of the user's exposure to previous similar systems, thus the term 'familiar' should be preferred. As an example: Two vertical lines "||" on media player buttons do not intuitively mean "pause"—they do so by convention. Aiming for "intuitive" interfaces (based on reusing existing skills with interaction systems) could lead designers to discard a better design solution only because it would require a novel approach. This position is sometimes illustrated with the remark that "The only intuitive interface is the nipple; everything else is learned." Bruce Tognazzini even denies the existence of "intuitive" interfaces, since such interfaces must be able to intuit, i.e., "perceive the patterns of the user's behavior and draw inferences." Instead, he advocates the term "intuitable," i.e., "that users could intuit the workings of an application by seeing it and using it." He continues, however, "But even that is a less than useful goal since only 25 percent of the population depends on intuition to perceive anything."

ISO standards

ISO/TR 16982:2002 standard

ISO/TR 16982:2002 ("Ergonomics of human-system interaction—Usability methods supporting human-centered design") is an International Standards Organization (ISO) standard that provides information on human-centered usability methods that can be used for design and evaluation. It details the advantages, disadvantages, and other factors relevant to using each usability method. It explains the implications of the stage of the life cycle and the individual project characteristics for the selection of usability methods and provides examples of usability methods in context. The main users of ISO/TR 16982:2002 are project managers. It therefore addresses technical human factors and ergonomics issues only to the extent necessary to allow managers to understand their relevance and importance in the design process as a whole. The guidance in ISO/TR 16982:2002 can be tailored for specific design situations by using the lists of issues characterizing the context of use of the product to be delivered. Selection of appropriate usability methods should also take account of the relevant life-cycle process. ISO/TR 16982:2002 is restricted to methods that are widely used by usability specialists and project managers. It does *not* specify the details of how to implement or carry out the usability methods described.

ISO 9241 standard

ISO 9241 is a multi-part standard that covers a number of aspects of people working with computers. Although originally titled *Ergonomic requirements for office work with visual display terminals (VDTs)*, it has been retitled to the more generic *Ergonomics of Human System Interaction*. As part of this change, ISO is renumbering some parts of the standard so that it can cover more topics, e.g. tactile and haptic interaction. The first part to be renumbered was part 10 in 2006, now part 110.

Designing for Usability

Any system or device designed for use by people should be easy to use, easy to learn, easy to remember (the instructions), and helpful to users. John Gould and Clayton Lewis recommend that designers striving for usability follow these three design principles

- Early focus on end users and the tasks they need the system/device to do

- Empirical measurement using quantitative or qualitative measures

- Iterative design, in which the designers work in a series of stages, improving the design each time

Early Focus on Users and Tasks

The design team should be user-driven and it should be in direct contact with potential users. Several evaluation methods, including personas, cognitive modeling, inspection, inquiry, prototyping, and testing methods may contribute to understanding potential users and their perceptions of how well the product or process works. Usability considerations, such as who the users are and their experience with similar systems must be examined. As part of understanding users, this knowledge must "...be played against the tasks that the users will be expected to perform." This includes the analysis of what tasks the users will perform, which are most important, and what decisions the users will make while using your system. Designers must understand how cognitive and emotional characteristics of users will relate to a proposed system. One way to stress the importance of these issues in the designers' minds is to use personas, which are made-up representative users. See below for further discussion of personas. Another more expensive but more insightful method is to have a panel of potential users work closely with the design team from the early stages.

Empirical Measurement

Test the system early on, and test the system on real users using behavioral measurements. This includes testing the system for both learnability and usability. (See Evaluation Methods). It is important in this stage to use quantitative usability specifications such as time and errors to complete tasks and number of users to test, as well as examine performance and attitudes of the users testing the system. Finally, "reviewing or demonstrating" a system before the user tests it can result in misleading results. The emphasis of empirical measurement is on measurement, both informal and formal, which can be carried out through a variety of evaluation methods.

Iterative Design

Iterative design is a design methodology based on a cyclic process of prototyping, testing, analyzing, and refining a product or process. Based on the results of testing the most recent iteration of a design, changes and refinements are made. This process is intended to ultimately improve the quality and functionality of a design. In iterative design, interaction with the designed system is used as a form of research for informing and evolving a project, as successive versions, or iterations of a design are implemented. The key requirements for Iterative Design are: identification of required changes, an ability to make changes, and a willingness to make changes. When a problem is encountered, there is no set method to determine the correct solution. Rather, there are empirical methods that can be used during system development or after the system is delivered, usually a more inopportune time. Ultimately, iterative design works towards meeting goals such as making the system user friendly, easy to use, easy to operate, simple, etc.

Evaluation Methods

There are a variety of usability evaluation methods. Certain methods use data from users, while others rely on usability experts. There are usability evaluation methods for all stages of design and development, from product definition to final design modifications. When choosing a method, consider cost, time constraints, and appropriateness. For a brief overview of methods, see Comparison of usability evaluation methods or continue reading below. Usability methods can be further classified into the subcategories below.

Cognitive Modeling Methods

Cognitive modeling involves creating a computational model to estimate how long it takes people to perform a given task. Models are based on psychological principles and experimental studies to determine times for cognitive processing and motor movements. Cognitive models can be used to improve user interfaces or predict problem errors and pitfalls during the design process. A few examples of cognitive models include:

Parallel Design

With parallel design, several people create an initial design from the same set of requirements. Each person works independently, and when finished, shares concepts with the group. The design team considers each solution, and each designer uses the best ideas to further improve their own solution. This process helps generate many different, diverse ideas, and ensures that the best ideas from each design are integrated into the final concept. This process can be repeated several times until the team is satisfied with the final concept.

GOMS

GOMS stands for *goals, operator, methods, and selection rules*. It is a family of techniques that analyzes the user complexity of interactive systems. Goals are what the user must accomplish. An operator is an action performed in pursuit of a goal. A method is a sequence of operators that accomplish a goal. Selection rules specify which method satisfies a given goal, based on context.

Human Processor Model

Sometimes it is useful to break a task down and analyze each individual aspect separately. This helps the tester locate specific areas for improvement. To do this, it is necessary to understand how the human brain processes information. A model of the human processor is shown below.

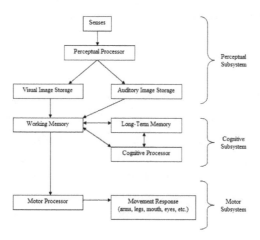

Many studies have been done to estimate the cycle times, decay times, and capacities of each of these processors. Variables that affect these can include subject age, aptitudes, ability, and the surrounding environment. For a younger adult, reasonable estimates are:

Parameter	Mean	Range
Eye movement time	230 ms	70–700 ms
Decay half-life of visual image storage	200 ms	90–1000 ms
Perceptual processor cycle time	100 ms	50–200 ms
Cognitive processor cycle time	70 ms	25–170 ms
Motor processor cycle time	70 ms	30–100 ms
Effective working memory capacity	2 items	2–3 items

Long-term memory is believed to have an infinite capacity and decay time.

Keystroke level modeling

Keystroke level modeling is essentially a less comprehensive version of GOMS that makes simplifying assumptions in order to reduce calculation time and complexity.

Inspection Methods

These usability evaluation methods involve observation of users by an experimenter, or the testing and evaluation of a program by an expert reviewer. They provide more quantitative data as tasks can be timed and recorded.

Card Sorts

Card sorting is a way to involve users in grouping information for a website's usability review. Participants in a card sorting session are asked to organize the content from a Web site in a way that makes sense to them. Participants review items from a Web site and then group these items into categories. Card sorting helps to learn how users think about the content and how they would organize the information on the Web site. Card sorting helps to build the structure for a Web site, decide what to put on the home page, and label the home page categories. It also helps to ensure that information is organized on the site in a way that is logical to users.

Tree Tests

Tree testing is a way to evaluate the effectiveness of a website's top-down organization. Participants are given "find it" tasks, then asked to drill down through successive text lists of topics and subtopics to find a suitable answer. Tree testing evaluates the findability and labeling of topics in a site, separate from its navigation controls or visual design.

Ethnography

Ethnographic analysis is derived from anthropology. Field observations are taken at a site of a possible user, which track the artifacts of work such as Post-It notes, items on desktop, shortcuts, and items in trash bins. These observations also gather the sequence of work and interruptions that determine the user's typical day.

Heuristic Evaluation

Heuristic evaluation is a usability engineering method for finding and assessing usability problems in a user interface design as part of an iterative design process. It involves having a small set of evaluators examining the interface and using recognized usability principles (the "heuristics"). It is the most popular of the usability inspection methods, as it is quick, cheap, and easy. Heuristic evaluation was developed to aid in the design of computer user-interface design. It relies on expert reviewers to discover usability problems and then categorize and rate them by a set of principles (heuristics.) It is widely used based on its speed and cost-effectiveness. Jakob Nielsen's list of ten heuristics is the most commonly used in industry. These are ten general principles for user interface design. They are called "heuristics" because they are more in the nature of rules of thumb than specific usability guidelines.

- *Visibility of system status*: The system should always keep users informed about what is going on, through appropriate feedback within reasonable time.

- *Match between system and the real world*: The system should speak the users' language, with words, phrases and concepts familiar to the user, rather than system-oriented terms. Follow real-world conventions, making information appear in a natural and logical order.

- *User control and freedom*: Users often choose system functions by mistake and will need a clearly marked "emergency exit" to leave the unwanted state without having to go through an extended dialogue. Support undo and redo.

- *Consistency and standards*: Users should not have to wonder whether different words, situations, or actions mean the same thing. Follow platform conventions.

- *Error prevention*: Even better than good error messages is a careful design that prevents a problem from occurring in the first place. Either eliminate error-prone conditions or check for them and present users with a confirmation option before they commit to the action.

- *Recognition rather than recall*: Minimize the user's memory load by making objects, actions, and options visible. The user should not have to remember information from one part of the dialogue to another. Instructions for use of the system should be visible or easily retrievable whenever appropriate.

- *Flexibility and efficiency of use*: Accelerators—unseen by the novice user—may often speed up the interaction for the expert user such that the system can cater to both inexperienced and experienced users. Allow users to tailor frequent actions.

- *Aesthetic and minimalist design*: Dialogues should not contain information that is irrelevant or rarely needed. Every extra unit of information in a dialogue competes with the relevant units of information and diminishes their relative visibility.

- *Help users recognize, diagnose, and recover from errors*: Error messages should be expressed in plain language (no codes), precisely indicate the problem, and constructively suggest a solution.

- *Help and documentation*: Even though it is better if the system can be used without documentation, it may be necessary to provide help and documentation. Any such information should be easy to search, focused on the user's task, list concrete steps to be carried out, and not be too large.

Thus, by determining which guidelines are violated, the usability of a device can be determined.

Usability Inspection

Usability inspection is a review of a system based on a set of guidelines. The review is conducted by a group of experts who are deeply familiar with the concepts of usability in design. The experts focus on a list of areas in design that have been shown to be troublesome for users.

Pluralistic Inspection

Pluralistic Inspections are meetings where users, developers, and human factors people meet together to discuss and evaluate step by step of a task scenario. As more people inspect the scenario for problems, the higher the probability to find problems. In addition, the more interaction in the team, the faster the usability issues are resolved.

Consistency Inspection

In consistency inspection, expert designers review products or projects to ensure consistency across multiple products to look if it does things in the same way as their own designs.

Activity Analysis

Activity analysis is a usability method used in preliminary stages of development to get a sense of situation. It involves an investigator observing users as they work in the field. Also referred to as user observation, it is useful for specifying user requirements and studying currently used tasks and subtasks. The data collected are qualitative and useful for defining the problem. It should be used when you wish to frame what is needed, or "What do we want to know?"

Inquiry Methods

The following usability evaluation methods involve collecting qualitative data from users. Although the data collected is subjective, it provides valuable information on what the user wants.

Task Analysis

Task analysis means learning about users' goals and users' ways of working. Task analysis can also mean figuring out what more specific tasks users must do to meet those goals and what steps they must take to accomplish those tasks. Along with user and task analysis, a third analysis is often used: understanding users' environments (physical, social, cultural, and technological environments).

Focus Groups

A focus group is a focused discussion where a moderator leads a group of participants through a set of questions on a particular topic. Although typically used as a marketing tool, Focus Groups are sometimes used to evaluate usability. Used in the product definition stage, a group of 6 to 10 users are gathered to discuss what they desire in a product. An experienced focus group facilitator is hired to guide the discussion to areas of interest for the developers. Focus groups are typically videotaped to help get verbatim quotes, and clips are often used to summarize opinions. The data gathered is not usually quantitative, but can help get an idea of a target group's opinion.

Questionnaires/Surveys

Surveys have the advantages of being inexpensive, require no testing equipment, and results reflect the users' opinions. When written carefully and given to actual users who have experience with the product and knowledge of design, surveys provide useful feedback on the strong and weak areas of the usability of a design. This is a very common method and often does not appear to be a survey, but just a warranty card.

Prototyping Methods

It is often very difficult for designers to conduct usability tests with the exact system being designed. Cost constraints, size, and design constraints usually lead the designer to creating a prototype of the system. Instead of creating the complete final system, the designer may test different sections of the system, thus making several small models of each component of the system. The types of usability prototypes may vary from using paper models, index cards, hand drawn models, or storyboards. Prototypes are able to be modified quickly, often are faster and easier to create with less time invested by designers and are more apt to change design; although sometimes are not an adequate representation of the whole system, are often not durable and testing results may not be parallel to those of the actual system.

Rapid Prototyping

Rapid prototyping is a method used in early stages of development to validate and refine the usability of a system. It can be used to quickly and cheaply evaluate user-interface designs without the need for an expensive working model. This can help remove hesitation to change the design, since it is implemented before any real programming begins. One such method of rapid prototyping is paper prototyping.

Testing Methods

These usability evaluation methods involve testing of subjects for the most quantitative data. Usually recorded on video, they provide task completion time and allow for observation of attitude. Regardless to how carefully a system is designed, all theories must be tested using usability tests. Usability tests involve typical users using the system (or product) in a realistic environment. Observation of the user's behavior, emotions, and difficulties while performing different tasks, often identify areas of improvement for the system.

Metrics

While conducting usability tests, designers must use usability metrics to identify what it is they are going to measure, or the usability metrics. These metrics are often variable, and change in conjunction with the scope and goals of the project. The number of subjects being tested can also affect usability metrics, as it is often easier to focus on specific demographics. Qualitative design phases, such as general usability (can the task be accomplished?), and user satisfaction are also typically done with smaller groups of subjects. Using inexpensive prototypes on small user groups provides more detailed information, because of the more interactive atmosphere, and the designer's ability to focus more on the individual user.

As the designs become more complex, the testing must become more formalized. Testing equipment will become more sophisticated and testing metrics become more quantitative. With a more refined prototype, designers often test effectiveness, efficiency, and subjective satisfaction, by asking the user to complete various tasks. These categories are measured by the percent that complete the task, how long it takes to complete the tasks, ratios of success to failure to complete the task, time spent on errors, the number of errors, rating scale of satisfactions, number of times user seems frustrated, etc. Additional observations of the users give designers insight on navigation difficulties, controls, conceptual models, etc. The ultimate goal of analyzing these metrics is to find/create a prototype design that users like and use to successfully perform given tasks. After conducting usability tests, it is important for a designer to record what was observed, in addition to why such behavior occurred and modify the model according to the results. Often it is quite difficult to distinguish the source of the design errors, and what the user did wrong. However, effective usability tests will not generate a solution to the problems, but provide modified design guidelines for continued testing.

Remote Usability Testing

Remote usability testing (also known as unmoderated or asynchronous usability testing) involves the use of a specially modified online survey, allowing the quantification of user testing studies by providing the ability to generate large sample sizes, or a deep qualitative analysis without the need for dedicated facilities. Additionally, this style of user testing also provides an opportunity to segment feedback by demographic, attitudinal and behavioral type. The tests are carried out in the user's own environment (rather than labs) helping further simulate real-life scenario testing. This approach also provides a vehicle to easily solicit feedback from users in remote areas. There are two types, quantitative or qualitative. Quantitative use large sample sized and task based surveys. These types of studies are useful for validating suspected usability issues. Qualitative studies are best used as exploratory research, in small sample sizes but frequent, even daily iterations. Qualitative usually allows for observing respondent's screens and verbal think aloud commentary (Screen Recording Video, SRV), and for a richer level of insight also include the webcam view of the respondent (Video-in-Video, ViV, sometimes referred to as Picture-in-Picture, PiP)

Remote Usability Testing for Mobile Devices

The growth in mobile and associated platforms and services (e.g.: Mobile gaming has experienced 20x growth in 2010-2012) has generated a need for unmoderated remote usability testing on mobile devices, both for websites but especially for app interactions. One methodology consists of shipping cameras and special camera holding fixtures to dedicated testers, and having them record the screens of the mobile smart-phone or tablet device, usually using an HD camera. A drawback of this approach is that the finger movements of the respondent can obscure the view of the screen, in addition to the bias and logistical issues inherent in shipping special hardware to selected respondents. A newer approach uses a wireless projection of the mobile device screen onto the computer desktop screen of the respondent, who can then be recorded through their webcam, and thus a combined Video-in-Video view of the participant and the screen interactions viewed simultaneously while incorporating the verbal think aloud commentary of the respondents.

Thinking aloud

The Think aloud protocol is a method of gathering data that is used in both usability and psychology studies. It involves getting a user to verbalize their thought processes as they perform a task or set of tasks. Often an instructor is present to prompt the user into being more vocal as they work. Similar to the Subjects-in-Tandem method, it is useful in pinpointing problems and is relatively simple to set up. Additionally, it can provide insight into the user's attitude, which can not usually be discerned from a survey or questionnaire.

RITE Method

Rapid Iterative Testing and Evaluation (RITE) is an iterative usability method similar to traditional "discount" usability testing. The tester and team must define a target population for testing, schedule participants to come into the lab, decide on how the users behaviors will be measured, construct a test script and have participants engage in a verbal protocol (e.g., think aloud). However it differs from these methods in that it advocates that changes to the user interface are made as soon as a problem is identified and a solution is clear. Sometimes this can occur after observing as few as 1 participant. Once the data for a participant has been collected the usability engineer and team decide if they will be making any changes to the prototype prior to the next participant. The changed interface is then tested with the remaining users.

Subjects-in-tandem or co-discovery

Subjects-in-tandem (also called co-discovery) is the pairing of subjects in a usability test to gather important information on the ease of use of a product. Subjects tend to discuss the tasks they have to accomplish out loud and through these discussions observers learn where the problem areas of a design are. To encourage co-operative problem-solving between the two subjects, and the attendant discussions leading to it, the tests can be designed to make the subjects dependent on each other by assigning them complementary areas of responsibility (e.g. for testing of software, one subject may be put in charge of the mouse and the other of the keyboard.)

Component-based Usability Testing

Component-based usability testing is an approach which aims to test the usability of elementary units of an interaction system, referred to as interaction components. The approach includes component-specific quantitative measures based on user interaction recorded in log files, and component-based usability questionnaires.

Other Methods

Cognitive Walk Through

Cognitive walkthrough is a method of evaluating the user interaction of a working prototype or final product. It is used to evaluate the system's ease of learning. Cognitive walk through is useful to understand the user's thought processes and decision making when interacting with a system, specially for first-time or infrequent users.

Benchmarking

Benchmarking creates standardized test materials for a specific type of design. Four key characteristics are considered when establishing a benchmark: time to do the core task, time to fix errors, time to learn applications, and the functionality of the system. Once there is a benchmark, other designs can be compared to it to determine the usability of the system. Many of the common objectives of usability studies, such as trying to understand user behavior or exploring alternative designs, must be put aside. Unlike many other usability methods or types of labs studies, benchmark studies more closely resemble true experimental psychology lab studies, with greater attention to detail on methodology, study protocol and data analysis.

Meta-analysis

Meta-analysis is a statistical procedure to combine results across studies to integrate the findings. This phrase was coined in 1976 as a quantitative literature review. This type of evaluation is very powerful for determining the usability of a device because it combines multiple studies to provide very accurate quantitative support.

PersonaW

Personas are fictitious characters created to represent a site or product's different user types and their associated demographics and technographics. Alan Cooper introduced the concept of using personas as a part of interactive design in 1998 in his book *The Inmates Are Running the Asylum*, but had used this concept since as early as 1975. Personas are a usability evaluation method that can be used at various design stages. The most typical time to create personas is at the beginning of designing so that designers have a tangible idea of who the users of their product will be. Personas are the archetypes that represent actual groups of users and their needs, which can be a general description of person, context, or usage scenario. This technique turns marketing data on target user population into a few physical concepts of users to create empathy among the design team, with the final aim of tailoring a product more closely to how the personas will use it. To gather the marketing data that personas require, several tools can be used, including online surveys, web analytics, customer feedback forms, and usability tests, and interviews with customer-service representatives.

Benefits

The key benefits of usability are:

- Higher revenues through increased sales
- Increased user efficiency and user satisfaction
- Reduced development costs
- Reduced support costs

Corporate Integration

An increase in usability generally positively affects several facets of a company's output quality. In particular, the benefits fall into several common areas:

- Increased productivity
- Decreased training and support costs
- Increased sales and revenues
- Reduced development time and costs
- Reduced maintenance costs
- Increased customer satisfaction

Increased usability in the workplace fosters several responses from employees: "Workers who enjoy their work do it better, stay longer in the face of temptation, and contribute ideas and enthusiasm to the evolution of enhanced productivity." To create standards, companies often implement experimental design techniques that create baseline levels. Areas of concern in an office environment include (though are not necessarily limited to):

- Working posture
- Design of workstation furniture
- Screen displays
- Input devices
- Organization issues
- Office environment
- Software interface

By working to improve said factors, corporations can achieve their goals of increased output at lower costs, while potentially creating optimal levels of customer satisfaction. There are numerous reasons why each of these factors correlates to overall improvement. For example, making software user interfaces easier to understand reduces the need for extensive training. The improved interface tends to lower the time needed to perform tasks, and so would both raise the productivity levels for employees and reduce development time (and thus costs). Each of the aforementioned factors are not mutually exclusive; rather they should be understood to work in conjunction to form the overall workplace environment. In the 2010s, usability is recognized as an important software quality attribute, earning its place among more traditional attributes such as performance, robustness and aesthetic appearance. Various academic programs focus on usability. Several usability consultancy companies have emerged, and traditional consultancy and design firms offer similar services.

Professional Development

Usability practitioners are sometimes trained as industrial engineers, psychologists, kinesiologists, systems design engineers, or with a degree in information architecture, information or library science, or Human-Computer Interaction (HCI). More often though they are people who are trained in specific applied fields who have taken on a usability focus within their organization. Anyone who aims to make tools easier to use and more effective for their desired function within the context of work or everyday living can benefit from studying usability principles and guidelines. For those seeking to extend their training, the Usability Professionals' Association offers online resources, reference lists, courses, conferences, and local chapter meetings. The UPA also sponsors World Usability Day each November. Related professional organizations include the Human Factors and Ergonomics Society (HFES) and the Association for Computing Machinery's special interest groups in Computer Human Interaction (SIGCHI), Design of Communication (SIGDOC) and Computer Graphics and Interactive Techniques (SIGGRAPH). The Society for Technical Communication also has a special interest group on Usability and User Experience (UUX). They publish a quarterly newsletter called *Usability Interface*.

Computer User Satisfaction

Computer user satisfaction (and closely related concepts such as *System Satisfaction, User Satisfaction, Computer System Satisfaction, End User Computing Satisfaction*) is the attitude of a user to the computer system (s)he employs in the context of his/her work environments. Doll and Torkzadeh's (1988) definition of user satisfaction is, *the opinion of the user about a specific computer application, which they use.* In a broader sense, the definition of user satisfaction can be extended to user satisfaction with any computer-based electronic appliance. However, scholars distinguish between user satisfaction and usability as part of Human-Computer Interaction. Successful organisations have systems in place which they believe help maximise profits and minimise overheads. It is therefore desirable that all their systems succeed and remain successful; and this includes their computer-based systems. According to key scholars such as DeLone and McLean (2002), user satisfaction is a key measure of computer system success, if not synonymous with it. However, the development of techniques for defining and measuring user satisfaction have been ad hoc and open to question. The term *Computer User Satisfaction* is abbreviated to *user satisfaction* in this article.

The Computer User Satisfaction Questionnaire and its Reduced Version, the User Information Satisfaction Short-form

Bailey and Pearson's (1983) 39Factor *Computer User Satisfaction (CUS)* questionnaire and its derivative, the *User Information Satisfaction (UIS)* short-form of Baroudi, Olson and Ives are typical of instruments which one might term as 'factor-based'. They consist of lists of factors, each of which the respondent is asked to rate on one or more multiple point scales. Bailey and Pearson's CUS asked for five ratings for each of 39 factors. The first four scales were for quality ratings and the fifth was an importance rating. From the fifth rating of each factor, they found that their sample of users rated as most important: *accuracy, reliability, timeliness, relevancy* and *confidence in the system.* The factors of least importance were found to be *feelings of control, volume of output, vendor support, degree of training,* and *organisational position of EDP* (the electronic data processing, or computing department). However, the CUS requires 39 x 5 = 195 individual sevenpoint scale responses. Ives, Olson and Baroudi (1983), amongst others, thought that so many responses could result in errors of attrition. This means, the respondent's failure to return the questionnaire or the increasing carelessness of the respondent as they fill in a long form. In psychometrics, such errors not only result in reduced sample sizes but can also distort the results, as those who return long questionnaires, properly completed, may have differing psychological traits from those who do not. Ives, et al. thus developed the UIS. This only requires the respondent to rate 13 factors, and so remains in significant use at the present time. Two sevenpoint scales are provided per factor (each for a quality), requiring 26 individual responses in all. But in a recent article, Islam, Mervi and Käkölä (2010) argued that it is difficult to measure user satisfaction in the industry settings as the response rate often remain low. Thus, a simpler version of user satisfaction measurement instrument is necessary.

The Problem with the Dating of Factors

An early criticism of these measures was that the factors date as computer technology evolves and changes. This suggested the need for updates and led to a sequence of other factor-based instruments. Doll and Torkzadeh (1988), for example, produced a factor-based instrument for a new type of user emerging at the time, called an end-user. They identified end-users as users who tend to interact with a computer interface only, while previously users interacted with developers and operational staff as well. McKinney, Yoon and Zahedi (2002) developed a model and instruments for measuring web-customer satisfaction during the information phase. Cheung and Lee (2005) in their development of an instrument to measure user satisfaction with e-portals, based their instrument on that of McKinney, Yoon and Zahedi (2002), which in turn was based primarily on instruments from prior studies.

The Problem of Defining User Satisfaction

As none of the instruments in common use really rigorously define their construct of user satisfaction, some scholars such as Cheyney, Mann and Amoroso (1986) have called for more research on the factors which influence the success of end-user computing. Little subsequent effort which sheds new light on the matter exists, however. All factor-based instruments run the risk of including factors irrelevant to the respondent, while omitting some that may be highly significant to him/her. Needless to say, this is further exacerbated by the ongoing changes in information technology.

In the literature there are two definitions for user satisfaction, 'User satisfaction' and 'User Information Satisfaction' are used interchangeably. According to Doll and Torkzadeh (1988) 'user satisfaction' is defined as the opinion of the user about a specific computer application, which they use. Ives et al. (1983) defined 'User Information Satisfaction' as "the extent to which users believe the information system available to them meets their information requirements." Other terms for User Information Satisfaction are "system acceptance" (Igersheim, 1976), "perceived usefulness" (Larcker and Lessig, 1980), "MIS appreciation" (Swanson, 1974) and "feelings about information system" (Maish, 1979). Ang en Koh (1997) have described user information satisfaction (UIS) as "a perceptual or subjective measure of system success". This means that user information satisfaction will differ in meaning and significance from person to person. In other words, users who are equally satisfied with the same system according to one definition and measure may not be equally satisfied according to another.

Several studies have investigated whether or not certain factors influence the UIS; for example, those by Yaverbaum (1988) and Ang and Soh (1997). Yaverbaum's (1988) study found that people who use their computer irregularly tend to be more satisfied than regular users. Ang en Soh's(1997)research, on the other hand, could find no evidence that computer background affects UIS.

Mullany, Tan and Gallupe (2006) do essay a definition of user satisfaction, claiming that it is based on memories of the past use of a system. Conversely motivation, they suggest, is based on beliefs about the future use of the system. (Mullany et al., 2006).

The large number of studies over the past few decades, as cited in this article, shows that user information satisfaction remains an important topic in research studies despite somewhat contradictory results.

A Lack of theoretical Underpinning

Another difficulty with most of these instruments is their lack of theoretical underpinning by psychological or managerial theory. Exceptions to this were the model of web site design success developed by Zhang and von Dran (2000), and a measure of user satisfaction with e-portals, developed by Cheung and Lee (2005). Both of these models drew upon Herzberg's two-factor theory of motivation. Consequently, their factors were designed to measure both 'satisfiers' and 'hygiene factors'. However, Herzberg's theory itself is criticized for failing to distinguish adequately between the terms *motivation, job motivation, job satisfaction*, and so on. Islam (2011) in a recent study found that the sources of dissatisfaction differs from the sources of satisfaction. He found that the environmental factors (e.g., system quality) were more critical to cause dissatisfaction while outcome specific factors (e.g., perceived usefulness) were more critical to cause satisfaction.

Computer User Satisfaction and Cognitive Style

A study by Mullany (2006) showed that during the life of a system, satisfaction from users will on average increase in time as the users' experiences with the system increase. Whilst the overall findings of the studies showed only a weak link between the gap in the users' and analysts' cognitive style (measured using the KAI scales) and user satisfaction, a more significant link was found in the regions of 85 and 652 days into the systems' usage. This link shows that a large absolute gap between user and analyst cognitive styles often yields a higher rate of user dissatisfaction than a smaller gap. Furthermore, an analyst with a more adaptive cognitive style than the user at the early and late stages (approximately days 85 and 652) of system usage tends to reduce user dissatisfaction.

Mullany, Tan and Gallupe (2006) devised an instrument (the System Satisfaction Schedule (SSS)), which utilizes user generated factors (that is, almost exclusively, and so avoids the problem of the dating of factors. Also aligning themselves to Herzberg, these authors argue that the perceived usefulness (or otherwise) of tools of the trade are contextually related, and so are special cases of hygiene factors. They consequently define user satisfaction as the absence of user dissatisfaction and complaint, as assessed by users who have had at least some experience of using the system. In other words, satisfaction is based on memories of the past use of a system. Motivation, conversely, is based on beliefs about the future use of the system. (Mullany et al., 2007, p. 464)

Future Developments

Currently, some scholars and practitioners are experimenting with other measurement methods and further refinements of the definition for *satisfaction* and *user satisfaction*. Others are replacing structured questionnaires by unstructured ones, where the respondent is asked simply to write down or dictate all the factors about a system which either satisfies or dissatisfies them. One problem with this approach, however, is that the instruments tend not to yield quantitative results, making comparisons and statistical analysis difficult. Also, if scholars cannot agree on the precise meaning of the term *satisfaction*, respondents will be highly unlikely to respond consistently to such instruments. Some newer instruments contain a mix of structured and unstructured items.

Gender HCI

Gender HCI is a subfield of human-computer interaction that focuses on the design and evaluation of interactive systems for humans, with emphasis on differences in how males and females interact with computers.

Examples

Gender HCI research has been conducted in the following areas (among others):

- Biases in perceptions of gendered computerized partners

- The effects of confidence and self-efficacy on both genders' interactions with software.

- The design of gender-specific software, such as video games created for females.

- The design of display screen sizes and how they affect both genders.

- The design of gender-neutral problem-solving software.

Overview

Gender HCI investigates ways in which attributes of software (or even hardware) can interact with gender differences. As with all of HCI, Gender HCI is a highly interdisciplinary area. Findings from fields such as psychology, computer science, marketing, neuroscience, education, and economics strongly suggest that males and females problem solve, communicate, and process information differently. Gender HCI investigates whether these differences need to be taken into account in the design of software and hardware.

History

The term *Gender HCI* was coined in 2004 by Laura Beckwith, a PhD candidate at Oregon State University, and her advisor Margaret Burnett. They discovered that, although there had been some activity that could be characterized as Gender HCI work, people did not know about each other's work. The relevant research reports were isolated and scattered about various fields. Since that time, they and others have worked to help researchers know about each other's work and practitioners to be aware of the findings, so as to allow this area to mature as a subarea of HCI.

The following are a brief set of milestones in the history of this emerging subarea.

- 1987: Games designed as "gender neutral" look like games designed for boys. (Chuck Huff).

- 1989: Ethnographic research exploring women, programming, and computers (Sherry Turkle).

- 1995: Gender differences in self-efficacy and attitudes toward computers (Tor Busch).

- 1998: Gender factors in the design of video games (Justine Cassell).

- 2002: Wider displays more beneficial to all users, especially females (Mary Czerwinski, Desney S. Tan, George G. Robertson).

- 2004: The concept Gender HCI made explicit (Laura Beckwith, Margaret Burnett).

- 2006: A research workshop on Gender HCI.

Selected Gender HCI Findings

Here are some results from the Gender HCI research conducted to date - ordered from most to least recent, within categories:

1. "Reward Expectations of Gendered Computers."

   o In one experiment, subjects worked on a task with a computerized partner that was named James or Julie. The task was gender-neutral, meaning that it was not directly relevant to being a man or woman. The results showed that subjects behaved the same way toward a computer named James or Julie. Despite these similarities in behavior, subjects estimated that a computer named James would cost them significantly more than one named Julie. The findings show gender shape user perceptions of their computers, which lack the human features that define the characteristic of gender.

2. *Confidence-Related Findings.*

   o For spreadsheet problem-solving tasks, (1) female end users had significantly lower self-efficacy than males and (2) females with low self-efficacy were significantly less likely to work effectively with problem-solving features available in the software. In contrast, males' self-efficacy did not impact their effectiveness with these features.

o   In a study of the computer attitudes and self-efficacy of 147 college students, gender differences existed in self-efficacy for complex tasks (such as word processing and spreadsheet software), but not simpler tasks. Also, male students had more experience working with computers and reported more encouragement from parents and friends.

3. *Software Feature Related Findings.*

o   In spreadsheet problem-solving tasks, female end users were significantly slower to try out unfamiliar features. Females significantly more often agreed with the statement, "I was afraid I would take too long to learn the [untaught feature]." Even if they tried it once, females were significantly less likely to adopt new features for repeated use. For females, unlike for males, self-efficacy predicted the amount of effective feature usage. There was no significant difference in the success of the two genders or in learning how the features worked, implying that females' low self-efficacy about their usage of new features was not an accurate assessment of their problem-solving potential, but rather became a self-fulfilling prophecy.

4. *Behavior Related Findings.*

o   In spreadsheet problem-solving tasks, tinkering (playfully experimenting) with features was adopted by males more often than females. While males were comfortable with this behavior, some did it to excess. For females, the amount of tinkering predicted success. Pauses after any action were predictive of better understanding for both genders.

o   Males viewed machines as a challenge, something to be mastered, overcome, and be measured against. They were risk-takers, and they demonstrated this by eagerly trying new techniques and approaches. Females rejected the image of the male hacker as alienating and depersonalizing. Their approach to computers was "soft;" tactile, artistic, and communicative.

5. *Hardware Interface Findings.*

o   Larger displays helped reduce the gender gap in navigating virtual environments. With smaller displays, males' performance was better than females'. With larger displays, females' performance improved and males' performance was not negatively affected.

6. *Video Games Findings.*

o   Several findings were reported about girls' interests that relate to video games, with interpretations for the video game software industry.

o   Several researchers explored what girls seek in video games, and implications for video game designers. Among the implications were collaboration vs. competition preferences, and use of non-violent rewards versus death and destruction as rewards. These works argue both sides of the question as to whether or not to design games specifically for girls.

7. *Other Related Findings About Gender and Computers.*

o   In a study of the way people interacted with conversational software agents in relation to the sex of the agent, the female virtual agent received many more violent and sexual overtures than either the male one or the gender-free one (a robot).

o   In the home, where many appliances are programmable to some extent, different categories of appliance were found to be more likely to be programmed by men (e.g. entertainment devices) and by women (e.g. kitchen appliances). There is often one member of a household who assumes responsibility for programming a particular device, with a "domestic economy" accounting for this task.

o   Males and females had different perceptions for whether a web page would be appropriate for his/her home country, and further, females more often than males preferred more information on all web pages viewed during a study.

o   Women who entered mathematics, science, and technology careers had high academic and social self-efficacy. Their self-efficacy was based on vicarious experiences and verbal persuasion of significant people around them.

o   Factors affecting low retention of women in computer science majors in college included women's lower previous experience in computing compared to men, their low self-perceived ability, discouragement by the dominant male peer culture, and lack of encouragement from faculty.

Interaction Technique

An interaction technique, user interface technique or input technique is a combination of hardware and software elements that provides a way for computer users to accomplish a single task. For example, one can go back to the previously visited page on a Web browser by either clicking a button, pressing a key, performing a mouse gesture or uttering a speech command. It is a widely used term in human-computer interaction.

In particular, the term "new interaction technique" is frequently used to introduce a novel user interface design idea.

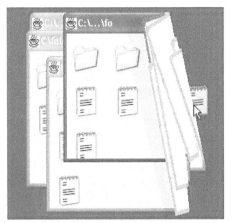

Fold n' Drop, a crossing-based interaction technique for dragging and dropping files between overlapping windows.

Definition

Although there is no general agreement on the exact meaning of the term "interaction technique", the most popular definition is from the computer graphics literature:

An interaction technique is a way of using a physical input/output device to perform a generic task in a human-computer dialogue.

A more recent variation is:

An interaction technique is the fusion of input and output, consisting of all software and hardware elements, that provides a way for the user to accomplish a task.

The Computing View

From the computer's perspective, an interaction technique involves:

- One or several input devices that capture user input,

- One or several output devices that display user feedback,

- A piece of software that:

    o interprets user input into commands the computer can understand,

    o produces user feedback based on user input and the system's state.

Consider for example the process of deleting a file using a contextual menu. This assumes the existence of a mouse (input device), a screen (output device), and a piece of code that paints a menu and updates its selection (user feedback) and sends a command to the file system when the user clicks on the "delete" item (interpretation). User feedback can be further used to confirm that the command has been invoked.

The user's view

From the user's perspective, an interaction technique is a way to perform a single computing task and can be informally expressed with user instructions or usage scenarios. For example, "to delete a file, right-click on the file you want to delete, then click on the delete item".

The Designer's View

From the user interface designer's perspective, an interaction technique is a well-defined solution to a specific user interface design problem. Interaction techniques as conceptual ideas can be refined, extended, modified and combined. For example, contextual menus are a solution to the problem of rapidly selecting commands. Pie menus are a radial variant of contextual menus. Marking menus combine pie menus with gesture recognition.

Level of Granularity

One extant cause of confusion in the general discussion of interaction is a lack of clarity about levels of granularity. Interaction techniques are usually characterized at a low level of granularity—not necessarily at the lowest level of physical events, but at a level that is technology-, platform-, and/or implementation-dependent. For example, interaction techniques exist that are specific to mobile devices, touch-based displays, traditional mouse/keyboard inputs, and other paradigms—in other words, they are dependent on a specific technology or platform. In contrast, viewed at higher levels of granularity, interaction is not tied to any specific technology or platform. The interaction of 'filtering', for example, can be characterized in a way that is technology-independent—e.g., performing an action such that some information is hidden and only a subset of the original information remains. Such an interaction could be implemented using any number of techniques, and on any number of platforms and technologies.

Interaction Tasks and Domain Objects

An interaction task is "the unit of an entry of information by the user", such as entering a piece of text, issuing a command, or specifying a 2D position. A similar concept is that of domain object, which is a piece of application data that can be manipulated by the user.

Interaction techniques are the glue between physical I/O devices and interaction tasks or domain objects. Different types of interaction techniques can be used to map a specific device to a specific domain object. For example, different gesture alphabets exist for pen-based text input.

In general, the less compatible the device is with the domain object, the more complex the interaction technique. For example, using a mouse to specify a 2D point involves a trivial interaction technique, whereas using a mouse to rotate a 3D object requires more creativity to design the technique and more lines of code to implement it.

A current trend is to avoid complex interaction techniques by matching physical devices with the task as close as possible, such as exemplified by the field of tangible computing. But this is not always a feasible solution. Furthermore, device/task incompatibilities are unavoidable in computer accessibility, where a single switch can be used to control the whole computer environment.

Interaction Style

Interaction techniques that share the same metaphor or design principles can be seen as belonging to the same interaction style. General examples are command line and direct manipulation user interfaces.

Interaction Patterns

While interaction techniques are typically technology-, platform-, and/or implementation-dependent, human-computer or human-information interactions can be characterized at higher levels of abstraction that are independent of particular technologies and platforms. At such levels of abstraction, the concern is not precisely how an interaction is performed; rather, the concern is a conceptual characterization of what the interaction is, and what the general utility of the interaction is for the user(s). Thus, any single interaction pattern may be instantiated by any number of interaction techniques, on any number of different technologies and platforms. Interaction patterns are more concerned with the timeless, invariant qualities of an interaction.

Visualization Technique

Interaction techniques essentially involve data entry and manipulation, and thus place greater emphasis on input than output. Output is merely used to convey affordances and provide user feedback. The use of the term *input technique* further reinforces the central role of input. Conversely, techniques that mainly involve data exploration and thus place greater emphasis on output are called visualization techniques. They are studied in the field of information visualization.

Research and Innovation

A large part of research in human-computer interaction involves exploring easier-to-learn or more efficient interaction techniques for common computing tasks. This includes inventing new (post-WIMP) interaction techniques, possibly relying on methods from user interface design, and assessing their efficiency with respect to existing techniques using methods from experimental psychology. Examples of scientific venues in these topics are the UIST and the CHI conferences. Other research focuses on the specification of interaction techniques, sometimes using formalisms such as Petri nets for the purposes of formal verification.

Look and Feel

In software design, *look and feel* is a term used in respect of a graphical user interface and comprises aspects of its design, including elements such as colors, shapes, layout, and typefaces (the "look"), as well as the behavior of dynamic elements such as buttons, boxes, and menus (the "feel"). The term can also refer to aspects of a non-graphical user interface (such as a command-line interface), as well as to aspects of an API – mostly to parts of an API that are not related to its functional properties. The term is used in reference to both software and websites.

Look and feel applies to other products. In documentation, for example, it refers to the graphical layout (document size, color, font, etc.) and the writing style. In the context of equipment, it refers to consistency in controls and displays across a product line.

Look and feel in operating system user interfaces serves two general purposes. First, it provides branding, helping to identify a set of products from one company. Second, it increases ease of use, since users will become familiar with how one product functions (looks, reads, etc.) and can translate their experience to other products with the same look and feel.

In Widget Toolkits

Contrary to operating system user interfaces, for which look and feel is a part of the product identification, widget toolkits often allow users to specialize their application look and feel, by deriving the default look and feel of the toolkit, or by completely defining their own. This specialization can go from skinning (that only deals with the look, or visual appearance of the graphical control elements to completely specializing the way the user interacts with the software (that is, the feel).

The definition of the look and feel to associate with the application is often done at initialization, but some Widget toolkits, such as the Swing widget toolkit that is part of the Java API, allow users to change the look and feel at runtime.

Some examples of Widget toolkits that support setting a specialized look and feel are:

- XUL (XML User Interface Language): The look and feel of the user interface can be specialized in a CSS file associated with the XUL definition files. Properties that can be specialized from the default are, for example, background or foreground colors of widgets, fonts, size of widgets, and so on.

- Swing supports specializing the look and feel of widgets by deriving from the default, another existing one, creating one from scratch, or, beginning with J2SE 5.0, in an XML property file called synth (skinnable look and feel).

Lawsuits Over

Some companies try to assert copyright of trade dress over their look and feel.

The *Broderbund v. Unison* (1986) case was an early software copyright case that attempted to apply U.S. copyright law to the look and feel presented by a software product.

Apple Computer was notable for its use of the term *look and feel* in reference to their Mac OS operating system. The firm tried, with some success, to block other software developers from creating software that had a similar look and feel. Apple argued that they had a copyright claim on the look and feel of their software, and even went so far as to sue Microsoft, alleging that the Windows operating system was illegally copying their look and feel.

Although provoking a vehement reaction from some in the software community, and causing Richard Stallman to form the League for Programming Freedom, the expected landmark ruling never happened, as most of the issues were resolved based on a license that Apple had granted Microsoft for Windows 1.0. The First Circuit Court of Appeals rejected a copyright claim on the feel of a user interface in *Lotus v. Borland*.

More recently, Apple Inc. has filed lawsuits against competing manufacturers of smartphones and tablet computers, claiming that those manufacturers copied the look and feel of Apple's popular iPhone and iPad products.

In APIs

An API, which is an interface to software which provides some sort of functionality, can also have a certain look and feel. Different parts of an API (e.g. different classes or packages) are often linked by common syntactic and semantic conventions (e.g. by the same asynchronous execution model, or by the same way object attributes are accessed). These elements are rendered either explicitly (i.e. are part of the syntax of the API), or implicitly (i.e. are part of the semantics of the API).

Mode (computer interface)

In user interface design, a mode is a distinct setting within a computer program or any physical machine interface, in which the same user input will produce perceived results different to those that it would in other settings. The best-known modal interface components are probably the Caps lock and Insert keys on the standard computer keyboard, both of which put the user's typing into a different mode after being pressed, then return it to the regular mode after being re-pressed.

An interface that uses no modes is known as a modeless interface. Modeless interfaces avoid mode errors by making it impossible for the user to commit them.

Definition

A precise definition is given by Jef Raskin in his book *The Humane Interface*:

"An human-machine interface is modal with respect to a given gesture when (1) the current state of the interface is not the user's locus of attention and (2) the interface will execute one among several different responses to the gesture, depending on the system's current state."

In Raskin's sense and according to his definition, an interface is not modal as long as the user is fully aware of its current state. Raskin refers to this as "locus of attention" (from the Latin word *locus* meaning "place" or "location"). Typically a user is aware of a system state if the state change was purposefully initiated by the user, or if the system gives some strong signals to notify the user of the state change in the place where inter- action occurs. If the user's locus of attention changes to a different area, the state of the interface may then represent a mode since the user is no longer aware of it.

Examples

Several examples of well-known software have been described as *modal* and/or using interface modes:

- Text editors – typically are in insert mode by default but can be toggled in and out of overtype mode by pressing the Insert key.

- vi – has one mode for inserting text, and a separate mode for entering com- mands. There is also an "ex" mode for issuing more complex commands (e.g. search and replace). Under normal circumstances, the editor automatically re- turns to the previous mode after a command has been issued; however, it is possible to permanently move into this mode using *Shift-Q*.

- Emacs – has the concept of "prefix keys", which trigger a modal state by press- ing the control key plus a letter key. Emacs then waits for additional keypresses that complete a keybinding. This differs from *vi* in that the mode always ends as soon as the command is called (when the sequence of key presses that activates it is completed). Emacs also has many "major and minor" modes that change the available commands, and may be automatically invoked based on file type to more easily edit files of that type. Emacs modes are not restricted to editing text files; modes exist for file browsing, web browsing, IRC and email and their interaction patterns are equivalent to application software within the Emacs environment. Modes are written in Emacs Lisp, and all modes may not be included with all versions.

- Cisco IOS – certain commands are executed in a "command mode".

- Tools chosen from a palette in photo-editing and drawing applications are examples of a modal interface. Some advanced image editors have a feature where the same tools can be accessed nonmodally by a keypress, and remain active as long as the key is held down. Releasing the key returns the interface to the modal tool activated by the palette.

- Video games can use game modes as a mechanic to enhance gameplay.

- Modal windows block all workflow in the top-level program until the modal window is closed.

Mode Errors

Modes are often frowned upon in interface design because they are likely to produce mode errors when the user forgets what state the interface is in, performs an action that is appropriate to a different mode, and gets an unexpected and undesired response. A mode error can be quite startling and disorienting as the user copes with the sudden violation of his or her user expectations.

Problems occur if a change in the system state happens unnoticed (initiated by the system, or by another person, such as the user who was previously using the machine), or if after some time the user forgets about the state change. Another typical problem is a sudden change of state that interrupts a user's activity, such as focus stealing. In such a situation it can easily happen that the user does some operations with the old state in mind, while the brain has not yet fully processed the signals indicating the state change.

A very frustrating type of modality is created by a mode where the user does not find a way out, in other words, where they cannot find how to restore the previous system state.

Examples of Mode Errors

- The most common source of mode errors may be the Caps Lock key. Other common modes available in PC keyboards are Insert and the other lock keys, Num lock and Scroll lock. Dead keys for diacritics also create a short-term mode, at least if they don't provide visual feedback that the next typed character will be modified.

- PC users whose language is not based on the Latin alphabet commonly have to interact using two different keyboard layouts: a local one and QWERTY. This gives rise to mode errors linked to the current keyboard layout: quite often, the synchronization of "current layout" mode between the human and the interface is lost, and text is typed in a layout which is not the intended one, producing meaningless text and confusion. Keyboard keys in UI elements like "(y/n)" can have opposite effect if a program is translated.

- A frequent example is the sudden appearance of a modal error dialog in an application while the user is typing, known as focus stealing; the user expects the typed text to be introduced into a text field, but the unexpected dialog may discard all the input, or may interpret some keystrokes (like "Y" for "yes" and "N" for "no") in a way that the user did not intend.

- The Unix text editor vi can be notoriously difficult for beginners precisely because it uses modes, and because earlier versions configured mode indication to be turned off by default.

- In many computer video games, the keyboard is used both for controlling the game and typing messages. A user may forget they are in "typing mode" as they attempt to react to something sudden in the game and find the controls unresponsive (and instead their text bar full of the command keys pressed).

In Aviation

According to the NTSB, one of the factors contributing to Asiana Airlines Flight 214 crash was *"the complexities of the autothrottle and autopilot flight director systems ... which increased the likelihood of mode error"*.

Assessment

Modes are intended to grab the user's full attention and to cause them to acknowledge the content present in them, in particular when critical confirmation from the user is required. This later use is criticised as ineffective for its intended use (protection against errors in destructive actions) due to habituation. Actually making the action reversible (providing an "undo" option) is recommended instead. Though modes can be successful in particular usages to restrict dangerous or undesired operations, especially when the mode is actively maintained by a user as a *quasimode*.

Modes are sometimes used to represent information pertinent to the task that doesn't fit well into the main visual flow. Modes can also work as well-understood conventions, such as painting tools.

Modal proponents may argue that many common activities are modal and users adapt to them. An example of modal interaction is that of driving motor vehicles. A driver may be surprised when pressing the acceleration pedal does not accelerate the vehicle in the forward direction, most likely because the vehicle has been placed in an operating mode like park, neutral, or reverse. Modal interfaces require training and experience to avoid mode errors like these.

Interface expert Jef Raskin came out strongly against modes, writing, "Modes are a significant source of errors, confusion, unnecessary restrictions, and complexity in interfaces." Later he notes, " 'It is no accident that swearing is denoted by #&%!#$&,' writes my colleague, Dr. James Winter; it is 'what a typewriter used to do when you typed numbers when the Caps Lock was engaged'." Raskin dedicated his book The Humane Interface to describe the principles of a modeless interface for computers. Those principles were implemented in the Canon Cat and Archy systems.

Some interface designers have recently taken steps to make modal windows more obvious and user friendly by darkening the background behind the window or allowing any mouse click outside of the modal window to force the window to close – a design called a Lightbox – thus alleviating the risk of modal errors. Jakob Nielsen states as an advantage of modal dialogs that it improves user awareness. "When something does need fixing, it's better to make sure that the user knows about it." For this goal, the Lightbox design provides strong visual contrast of the dialog over the rest of the visuals. However, while such a method may reduce the risk of inadvertent wrong interactions, it does not solve the problem that the modal window blocks use of the application's normal features and so prevents the user from taking any action to fix the difficulty, or even from scrolling the screen to bring into view information which they need to correctly choose from the options the modal window presents, and it does nothing to alleviate the user's frustration at having blundered into a dead end from which they cannot escape without some more or less destructive consequence.

Larry Tesler, of Xerox PARC and Apple Computer, disliked modes sufficiently to get a personalized license plate for his car that reads: "NO MODES". He has used this plate from the early 1980s to the present, on various cars. Along with others, he has also been using the phrase "Don't Mode Me In" for years as a rally cry to eliminate or reduce modes.

Bruce Wyman, the designer of a multi-touch table for a Denver Art Museum art exhibition argues that interfaces for several simultaneous users must be modeless, in order to avoid bringing any single user into focus.

Design Recommendations

Avoid When Possible

Alternatives to modes such as the undo command and the recycle bin are recommended when possible. HCI researcher Donald Norman argues that the best way to avoid mode errors, in addition to clear indications of state, is helping the users to construct an accurate mental model of the system which will allow them to predict the mode accurately.

Small signs make explicit the mappings from signal to roads

This is demonstrated, for example, by some stop signs at road intersections. A driver may be conditioned by a four-way stop sign near his or her home to assume that similar intersections will also be four way stops. If it happens to be only two way, the driver could proceed through if he or she sees no other cars. Especially if there is an obstructed view, a car could come though and hit the first car broadside. An improved design alleviates the problem by including a small diagram showing which of the directions have a stop sign and which don't, thus improving the situational awareness of drivers.

Proper Placement

Modal controls are best placed where the focus is in the task flow. For example, a modal window can be placed next to the graphical control element that triggers its activation. Modal controls can be disruptive, so efforts should be made to reduce their capacity to block user work. After completing the task for which the mode was activated, or after a cancel action such as the Escape key, returning to the previous state when a mode is dismissed will reduce the negative impact.

Quasimodes

In the book *The Humane Interface*, Jef Raskin championed what he termed *quasimodes*, which are modes that are kept in place only through some constant action on the part of the user; such modes are also called *spring-loaded modes*. The term *quasimode* is a composite of the Latin prefix *quasi-* (which means *almost, to some degree*) and the English word "mode".

Modifier keys on the keyboard, such as the Shift key, the Alt key and the Control key, are all examples of a quasimodal interface.

The application enters into that mode as long as the user is performing a conscious action, like pressing a key and keeping it pressed while invoking a command. If the sustaining action is stopped without executing a command, the application returns to a neutral status.

The purported benefit of this technique is that the user doesn't have to remember the current state of the application when invoking a command: the same action will always produce the same perceived result. An interface that uses quasimodes only and has no full modes is still modeless according to Raskin's definition.

The StickyKeys feature turns a quasimode into a mode by serializing keystrokes of modifier keys with normal keys, so that they don't have to be pressed simultaneously. In this case the increased possibility of a mode error is largely compensated for by the improved accessibility for users with physical disabilities.

References

- Holm, Ivar (2006). Ideas and Beliefs in Architecture and Industrial design: How attitudes, orientations, and underlying assumptions shape the built environment. Oslo School of Architecture and Design. ISBN 82-547-0174-1.

- Nielsen, Jakob (4 January 2012). "Usability 101: Introduction to Usability". Nielsen Norman Group. Retrieved 7 August 2016.

- Timothy B. Lee (2011-10-25). "Yes, Google "Stole" From Apple, And That's A Good Thing". Forbes. Retrieved 2015-08-13.

- Richard Stallman. "Is Digital Inclusion a Good Thing? How Can We Make Sure It Is?". gnu.org. Retrieved 2015-08-13.

- Josh Lowensohn (March 31, 2014). "Round two: Apple and Samsung suit up for another billion dollar patent war". The Verge. Retrieved 2015-08-13.

- Bohannon, John (December 19, 2013). "Click here to improve your motor skills". Science. Retrieved 23 December 2013.

3

Practices of Human-computer Interaction

The practices of human-computer interaction are user experience, first-time user experience, 3D interaction and 3D user interaction. User experience is the experience of users when they are using particular products or systems whereas first time user experience is the initial stage of using a particular software. The major practices of human-computer interactions are discussed in this chapter.

User Experience

User experience (UX) is a person's entire experience using a particular product, system or service. It includes the practical, experiential, affective, meaningful and valuable aspects of human–computer interaction and product ownership. Additionally, it includes a person's perceptions of system aspects such as utility, ease of use and efficiency. User experience may be considered subjective in nature to the degree that it is about individual perception and thought with respect to the system. User experience is dynamic as it is constantly modified over time due to changing usage circumstances and changes to individual systems as well as the wider usage context in which they can be found.

Definitions

The international standard on *ergonomics of human system interaction*, ISO 9241-210, defines user experience as "a person's perceptions and responses that result from the use or anticipated use of a product, system or service". According to the ISO definition, user experience includes all the users' emotions, beliefs, preferences, perceptions, physical and psychological responses, behaviors and accomplishments that occur before, during and after use. The ISO also list three factors that influence user experience: system, user and the context of use.

Note 3 of the standard hints that usability addresses aspects of user experience, e.g. "usability criteria can be used to assess aspects of user experience". The standard does not go further in clarifying the relation between user experience and usability. Clearly, the two are overlapping concepts, with usability including pragmatic aspects (getting a task done) and user experience focusing on users' feelings stemming both from pragmatic and hedonic aspects of the system. Many practitioners use the terms interchangeably. The term usability pre-dates the term user experience. Part of the reason the terms are often used interchangeably is that, as a practical matter, a user will at minimum require sufficient usability to accomplish a task, while the feelings of the user may be less important, even to the user herself. Since usability is about getting a task done, aspects of user experience like information architecture and user interface can help or hinder a user's experience. If a website has "bad" information architecture and a user has a difficult time finding what they are looking for, then a user will not have an effective, efficient and satisfying search.

In addition to the ISO standard, there exist several other definitions for user experience. Some of them have been studied by Law et al.

History

Early developments in User Experience can be traced back to the machine age that includes the 19th and early 20th centuries. Inspired by the machine age intellectual framework, a quest for improving assembly processes to increase production efficiency and output led to the development of major technological advancements, such as mass production of high-volume goods on moving assembly lines, high-speed printing press, large hydroelectric power production plants, and radio technology to name a few.

Frederick Winslow Taylor and Henry Ford were in the forefront of exploring new ways to make human labor more efficient and productive. Taylor's pioneering research into the efficiency of interactions between workers and their tools is the earliest example that resembles today's user experience fundamentals.

The term *user experience* was brought to wider knowledge by Donald Norman in the mid-1990s. He never intended the term "user experience" to be applied only to the affective aspects of usage. A review of his earlier work suggests that the term "user experience" was used to signal a shift to include affective factors, along with the pre-requisite behavioral concerns, which had been traditionally considered in the field. Many usability practitioners continue to research and attend to affective factors associated with end-users, and have been doing so for years, long before the term "user experience" was introduced in the mid-1990s. In an interview in 2007, Norman discusses the widespread use of the term "user experience" and its imprecise meaning as a consequence thereof.

Several developments affected the rise of interest in the user experience

1. Recent advances in mobile, ubiquitous, social, and tangible computing technologies have moved human-computer interaction into practically all areas of human activity. This has led to a shift away from usability engineering to a much richer scope of user experience, where users' feelings, motivations, and values are given as much, if not more, attention than efficiency, effectiveness and basic subjective satisfaction (i.e. the three traditional usability metrics).

2. In website design, it was important to combine the interests of different stake-holders: marketing, branding, visual design, and usability. Marketing and branding people needed to enter the interactive world where usability was important. Usability people needed to take marketing, branding, and aesthetic needs into account when designing websites. User experience provided a platform to cover the interests of all stakeholders: making web sites easy to use, valuable, and effective for visitors. This is why several early user experience publications focus on website user experience.

The field of user experience represents an expansion and extension of the field of usability, to include the holistic perspective of how a person feels about using a system. The focus is on pleasure and value as well as on performance. The exact definition, framework, and elements of user experience are still evolving.

User Experience of an interactive product or a web site is usually measured by a number of methods, including questionnaires, focus groups, and other methods. A freely available questionnaire (available in several languages) is the User Experience Questionnaire (UEQ). The development and validation of this questionnaire is described in

Google Ngram Viewer shows wide use of the term starting in the 1930s., "He suggested that more follow-up in the field would be welcomed by the user, and would be a means of incorporating the results of user's experience into the design of new machines." Use of the term in relation to computer software also pre-dates Norman.

Influences on User Experience

Many factors can influence a user's experience with a system. To address the variety, factors influencing user experience have been classified into three main categories: user's state and previous experience, system properties, and the usage context (situation). Understanding representative users, working environments, interactions and emotional reactions help in designing the system.

Momentary Emotion or Overall User Experience

Single experiences influence the overall user experience: the experience of a key click affects the experience of typing a text message, the experience of typing a message affects the experience of text messaging, and the experience of text messaging affects the overall user experience with the phone. The overall user experience is not simply a sum of smaller interaction experiences, because some experiences are more salient than others. Overall user experience is also influenced by factors outside the actual interaction episode: brand, pricing, friends' opinions, reports in media, etc.

One branch in user experience research focuses on emotions. This includes momentary experiences during interaction: designing affective interaction and evaluating emotions. Another branch is interested in understanding the long-term relation between user experience and product appreciation. The industry sees good overall user experience with a company's products as critical for securing brand loyalty and enhancing the growth of customer base. All temporal levels of user experience (momentary, episodic, and long-term) are important, but the methods to design and evaluate these levels can be very different.

First-time User Experience

In computer science, a first-time user experience (FTUE) refers to the initial stages of using a piece of software. Of particular importance are the configuration steps, such as signing up for an email account, or configuring a DVR. Every user of a service has his/her own FTUE, even if he/she has extensive experience with using a similar product. Patience, time investment, and intuitiveness are factors for a user's FTUE. Software services generally have different layouts, styles, graphics, and hotkeys which must be identified to contribute to a user's learning, mastery, and efficiency of the software. The FTUE is responsible for setting the stage for the experience of the user when interacting with a product down the line. This differs from the out-of-box experience (OOBE), which is specifically about packaging, information presentation, and setup of the system out of the box.

Relation to the Cold Start Problem

FTUEs are directly related to the well-known cold start problem in recommender systems, which attempts to balance the ease of the initial experience with the difficulty of gathering the needed information to make quality recommendations to the user. Generally, an effort is made to increase user retention by minimizing the barriers to entry while maximizing the quality of the recommendations for the user. For example, it was found that by changing the FTUE task from rating 15 *individual* items to rating a smaller number of *groups* of items, the time taken to complete the initial task was reduced by more than 50% and user satisfaction with the resulting recommendations increased.

However, there is evidence that steeper entry requirements can lead to more dedicated users. Furthermore, in a study at the University of Minnesota, it was found that increasing the barriers to entry can increase the amount of user-generated content produced during the FTUE without sacrificing the quality of the content. Users subjected to a more difficult FTUE may also be more likely to produce more content in the future. This comes at a tradeoff, as the user attrition rate gradually increases with a higher barrier to entry. In this light, the idea of the FTUE becomes one of maximizing the benefit to the online community and the quality of the recommendations while minimizing the increase in the rate of user attrition.

User Retention

Preventing customers from abandoning software after the initial exposure is a goal of good FTUE design. The following are examples of efforts in user retention.

- *Speed vs Quality*: First impressions on the initial user interface (UI) of an interactive application depend on multiple factors; most notably speed and quality. Speed and quality are not necessarily inversely related, but if there is a limit on the amount of development hours available for a project, one of the two will generally suffer. Depending on the application, a sacrifice in either speed or quality must usually be made. Sacrifices in quality can include fewer luxury features, less intuitive/advanced UI features, or minimal customization. Sacrifices in speed can result in overall sluggish performance or delayed responsiveness when interacting with external clients or servers. Both are important to the "feel" of the application, and thus factor into the FTUE.

- *Negative first time user experiences:* Negative FTUEs can severely impact user retention. Negative experiences can be related to over-complicated initial registration procedures. Requiring multiple stages of registration and email/phone verification can result in users abandoning the registration completely.

- *Social login:* This allows users to create an account based on pre-obtained information from social networking profiles such as Facebook. Popular applications such as Spotify, Quora, Pinterest and more offer this method of registration. Up to 92% of people have reported leaving websites permanently instead of recovering lost login information; social login can help combat this by converting monthly unique users to monthly active users. Social login also allows access to the user's friends or contacts. This offers up more opportunity personalization and potential virality considering up to 78% of people claim to have visited a website after seeing it mentioned on their social network, and that they heavily weigh their friends recommendations for purchases of products mentioned via social media.

- *Structured setup:* A set of clearly outlined steps to completion/registration is key for a successful FTUE. For example, Facebook registration clearly displays the number of steps remaining before the creation of a new profile is complete. This type of transparency is favorable because "uncertain, unexplained waits feel longer than known, finite waits." The more structured and clear the remaining time and number of steps remaining are, the more likely a user will be patient enough to go through and complete all of the steps required to get through the FTUE.

- *Paid upgrades:* Offering an opportunity to purchase an upgrade in the FTUE process can be advantageous considering that new users tend to be more motivated or enthusiastic. They will thereby be more likely to become paying customers instead of freemium users. After spending the time to install software and register, a user has shown at least moderate dedication to the technology and may be invested enough to pay for an upgrade they had not originally considered. Dropbox does this by offering more storage for a dollar amount per month with a simple, non-invasive question. Vimeo offers a professional package, as is common with many online services.

Prolonged User Experience

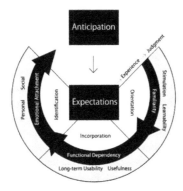

An illustration describing the temporality of experience for extended interaction with products.

While desired early experiences commonly seem to relate to pleasant sensational aspects of software and product use, prolonged experiences are significantly more tied to aspects that reflect how the product may become meaningful in the user's life. Social products are not solely responsible for mediating goal achievement; they fulfill an inner need for personal growth and communicating messages about the user's self-identity in a social setting. As a user's familiarity with a product strengthens over time, it is expected that they would experience less frustration, as well as less excitement. As a result, the perceived quality of the product is expected to change, and therefore the relative importance of different qualities in the product can also change over time. It is widely accepted that learnability and novelty are critical during initial phases of product use, however, other aspects such as a product's social capital are likely to motivate prolonged use.

The experience of a service or product's use is consistent of three main forces: *familiarity, functional dependency,* and *emotional attachment.* These three forces are responsible for shifting a users' experience across three phases: *orientation, incorporation,* and *identification,* respectively. The incorporation factor is the most significant user experience phase of the three. Incorporation makes long-term usability become much more important than the initial learnability, and the product's usefulness becomes the main factor impacting the product's overall value in the eye of the user. As the user accepts the product into their lives, it participates in normal social interactions, and integrates with part of the users self-identity that connects to others and creates a sense of community, building identification. The actual experience with the product has been found to be more influential to users' satisfaction than their prior expectations, though the act of anticipation and creation of expectations is a crucial part of the primary user experience. Sometimes anticipating experiences with a product becomes even more important, emotional, and memorable than the experiences itself.

Effective and successful services and products are *designed for daily rituals* and *designed for the self*. Users become attached to products that support a self-identity that they wish to communicate in certain settings. Products and self-identity have been a major part of consumer behavior research, but still remain largely unexplored in CHI and design research.

3D Interaction

In computing, 3D interaction is a form of human-machine interaction where users are able to move and perform interaction in 3D space. Both human and machine process information where the physical position of elements in the 3D space is relevant.

The 3D space used for interaction can be the real physical space, a virtual space representation simulated in the computer, or a combination of both. When the real space is used for data input, humans perform actions or give commands to the machine using an input device that detects the 3D position of the human action. When it is used for data output, the simulated 3D virtual scene is projected onto the real environment through one output device or a combination of them.

Background

3D's early beginnings can be traced back to 1962 when Morton Heilig invented the *Sensorama* simulator. It provided 3D video feedback, as well motion, audio, and haptic feedbacks to produce a virtual environment. The next stage of development was Dr. Ivan Sutherland's completion of his pioneering work in 1968. He created a head-mounted display that produced a 3D, virtual environment by presenting a left and right still image of that environment.

Availability of technology as well as impractical costs held back the development and application of virtual environments until the 1980s. Applications were limited to military ventures in the United States. Since then, further research and technological advancements have allowed new doors to be opened to application in various other areas such as education, entertainment, and manufacturing.

In 3D interaction, users carry out their tasks and perform functions by exchanging information with computer systems in 3D space. It is an intuitive type of interaction because humans interact in three dimensions in the real world. The tasks that users perform have been classified as selection and manipulation of objects in virtual space, navigation, and system control. Tasks can be performed in virtual space through interaction techniques and by utilizing interaction devices. 3D interaction techniques were classified according to the task group it supports. Techniques that support navigation tasks are classified as *navigation techniques*. Techniques that support object selection and manipulation are labeled *selection and manipulation techniques*. Lastly, *system control techniques* support tasks that have to do with controlling the application itself. A consistent and efficient mapping between techniques and interaction devices must be made in order for the system to be usable and effective. Interfaces associated with 3D interaction are called *3D interfaces*. Like other types of user interfaces, it involves two-way communication between users and system, but allows users to perform action in 3D space. Input devices permit the users to give directions and commands to the system, while output devices allow the machine to present information back to them.

3D interfaces have been used in applications that feature virtual environments, and augmented and mixed realities. In virtual environments, users may interact directly with the environment or use tools with specific functionalities to do so. 3D interaction occurs when physical tools are controlled in 3D spatial context to control a corresponding virtual tool.

Users experience a sense of presence when engaged in an immersive virtual world. Enabling the users to interact with this world in 3D allows them to make use of natural and intrinsic knowledge of how information exchange takes place with physical objects in the real world. Texture, sound, and speech can all be used to augment 3D interaction. Currently, users still have difficulty in interpreting 3D space visuals and understanding how interaction occurs. Although it's a natural way for humans to move around in a three-dimensional world, the difficulty exists because many of the cues present in real environments are missing from virtual environments. Perception and occlusion are the primary perceptual cues used by humans. Also, even though scenes in virtual space appear three-dimensional, they are still displayed on a 2D surface so some inconsistencies in depth perception will still exist.

3D User Interfaces

User interfaces are the means for communication between users and systems. 3D interfaces include media for 3D representation of system state, and media for 3D user input or manipulation. Using 3D representations is not enough to create 3D interaction. The users must have a way of performing actions in 3D as well. To that effect, special input and output devices have been developed to support this type of interaction. Some, such as the 3D mouse, were developed based on existing devices for 2D interaction.

Input Devices

Input devices are instruments used to manipulate objects, and send control instructions to the computer system. They vary in terms of degrees of freedom available to them and can be classified into standard input devices, trackers, control devices, navigation equipment, and gesture interfaces.

Standard input devices include keyboards, tablets and stylus, joysticks, mice, touch screens, knobs, and trackballs.

Trackers detect or monitor head, hand or body movements and send that information to the computer. The computer then translates it and ensures that position and orientation are reflected accurately in the virtual world. Tracking is important in presenting the correct viewpoint, coordinating the spatial and sound information presented to users as well the tasks or functions that they could perform. 3D trackers have been identified as mechanical, magnetic, ultrasonic, optical, and hybrid inertial. Examples of trackers include motion trackers, eye trackers, and data gloves.

A simple 2D mouse may be considered a navigation device if it allows the user to move to a different location in a virtual 3D space. Navigation devices such as the treadmill and bicycle make use of the natural ways that humans travel in the real world. Treadmills simulate walking or running and bicycles or similar type equipment simulate vehicular travel. In the case of navigation devices, the information passed on to the machine is the user's location and movements in virtual space.

Wired gloves and bodysuits allow gestural interaction to occur. These send hand or body position and movement information to the computer using sensors.

Output Devices

Output devices allow the machine to provide information or feedback to the user. They include visual displays, auditory displays, and haptic displays. Visual displays provide feedback to users in 3D visual form. Virtual reality headsets and CAVEs (Cave Automatic Virtual Environment) are examples of a fully immersive visual display, where the user can see only the virtual world and not the real world. Semi-immersive displays allow users to see both. Monitors and workbenches are examples of semi-immersive displays. Auditory displays provide information in auditory form. This is especially useful when supplying location and spatial information to the users. Adding background audio component to a display adds to the sense of realism. Haptic displays send tactile feedback or feeling back to the user.

3D Interaction Techniques

3D interaction techniques are methods used in order to execute different types of task in 3D space. Techniques are classified according to the tasks that they support.

Selection and Manipulation

Users need to be able to manipulate virtual objects. Manipulation tasks involve selecting and moving an object. Sometimes, rotation of the object is involved as well. Direct-hand manipulation is the most natural technique because manipulating physical objects with the hand is intuitive for humans. However, this is not always possible. A virtual hand that can select and re-locate virtual objects will work as well. 3D widgets can be used to put controls on objects: these are usually called 3D Gizmos or Manipulators (a good example are the ones from Blender). Users can employ these to re-locate, re-scale or re-orient an object (Translate, Scale, Rotate). Other techniques include the Go-Go technique and ray casting, where a virtual ray is used to point to, and select and object. More recently there has been user interface development and research by Richard White in Kansas over the past 3 years regarding interactive surfaces & classroom interactive whiteboards, grade school students, and 3D natural user interfaces known as Edusim.

Navigation

The computer needs to provide the user with information regarding location and movement. Navigation tasks have two components. Travel involves moving from the current location to the desired point. Wayfinding refers to finding and setting routes to get to a travel goal within the virtual environment.

- Wayfinding : Wayfinding in virtual space is different and more difficult to do than in the real world because synthetic environments are often missing perceptual cues and movement constraints. It can be supported using user-centred techniques such as using a larger field of view and supplying motion cues, or environment-centred techniques like structural organization and wayfinding principles.

- Travel : Good travel techniques allow the user to easily move through the environment. There are three types of travel tasks namely, exploration, search, and manoeuvring. Travel techniques can be classified into the following five categories:

  o Physical movement – user moves through the virtual world

  o Manual Viewpoint manipulation – use hand motions to achieve movement

  o Steering – direction specification

  o Target-based travel – destination specification

  o Route planning – path specification

System Control

Tasks that involve issuing commands to the application in order to change system mode or activate some functionality fall under the category of system control. Techniques that support system control tasks in three-dimensions are classified as:

- Graphical menus

- Voice commands

- Gestural interaction

- Virtual tools with specific functions

Symbolic Input

This task allows the user to enter and/or edit, for example, text, making it possible to annotate 3D scenes or 3D objects.

3D User Interaction

In 3D user interaction (3DUI) the humans interacts with a computer or other device with an aspect of three-dimensional space. This interaction is created thanks to the interfaces, which they will be the intermediaries between human and machine.

The 3D space used for interaction can be the real physical space, a virtual space representation simulated in the computer, or a combination of both. When the real physical space is used for data input, human interacts with machine performing actions using input device that should know the relative position and distance of the user action among other things. When it is used for data output, the simulated 3D virtual scene is projected onto the real environment through one output device.

History

Research in 3D interaction and 3D display began in the 1960s, pioneered by researchers like Ivan Sutherland, Fred Brooks, Bob Sproull, Andrew Ortony and Richard Feldman. But it was not until 1962 when Morton Heilig invented the Sensorama simulator. It provided 3D video feedback, as well motion, audio, and feedbacks to produce a virtual environment. The next stage of development was Dr. Ivan Sutherland's completion of his pioneering work in 1968, the Sword of Damocles. He created a head-mounted display that produced 3D virtual environment by presenting a left and right still image of that environment.

Availability of technology as well as impractical costs held back the development and application of virtual environments until the 1980s. Since then, further research and technological advancements have allowed new doors to be opened to application in various other areas such as education, entertainment, and manufacturing.

3D User Interfaces

3D user interfaces, are user interfaces where 3D interaction takes place, this means that the user's tasks occur directly within a three-dimensional space. The user must communiᴄᴀᴛᴇ ᴄᴏᴍᴍᴀɴᴅs, requests, questions, intent, and goals to the system, and in turn this one has to provide feedback, requests for input, information about their status, and so on.

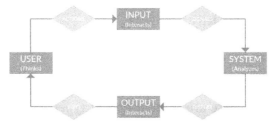

Scheme of 3D User Interaction phases

Both the user and the system do not have the same type of language, therefore to make possible the communication process, the interfaces must serve as intermediaries or translators between them.

The way the user transforms perceptions into actions is called Human transfer function, and the way the system transforms signals into display information is called System transfer function. 3D user interfaces are actually physical devices that communicate the user and the system with the minimum delay, in this case there are two types: 3D User Interface Output Hardware and 3D User Interface Input Hardware.

3D User Interface Output Hardware

These hardware devices are usually called display devices or output devices and their aim is to present information to one or more users through the human perceptual system. Most of them are focused on stimulating the visual, auditory, or haptic senses. However, in some unusual cases they also can stimulate the user's olfactory system.

3D Visual Displays

This type of devices are the most popular and its goal is to present the information produced by the system through the human visual system in a three-dimensional way. The main features that distinguish these devices are: field of regard and field of view, spatial resolution, screen geometry, light transfer mechanism, refresh rate and ergonomics.

Another way to characterize these devices is according to the different categories of depth perception cues used to achieve that the user can understand the three-dimensional information. The main types of displays used in 3D UIs are: monitors, surround-screen displays, workbenches, hemispherical displays, head-mounted displays, arm-mounted displays and autostereoscopic displays.

3D Audio Displays

3D Audio displays are devices that present information (in this case sound) through the human auditory system, its objective is to generate and display a spatialized 3D sound so the user can use its psychoacoustic skills and be able to determine the location and direction of the sound. There are different localizations cues: binaural cues, spectral and dynamic cues, head-related transfer functions, reverberation, sound intensity and vision and environment familiarity.

3D Haptic Displays

These devices use the sense of touch to simulate the physical interaction between the user and a virtual object. There are three different types of 3D Haptic displays: those that provide the user a sense of force, the ones that simulate the sense of touch and those that use both. The main features that distinguish these devices are: haptic presentation capability, resolution and ergonomics. The human haptic system has 2 fundamental kinds of cues, tactile and kinesthetic. Tactile cues are a type of human touch cues that have a wide variety of skin receptors located below the surface of the skin that provide information about the texture, temperature, pressure and damage. Kinesthetic cues are a type of human touch cues that have many receptors in the muscles, joints and tendons that provide information about the angle of joints and stress and length of muscles.

3D User Interface Input Hardware

These hardware devices are called input devices and their aim is to capture and interpret the actions performed by the user. The degrees of freedom (DOF) are one of the main features of these systems. These systems are also differentiated according to how much physical interaction is needed to use the device, purely active need to be manipulated to produce information, purely passive do not need to. The main categories of these devices are desktop input devices, tracking devices, 3D mice, brain-computer interface.

Desktop Input Devices

This type of devices are designed for an interaction 3D on a desktop, many of them have an initial design thought in a traditional interaction in two dimensions, but with an appropriate mapping between the system and the device, this can work perfectly in a three-dimensional way. There are different types of them: keyboards, 2D mice and trackballs, pen-based tablets and joysticks.

Tracking Devices

3D user interaction systems are based primarily on tracking technologies, to obtain all the necessary information from the user through the analysis of their movements or gestures, these technologies are called, tracking technologies.

For the full development of a 3D User Interaction system, is required to have access to a few basic parameters, all this technology-based system should know, or at least partially, as the relative position of the user, the absolute position, angular velocity, rotation data, orientation or height.

The collection of these data is achieved through systems of space tracking and sensors in multiple forms, as well as the use of different techniques to obtain. The ideal system for this type of interaction is a system based on the tracking of the position, using six degrees of freedom (6-DOF), these systems are characterized by the ability to obtain absolute 3D position of the user, in this way will get information on all possible three-dimensional field angles.

The implementation of these systems can be achieved by using various technologies, such as electromagnetic fields, optical, or ultrasonically tracking, but all share the main limitation, they should have a fixed external reference, either a base, an array of cameras, or a set of visible markers, so this single system can be carried out in prepared areas.

Inertial tracking systems do not require external reference such as those based on movement, are based on the collection of data using accelerometers, gyroscopes, or video cameras, without a fixed reference mandatory, in the majority of cases, the main problem of this system, is based on not obtaining the absolute position, since not part of any pre-set external reference point so it always gets the relative position of the user, aspect that causes cumulative errors in the process of sampling data.

The goal to achieve in a 3D tracking system would be based on obtaining a system of 6-DOF able to get absolute positioning and precision of movement and orientation, with a precision and an uncut space very high, a good example of a rough situation would be a mobile phone, since it has all the motion capture sensors and also GPS tracking of latitude, but currently these systems are not so accurate to capture data with a precision of centimeters and therefore would be invalid.

However, there are several systems that are closely adapted to the objectives pursued, the determining factor for them is that systems are auto content, i.e., all-in-one and does not require a fixed prior reference, these systems are as follows:

Nintendo Wii Remote ("Wiimote")

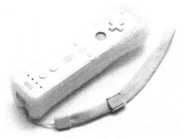

Wiimote device

The Wii Remote device does not offer a technology based on 6-DOF since again, cannot provide absolute position, in contrast, is equipped with a multitude of sensors, which convert a 2D device in a great tool of interaction in 3D environments.

This device has gyroscopes to detect rotation of the user, accelerometers ADXL3000, for obtaining speed and movement of the hands, optical sensors for determining orientation and electronic compasses and infra-red devices to capture the position.

Should be noted that this type of device can be affected by external references of infra-red light bulbs or candles, causing errors in the accuracy of the position.

Microsoft KINECT

Kinect Sensor

The Microsoft Kinect device offers us a different motion capture technology for tracking.

Instead of basing its operation on sensors, this is based on a structured light scanner, located in a bar, which allows tracking of the entire body through the detection of about 20 spatial points, of which 3 different degrees of freedom are measured to obtain position, velocity and rotation of each point.

Its main advantage is ease of use, and the no requirement of an external device attached by the user, and its main disadvantage lies in the inability to detect the orientation of the user, thus limiting certain space and guidance functions.

Leap Motion

Leap Motion Controller

The Leap Motion is a new system of tracking of hands, designed for small spaces, allowing a new interaction in 3D environments for desktop applications, so it offers a great fluidity when browsing through three-dimensional environments in a realistic way.

It is a small device that connects via USB to a computer, and used two cameras with infra-red light LED, allowing the analysis of a hemispheric area about 1 meter on its surface, thus recording responses from 300 frames per second, information is sent to the computer to be processed by the specific software company.

3D Interaction Techniques

3D Interaction Techniques are the different ways that the user can interact with the 3D virtual environment to execute different kind of tasks. The quality of these techniques has a profound effect on the quality of the entire 3D User Interfaces. They can be classified into three different groups: Navigation, Selection and manipulation and System control.

Navigation

Navigation is the most used by the user in big 3D environments and presents different challenges as supporting spatial awareness, giving efficient movements between distant places and making navigation bearable so the user can focus on more important tasks. These techniques can be divided into two components: travel and wayfinding.

Travel

Travel is a conceptual technique that consists in the movement of the viewpoint from one location to another. This orientation is usually handled in immersive virtual environments by head tracking. Exists five types of travel interaction techniques:

- Physical movement: uses the user's body motion to move through the virtual environment. Is an appropriate technique when is required an augmented perception of the feeling of being present or when is required physical effort form the user.

- Manual viewpoint manipulation: the user's hands movements determine the displacement on the virtual environment. One example could be when the user moves their hands in a way that seems like is grabbing a virtual rope and pulls his self up. This technique could be easy to learn and efficient, but can cause fatigue.

- Steering: the user has to constantly indicate where to move. Is a common and efficient technique. One example of this are the gaze-directed steering, where the head orientation determines the direction of travel.

- Target-based travel: user specifies a destination point and the system effectuates the displacement. This travel can be executed by teleport, where the user is instantly moved to the destination point or the system can execute some transition movement to the destiny. These techniques are very simple from the user's point of view because he only has to indicate the destination.

- Route planning: the user specifies the path that should be taken through the environment and the system executes the movement. The user may draw a path on a map of the virtual environment to plan a route. This technique allows users to control travel while they have the ability to do other tasks during motion.

Wayfinding

Is the cognitive process of defining a route for the virtual environment, using and acquiring spatial knowledge to construct a cognitive map of the virtual environment.

In order for a good wayfinding, users should receive wayfinding supports during the virtual environment travel to facilitate it because of the constraints from the virtual world.

These supports can be user-centered supports such as a large field-of-view or even non-visual support such as audio, or environment-centered support, artificial cues and structural organization to define clearly different parts of the environment. Some of the most used artificial cues are maps, compasses and grids, or even architectural cues like lighting, color and texture.

Selection and Manipulation

Selection and Manipulation techniques for 3D environments must accomplish at least one of three basic tasks: object selection, object positioning and object rotation.

To accomplish these tasks usually the system provides the user a 3D cursor represented as a human hand whose movements correspond to the motion of the hand tracker. This virtual hand technique is rather intuitive because simulates a real-world interaction with objects but with the limit of objects that we can reach inside a reach-area.

To avoid this limit, there are many techniques that have been suggested, like the Go-Go technique. This technique allows the user to extend the reach-area using a non-linear mapping of the hand: when the user extends the hand beyond a fixed threshold distance, the mapping becomes non-linear and the hand grows.

There is another way to select and manipulate objects in 3D virtual spaces and that is pointing objects using a virtual-ray emanating from the virtual hand. When the ray intersects with the objects, it can be manipulated. Several variations of this technique has been made, like the aperture technique, which uses a conic pointer addressed for the user's eyes, estimated from the head location, to select distant objects. This technique also uses a hand sensor to adjust the conic pointer size.

System Control

System control techniques allows the user to send commands to an application, change the interaction mode or modify a parameter. The command sender always includes the selection of an element from a set. System control techniques can be categorized into four groups:

- Graphical menus: visual representations of commands.

- Voice commands: menus accessed via voice.

- Gestural interaction: command accessed via body gesture.

- Tools: virtual objects with an implicit function or mode.

Also exists different hybrid techniques that combine some of the types.

Wizard of Oz experiment

In the field of human–computer interaction, a Wizard of Oz experiment is a research experiment in which subjects interact with a computer system that subjects believe to be autonomous, but which is actually being operated or partially operated by an unseen human being.

Concept

The phrase *Wizard of Oz* (originally *OZ Paradigm*) has come into common usage in the fields of experimental psychology, human factors, ergonomics, linguistics, and usability engineering to describe a testing or iterative design methodology wherein an experimenter (the "wizard"), in a laboratory setting, simulates the behavior of a theoretical intelligent computer application (often by going into another room and intercepting all communications between participant and system). Sometimes this is done with the participant's a-priori knowledge and sometimes it is a low-level deceit employed to manage the participant's expectations and encourage natural behaviors.

For example, a test participant may think he or she is communicating with a computer using a speech interface, when the participant's words are actually being secretly entered into the computer by a person in another room (the "wizard") and processed as a text stream, rather than as an audio stream. The missing system functionality that the wizard provides may be implemented in later versions of the system (or may even be speculative capabilities that current-day systems do not have), but its precise details are generally considered irrelevant to the study. In testing situations, the goal of such experiments may be to observe the use and effectiveness of a proposed user interface by the test participants, rather than to measure the quality of an entire system.

Origin

John F. ("Jeff") Kelley coined the phrases "Wizard of OZ" and "OZ Paradigm" for this purpose circa 1980 to describe the method he developed during his dissertation work at Johns Hopkins University. (His dissertation advisor was the late professor Alphonse Chapanis, the "Godfather of Human Factors and Engineering Psychology".) Amusingly enough, in addition to some one-way mirrors and such, there literally was a blackout curtain separating Jeff, as the "Wizard", from view by the participant during the study.

The "Experimenter-in-the-Loop" technique had been pioneered at Chapanis' Communications Research Lab at Johns Hopkins as early as 1975 (J. F. Kelley arrived in 1978). W. Randolph Ford used the experimenter-in-the-loop technique with his innovative CHECKBOOK program wherein he obtained language samples in a naturalistic setting. In Ford's method, a preliminary version of the natural language processing system would be placed in front of the user. When the user entered a syntax that was not recognized, they would receive a "Could you rephrase that?" prompt from the software. After the session, the algorithms for processing the newly obtained samples would be created or enhanced and another session would take place. This approach led to the eventual development of his natural language processing technique, "Multi-Stage Pattern Reduction". Dr. Ford's recollection was that Dr. Kelley did in fact coin the phrase "Wizard of Oz Paradigm" but that the technique had been employed in at least two separate studies before Dr. Kelley had started conducting studies at the Johns Hopkins Telecommunications Lab.

In that employment the experimenter (the "Wizard") sat at a terminal in an adjacent room separated by a one-way mirror so the subject could be observed. Every input from the user was processed correctly by a combination of software processing and real-time experimenter intervention. As the process was repeated in subsequent sessions, more and more software components were added so that the experimenter had less and less to do during each session until asymptote was reached on phrase/word dictionary growth and the experimenter could "go get a cup of coffee" during the session (which at this point was a cross-validation of the final system's unattended performance).

A final point: Dr. Kelley's recollection of the coinage of the term is backed up by that of the late professor Al Chapanis. In their 1985 University of Michigan technical report, Green and Wei-Haas state the following: *The first appearance of the "Wizard of Oz" name in print was in Jeff Kelley's thesis (Kelley, 1983a, 1983b, 1984a). It is thought the name was coined in response to a question at a graduate seminar at Hopkins (Chapanis, 1984; Kelley, 1984b). "What happens if the subject sees the experimenter [behind the "curtain" in an adjacent room acting as the computer]?" Kelley answered: "Well, that's just like what happened to Dorothy in the Wizard of Oz." And so the name stuck.* (Cited by permission.)

There is also a passing reference to planned use of the "Wizard of Oz experiments" in a 1982 proceedings paper by Ford and Smith.

One fact, presented in Kelley's dissertation, about the etymology of the term in this context: Dr. Kelley did originally have a definition for the "OZ" acronym (aside from the obvious parallels with the 1900 book The Wonderful Wizard of Oz by L. Frank Baum). "Offline Zero" was a reference to the fact that an experimenter (the "Wizard") was interpreting the users' inputs in real time during the simulation phase.

Similar experimental setups had occasionally been used earlier, but without the "Wizard of Oz" name. Design researcher Nigel Cross conducted studies in the 1960s with "simulated" computer-aided design systems where the purported simulator was actually a human operator, using text and graphical communication via CCTV. As he explained, "All that the user perceives of the system is this remote-access console, and the remainder is a black box to him. ... one may as well fill the black box with people as with machinery. Doing so provides a comparatively cheap simulator, with the remarkable advantages of the human operator's flexibility, memory, and intelligence, and which can be reprogrammed to give a wide range of computer roles merely by changing the rules of operation. It sometimes lacks the real computer's speed and accuracy, but a team of experts working simultaneously can compensate to a sufficient degree to provide an acceptable simulation." Cross later referred to this as a kind of Reverse Turing test.

Significance

The Wizard of OZ method (unlike the eponymous "wizard" in the film) *is* very powerful. In its original application, Dr. Kelley was able to create a simple keyboard-input natural language recognition system that far exceeded the recognition rates of any of the far more complex systems of the day.

The thinking current among many computer scientists and linguists at the time was that, in order for a computer to be able to "understand" natural language enough to be able to assist in useful tasks, the software would have to be attached to a formidable "dictionary" having a large number of categories for each word. The categories would enable a very complex parsing algorithm to unravel the ambiguities inherent in naturally produced language. The daunting task of creating such a dictionary led many to believe that computers simply would never truly "understand" language until they could be "raised" and "experience life" as humans, since humans seem to apply a life's worth of experiences to the interpretation of language.

The key enabling factor for the first use of the OZ method was that the system was designed to work in a single context (calendar-keeping), which constrained the complexity of language encountered from users to the extent where a simple language processing model was sufficient to meet the goals of the application. The processing model was a two-pass keyword/keyphrase matching approach, based loosely on the algorithms employed in Weizenbaum's famous Eliza program. By inducing participants to generate language samples in the context of solving an actual task (using a computer that they believed actually understood what they were typing), the variety and complexity of the lexical structures gathered was greatly reduced and simple keyword matching algorithms could be developed to address the actual language collected.

This first use of OZ was in the context of an iterative design approach. In the early development sessions, the experimenter simulated the system *in toto*, performing all the database queries and composing all the responses to the participants by hand. As the process matured, the experimenter was able to replace human interventions, piece by piece, with newly created developed code (which, at each phase, was designed to accurately process all the inputs that were generated in preceding steps). By the end of the process, the experimenter was able to observe the sessions in a "hands-off" mode (and measure the recognition rates of the completed program).

OZ was important because it addressed the obvious criticism:

> *Who can afford to use an iterative method to build a separate natural language system (dictionaries, syntax) for each new context? Wouldn't you be forever adding new structures and algorithms to handle each new batch of inputs?*

The answer turned out to be:

By using an empirical approach like OZ, anyone can afford to do this; Dr. Kelley's dictionary and syntax growth reached asymptote (achieving from 86% to 97% recognition rates, depending on the measurements employed) after only 16 experimental trials and the resulting program, with dictionaries, was less than 300k of code.

In the 23 years that followed initial publication, the OZ method has been employed in a wide variety of settings, notably in the prototyping and usability testing of proposed user interface designs in advance of having actual application software in place.

Fictional References

The name of the experiment comes from *The Wonderful Wizard of Oz* story, in which an ordinary man hides behind a curtain and pretends, through the use of "amplifying" technology, to be a powerful wizard.

In David Lodge's novel *Small World*, a university lecturer in English literature is introduced to a computer program named ELIZA, which he believes is capable of conducting a coherent conversation with him. It transpires that a computer lecturer is operating the computer and providing all the responses. The original ELIZA program, providing basic but often surprisingly human-like responses to questions, was written at MIT by Joseph Weizenbaum in the 1960s.

References

- Chang; Harper; Terveen (2015). "Using Groups of Items for Preference Elicitation in Recommender Systems" (PDF). Retrieved April 22, 2015.

- Drenner, Sara; Sen, Shilad; Terveen, Loren (2008). "Crafting The Initial User Experience to Achieve Community Goals" (PDF). Retrieved April 22, 2015.

- Belk, Russell (1988). "Possessions and the Extended Self" (PDF). The Journal of Consumer Research, Vol. 15, No. 2. 15: 139. doi:10.1086/209154. Retrieved April 21, 2015.

- Karapanos; Zimmerman; Forlizzi; Martens (2009). "User Experience Over Time: An Initial Framework" (PDF). Retrieved April 21, 2015.

4

Methods and Techniques in Human-computer Interaction

Methods and techniques are important components of any field of study. Some of the techniques discussed within this text are usability testing, heuristic evaluation, card sorting, drag and drop and point and click. Usability testing is the method that is used to evaluate a product by testing it on users. The following section elucidates the various techniques that are related to human-computer interaction.

Usability Testing

Usability testing is a technique used in user-centered interaction design to evaluate a product by testing it on users. This can be seen as an irreplaceable usability practice, since it gives direct input on how real users use the system. This is in contrast with usability inspection methods where experts use different methods to evaluate a user interface without involving users.

Usability testing focuses on measuring a human-made product's capacity to meet its intended purpose. Examples of products that commonly benefit from usability testing are foods, consumer products, web sites or web applications, computer interfaces, documents, and devices. Usability testing measures the usability, or ease of use, of a specific object or set of objects, whereas general human-computer interaction studies attempt to formulate universal principles.

What It is not

Simply gathering opinions on an object or document is market research or qualitative research rather than usability testing. Usability testing usually involves systematic observation under controlled conditions to determine how well people can use the product. However, often both qualitative and usability testing are used in combination, to better understand users' motivations/perceptions, in addition to their actions.

Rather than showing users a rough draft and asking, "Do you understand this?", usability testing involves watching people trying to *use* something for its intended purpose. For example, when testing instructions for assembling a toy, the test subjects should be given the instructions and a box of parts and, rather than being asked to comment on the parts and materials, they are asked to put the toy together. Instruction phrasing, illustration quality, and the toy's design all affect the assembly process.

Methods

Setting up a usability test involves carefully creating a scenario, or realistic situation, wherein the person performs a list of tasks using the product being tested while observers watch and take notes. Several other test instruments such as scripted instructions, paper prototypes, and pre- and post-test questionnaires are also used to gather feedback on the product being tested. For example, to test the attachment function of an e-mail program, a scenario would describe a situation where a person needs to send an e-mail attachment, and ask him or her to undertake this task. The aim is to observe how people function in a realistic manner, so that developers can see problem areas, and what people like. Techniques popularly used to gather data during a usability test include think aloud protocol, co-discovery learning and eye tracking.

Hallway Testing

Hallway testing is a quick, cheap method of usability testing in which randomly-selected people—e.g., those passing by in the hallway—are asked to try using the product or service. This can help designers identify "brick walls," problems so serious that users simply cannot advance, in the early stages of a new design. Anyone but project designers and engineers can be used (they tend to act as "expert reviewers" because they are too close to the project). The idea behind hallway usability testing began as an alternative to hiring trained or certified personnel to test a particular software or technology product. The idea is that you can go out and grab random individuals passing by an office in a hallway and get them to test a product being developed. Another way to think of it is that random individuals are gathered from the street and then assembled in the hallway before having them test a product under development.

Some experts believe that using hallway usability testing can reveal up to 95% of usability problems with a given interface or product. In some ways, the principle of hallway usability testing is similar to the old idea of "putting 1000 monkeys at 1000 typewriters"—there is the commonly acknowledged suggestion that, by doing this, companies can effectively test systems without investing in a core group of certified testers or other users whose skillset or experience may be expensive. In a lot of ways, hallway usability testing is like developing a beta testing phase, where the product or interface is constrained to a random sample group before it is released to the public.

Remote Usability Testing

In a scenario where usability evaluators, developers and prospective users are located in different countries and time zones, conducting a traditional lab usability evaluation creates challenges both from the cost and logistical perspectives. These concerns led to research on remote usability evaluation, with the user and the evaluators separated over space and time. Remote testing, which facilitates evaluations being done in the context of the user's other tasks and technology, can be either synchronous or asynchronous. The former involves real time one-on-one communication between the evaluator and the user, while the latter involves the evaluator and user working separately. Numerous tools are available to address the needs of both these approaches.

Synchronous usability testing methodologies involve video conferencing or employ remote application sharing tools such as WebEx. WebEx and GoToMeeting are the most commonly used technologies to conduct a synchronous remote usability test. However, synchronous remote testing may lack the immediacy and sense of "presence" desired to support a collaborative testing process. Moreover, managing inter-personal dynamics across cultural and linguistic barriers may require approaches sensitive to the cultures involved. Other disadvantages include having reduced control over the testing environment and the distractions and interruptions experienced by the participants' in their native environment. One of the newer methods developed for conducting a synchronous remote usability test is by using virtual worlds.

Asynchronous methodologies include automatic collection of user's click streams, user logs of critical incidents that occur while interacting with the application and subjective feedback on the interface by users. Similar to an in-lab study, an asynchronous remote usability test is task-based and the platforms allow you to capture clicks and task times. Hence, for many large companies this allows you to understand the WHY behind the visitors' intents when visiting a website or mobile site. Additionally, this style of user testing also provides an opportunity to segment feedback by demographic, attitudinal and behavioral type. The tests are carried out in the user's own environment (rather than labs) helping further simulate real-life scenario testing. This approach also provides a vehicle to easily solicit feedback from users in remote areas quickly and with lower organizational overheads. In recent years, conducting usability testing asynchronously has also become prevalent and allows testers to provide their feedback at their free time and in their own comfort at home.

Expert Review

Expert review is another general method of usability testing. As the name suggests, this method relies on bringing in experts with experience in the field (possibly from companies that specialize in usability testing) to evaluate the usability of a product.

A heuristic evaluation or usability audit is an evaluation of an interface by one or more human factors experts. Evaluators measure the usability, efficiency, and effectiveness of the interface based on usability principles, such as the 10 usability heuristics originally defined by Jakob Nielsen in 1994.

Nielsen's usability heuristics, which have continued to evolve in response to user research and new devices, include:

- Visibility of system status
- Match between system and the real world
- User control and freedom
- Consistency and standards
- Error prevention
- Recognition rather than recall
- Flexibility and efficiency of use
- Aesthetic and minimalist design
- Help users recognize, diagnose, and recover from errors
- Help and documentation

Automated Expert Review

Similar to expert reviews, automated expert reviews provide usability testing but through the use of programs given rules for good design and heuristics. Though an automated review might not provide as much detail and insight as reviews from people, they can be finished more quickly and consistently. The idea of creating surrogate users for usability testing is an ambitious direction for the artificial intelligence community.

A/B Testing

In web development and marketing, A/B testing or split testing is an experimental approach to web design (especially user experience design), which aims to identify changes to web pages that increase or maximize an outcome of interest (e.g., click-through rate for a banner advertisement). As the name implies, two versions (A and B) are compared, which are identical except for one variation that might impact a user's behavior. Version A might be the one currently used, while version B is modified in some respect. For instance, on an e-commerce website the purchase funnel is typically a good candidate for A/B testing, as even marginal improvements in drop-off rates can represent a significant gain in sales. Significant improvements can be seen through testing elements like copy text, layouts, images and colors.

Multivariate testing or bucket testing is similar to A/B testing but tests more than two versions at the same time.

Number of Test Subjects

In the early 1990s, Jakob Nielsen, at that time a researcher at Sun Microsystems, popularized the concept of using numerous small usability tests—typically with only five test subjects each—at various stages of the development process. His argument is that, once it is found that two or three people are totally confused by the home page, little is gained by watching more people suffer through the same flawed design. "Elaborate usability tests are a waste of resources. The best results come from testing no more than five users and running as many small tests as you can afford." Nielsen subsequently published his research and coined the term heuristic evaluation.

The claim of "Five users is enough" was later described by a mathematical model which states for the proportion of uncovered problems U

$$U = 1 - (1 - p)^n$$

where p is the probability of one subject identifying a specific problem and n the number of subjects (or test sessions). This model shows up as an asymptotic graph towards the number of real existing problems (see figure below).

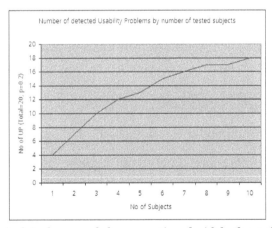

In later research Nielsen's claim has eagerly been questioned with both empirical evidence and more advanced mathematical models. Two key challenges to this assertion are:

1. Since usability is related to the specific set of users, such a small sample size is unlikely to be representative of the total population so the data from such a small sample is more likely to reflect the sample group than the population they may represent

2. Not every usability problem is equally easy-to-detect. Intractable problems happen to decelerate the overall process. Under these circumstances the progress of the process is much shallower than predicted by the Nielsen/Landauer formula.

It is worth noting that Nielsen does not advocate stopping after a single test with five users; his point is that testing with five users, fixing the problems they uncover, and then testing the revised site with five different users is a better use of limited resources than running a single usability test with 10 users. In practice, the tests are run once or twice per week during the entire development cycle, using three to five test subjects per round, and with the results delivered within 24 hours to the designers. The number of users actually tested over the course of the project can thus easily reach 50 to 100 people.

In the early stage, when users are most likely to immediately encounter problems that stop them in their tracks, almost anyone of normal intelligence can be used as a test subject. In stage two, testers will recruit test subjects across a broad spectrum of abilities. For example, in one study, experienced users showed no problem using any design, from the first to the last, while naive user and self-identified power users both failed repeatedly. Later on, as the design smooths out, users should be recruited from the target population.

When the method is applied to a sufficient number of people over the course of a project, the objections raised above become addressed: The sample size ceases to be small and usability problems that arise with only occasional users are found. The value of the method lies in the fact that specific design problems, once encountered, are never seen again because they are immediately eliminated, while the parts that appear successful are tested over and over. While it's true that the initial problems in the design may be tested by only five users, when the method is properly applied, the parts of the design that worked in that initial test will go on to be tested by 50 to 100 people.

Example

A 1982 Apple Computer manual for developers advised on usability testing:

1. "Select the target audience. Begin your human interface design by identifying your target audience. Are you writing for businesspeople or children?"

2. Determine how much target users know about Apple computers, and the subject matter of the software.

3. Steps 1 and 2 permit designing the user interface to suit the target audience's needs. Tax-preparation software written for accountants might assume that its users know nothing about computers but are expert on the tax code, while such software written for consumers might assume that its users know nothing about taxes but are familiar with the basics of Apple computers.

Apple advised developers, "You should begin testing as soon as possible, using drafted friends, relatives, and new employees":

Our testing method is as follows. We set up a room with five to six computer systems. We schedule two to three groups of five to six users at a time to try out the systems (often without their knowing that it is the software rather than the system that we are testing). We have two of the designers in the room. Any fewer, and they miss a lot of what is going on. Any more and the users feel as though there is always someone breathing down their necks.

Designers must watch people use the program in person, because

Ninety-five percent of the stumbling blocks are found by watching the body language of the users. Watch for squinting eyes, hunched shoulders, shaking heads, and deep, heart-felt sighs. When a user hits a snag, he will assume it is "on account of he is not too bright": he will not report it; he will hide it ... Do not make assumptions about why a user became confused. Ask him. You will often be surprised to learn what the user thought the program was doing at the time he got lost.

Education

Usability testing has been a formal subject of academic instruction in different disciplines.

Heuristic Evaluation

A heuristic evaluation is a usability inspection method for computer software that helps to identify usability problems in the user interface (UI) design. It specifically involves evaluators examining the interface and judging its compliance with recognized usability principles (the "heuristics"). These evaluation methods are now widely taught and practiced in the new media sector, where UIs are often designed in a short space of time on a budget that may restrict the amount of money available to provide for other types of interface testing.

Introduction

The main goal of heuristic evaluations is to identify any problems associated with the design of user interfaces. Usability consultant Jakob Nielsen developed this method on the basis of several years of experience in teaching and consulting about usability engineering.

Heuristic evaluations are one of the most informal methods of usability inspection in the field of human-computer interaction. There are many sets of usability design heuristics; they are not mutually exclusive and cover many of the same aspects of user interface design.

Quite often, usability problems that are discovered are categorized—often on a numeric scale—according to their estimated impact on user performance or acceptance. Often the heuristic evaluation is conducted in the context of use cases (typical user tasks), to provide feedback to the developers on the extent to which the interface is likely to be compatible with the intended users' needs and preferences.

The simplicity of heuristic evaluation is beneficial at the early stages of design. This usability inspection method does not require user testing which can be burdensome due to the need for users, a place to test them and a payment for their time. Heuristic evaluation requires only one expert, reducing the complexity and expended time for evaluation. Most heuristic evaluations can be accomplished in a matter of days. The time required varies with the size of the artifact, its complexity, the purpose of the review, the nature of the usability issues that arise in the review, and the competence of the reviewers. Using heuristic evaluation prior to user testing will reduce the number and severity of design errors discovered by users. Although heuristic evaluation can uncover many major usability issues in a short period of time, a criticism that is often leveled is that results are highly influenced by the knowledge of the expert reviewer(s). This "one-sided" review repeatedly has different results than software performance testing, each type of testing uncovering a different set of problems.

Nielsen's Heuristics

Jakob Nielsen's heuristics are probably the most-used usability heuristics for user interface design. Nielsen developed the heuristics based on work together with Rolf Molich in 1990. The final set of heuristics that are still used today were released by Nielsen in 1994. The heuristics as published in Nielsen's book *Usability Engineering* are as follows:

1. Visibility of system status: The system should always keep users informed about what is going on, through appropriate feedback within reasonable time.

2. Match between system and the real world: The system should speak the user's language, with words, phrases and concepts familiar to the user, rather than system-oriented terms. Follow real-world conventions, making information appear in a natural and logical order.

3. User control and freedom: Users often choose system functions by mistake and will need a clearly marked "emergency exit" to leave the unwanted state without having to go through an extended dialogue. Support undo and redo.

4. Consistency and standards: Users should not have to wonder whether different words, situations, or actions mean the same thing. Follow platform conventions.

5. Error prevention: Even better than good error messages is a careful design which prevents a problem from occurring in the first place. Either eliminate error-prone conditions or check for them and present users with a confirmation option before they commit to the action.

6. Recognition rather than recall: Minimize the user's memory load by making objects, actions, and options visible. The user should not have to remember

information from one part of the dialogue to another. Instructions for use of the system should be visible or easily retrievable whenever appropriate.

7. Flexibility and efficiency of use: Accelerators—unseen by the novice user—may often speed up the interaction for the expert user such that the system can cater to both inexperienced and experienced users. Allow users to tailor frequent actions.

8. Aesthetic and minimalist design: Dialogues should not contain information which is irrelevant or rarely needed. Every extra unit of information in a dialogue competes with the relevant units of information and diminishes their relative visibility.

9. Help users recognize, diagnose, and recover from errors: Error messages should be expressed in plain language (no codes), precisely indicate the problem, and constructively suggest a solution.

10. Help and documentation: Even though it is better if the system can be used without documentation, it may be necessary to provide help and documentation. Any such information should be easy to search, focused on the user's task, list concrete steps to be carried out, and not be too large.

Gerhardt-Powals' Cognitive Engineering Principles

Although Nielsen is considered the expert and field leader in heuristics, Jill Gerhardt-Powals also developed a set of cognitive principles for enhancing computer performance. These heuristics, or principles, are similar to Nielsen's heuristics but take a more holistic approach to evaluation. Gerhardt Powals' principles are listed below.

- Automate unwanted workload:

    o   free cognitive resources for high-level tasks.

    o   eliminate mental calculations, estimations, comparisons, and unnecessary thinking.

- Reduce uncertainty:

    o   display data in a manner that is clear and obvious.

- Fuse data:

    o   reduce cognitive load by bringing together lower level data into a higher-level summation.

- Present new information with meaningful aids to interpretation:

    o   use a familiar framework, making it easier to absorb.

- o   use everyday terms, metaphors, etc.
- Use names that are conceptually related to function:
    - o   Context-dependent.
    - o   Attempt to improve recall and recognition.
    - o   Group data in consistently meaningful ways to decrease search time.
- Limit data-driven tasks:
    - o   Reduce the time spent assimilating raw data.
    - o   Make appropriate use of color and graphics.
- Include in the displays only that information needed by the user at a given time.
- Provide multiple coding of data when appropriate.
- Practice judicious redundancy.

Weinschenk and Barker classification

Susan Weinschenk and Dean Barker created a categorization of heuristics and guidelines by several major providers into the following twenty types:

1. User Control: heuristics that check whether the user has enough control of the interface.

2. Human Limitations: the design takes into account human limitations, cognitive and sensorial, to avoid overloading them.

3. Modal Integrity: the interface uses the most suitable modality for each task: auditory, visual, or motor/kinesthetic.

4. Accommodation: the design is adequate to fulfill the needs and behaviour of each targeted user group.

5. Linguistic Clarity: the language used to communicate is efficient and adequate to the audience.

6. Aesthetic Integrity: the design is visually attractive and tailored to appeal to the target population.

7. Simplicity: the design will not use unnecessary complexity.

8. Predictability: users will be able to form a mental model of how the system will behave in response to actions.

9. Interpretation: there are codified rules that try to guess the user intentions and anticipate the actions needed.

10. Accuracy: There are no errors, i.e. the result of user actions correspond to their goals.

11. Technical Clarity: the concepts represented in the interface have the highest possible correspondence to the domain they are modeling.

12. Flexibility: the design can be adjusted to the needs and behaviour of each particular user.

13. Fulfillment: the user experience is adequate.

14. Cultural Propriety: user's cultural and social expectations are met.

15. Suitable Tempo: the pace at which users works with the system is adequate.

16. Consistency: different parts of the system have the same style, so that there are no different ways to represent the same information or behavior.

17. User Support: the design will support learning and provide the required assistance to usage.

18. Precision: the steps and results of a task will be what the user wants.

19. Forgiveness: the user will be able to recover to an adequate state after an error.

20. Responsiveness: the interface provides enough feedback information about the system status and the task completion.

Card Sorting

Card sorting is a technique in user experience design in which a person tests a group of subject experts or users to generate a dendrogram (category tree) or folksonomy. It is a useful approach for designing information architecture, workflows, menu structure, or web site navigation paths.

Card sorting uses a relatively low-tech approach. The person conducting the test (usability analyst, user experience designer, etc.) first identifies key concepts and writes them on index cards or Post-it notes. Test subjects, individually or sometimes as a group, then arrange the cards to represent how they see the structure and relationships of the information.

Groups can be organised as collaborative groups (focus groups) or as repeated individual sorts. The literature discusses appropriate numbers of users needed to produce trustworthy results.

A card sort is commonly undertaken when designing a navigation structure for an environment that offers a variety of content and functions, such as a web site. In that context, the items to organize are those significant in the environment. The way the items are organized should make sense to the target audience and cannot be determined from first principles.

The field of information architecture is founded on the study of the structure of information. If an accepted and standardized taxonomy exists for a subject, it would be natural to apply that taxonomy to organize both the information in the environment, and any navigation to particular subjects or functions. Card sorting is useful when:

- The variety of items to organize is so great that no existing taxonomy is accepted as organizing the items.

- Similarities among the items make them difficult to divide clearly into categories.

- Members of the audience that uses the environment differ significantly in how they view the similarities among items and the appropriate groupings of items.

Basic Method

To perform a card sort:

1. A person representative of the audience receives a set of index cards with terms written on them.

2. This person groups the terms in whatever way they think is logical, and gives each group a category name, either from an existing card or by writing a name on a blank card.

3. Testers repeat this process across a group of test subjects.

4. The testers later analyze the results to discover patterns.

Variants

Open Card Sorting

In an open card sort, participants create their own names for the categories. This helps reveal not only how they mentally classify the cards, but also what terms they use for the categories. Open sorting is generative; it is typically used to discover patterns in how participants classify, which in turn helps generate ideas for organizing information.

Closed Card Sorting

In a closed card sort, participants are provided with a predetermined set of category names. They then assign the index cards to these fixed categories. This helps reveal the degree to which the participants agree on which cards belong under each category. Closed sorting is evaluative; it is typically used to judge whether a given set of category names provides an effective way to organize a given collection of content.

Reverse Card Sorting

In a reverse card sort (more popularly called tree testing), an existing structure of categories and sub-categories is tested. Users are given tasks and are asked to complete them navigating a collection of cards. Each card contains the names of subcategories related to a category, and the user should find the card most relevant to the given task starting from the main card with the top-level categories. This ensures that the structure is evaluated in isolation, nullifying the effects of navigational aids, visual design, and other factors. Reverse card sorting is evaluative—it judges whether a predetermined hierarchy provides a good way to find information.

Analysis

Various methods can be used to analyze the data. The purpose of the analysis is to extract patterns from the population of test subjects, so that a common set of categories and relationships emerges. This common set is then incorporated into the design of the environment, either for navigation or for other purposes. Card sorting is also evaluated through dendrograms. There is some indication that different evaluation methods for card sorting provide different results.

Card sorting is an established technique with an emerging literature.

Online (Remote) Card Sorting

A number of web-based tools are available to perform card sorting. The perceived advantage of web-based card sorting is that it reaches a larger group of participants at a lower cost. The software can also help analyze the sort results. A perceived disadvantage of a remote card sort is the lack of personal interaction between card sort participants and the card sort administrator, which may produce valuable insights.

Cut, Copy, and Paste

In human–computer interaction, cut and paste and copy and paste are related commands that offer a user-interface interprocess communication technique for transferring data. The cut command removes the selected data from its original position, while the copy command creates a duplicate; in both cases the selected data is kept in a temporary place called the clipboard. The data in the clipboard is later inserted in the position where the paste command is issued.

The command names are an interface metaphor based on the physical procedure used in manuscript editing to create a page layout.

This interaction technique has close associations with related techniques in graphical user interfaces that use pointing devices such as a computer mouse (by drag and drop, for example).

The capability to replicate information with ease, changing it between contexts and applications, involves privacy concerns because of the risks of disclosure when handling sensitive information. Terms like *cloning, copy forward, carry forward,* or *re-use* refer to the dissemination of such information through documents, and may be subject to regulation by administrative bodies.

History

Origins

The term *"cut and paste"* comes from the traditional practice in manuscript-editings whereby people would cut paragraphs from a page with scissors and paste them onto another page. This practice remained standard into the 1980s. Stationery stores formerly sold "editing scissors" with blades long enough to cut an 8½"-wide page. The advent of photocopiers made the practice easier and more flexible.

The act of copying/transferring text from one part of a computer-based document ("buffer") to a different location within the same or different computer-based document was a part of the earliest on-line computer editors. As soon as computer data entry moved from punch-cards to online files (in the mid/late 1960s) there were "commands" for accomplishing this operation. This mechanism was often used to transfer frequently-used commands or text snippets from additional buffers into the document, as was the case with the QED editor.

Early Methods

The earliest editors, since they were designed for teleprinter terminals, provided keyboard commands to delineate contiguous regions of text, remove such regions, or move them to some other location in the file. Since moving a region of text required first removing it from its initial location and then inserting it into its new location various schemes had to be invented to allow for this multi-step process to be specified by the user.

Often this was done by the provision of a 'move' command, but some text editors required that the text be first put into some temporary location for later retrieval/placement. In 1983, the Apple Lisa became the first text editing system to call that temporary location "the clipboard".

Earlier control schemes such as NLS used a verb-object command structure, where the command name was provided first and the object to be copied or moved was second. The inversion from verb-object to object-verb on which copy and paste are based, where the user selects the object to be operated before initiating the operation, was an innovation crucial for the success of the desktop metaphor as it allowed copy and move operations based on direct manipulation.

Popularization

Inspired by early line and character editors that broke a move or copy operation into two steps—between which the user could invoke a preparatory action such as navigation—Lawrence G. Tesler (Larry Tesler) proposed the names "cut" and "copy" for the first step and "paste" for the second step. Beginning in 1974, he and colleagues at Xerox Corporation Palo Alto Research Center (PARC) implemented several text editors that used cut/copy-and-paste commands to move/copy text.

Apple Computer widely popularized the computer-based cut/copy-and-paste paradigm through the Lisa (1983) and Macintosh (1984) operating systems and applications. Apple mapped the functionalities to key combinations consisting of the Command key (a special modifier key) held down while typing the letters X (for cut), C (for copy), and V (for paste), choosing a handful of keyboard shortcuts to control basic editing operations. The keys involved all cluster together at the left end of the bottom row of the standard QWERTY keyboard, and each key is combined with a special modifier key to perform the desired operation:

- Z to undo

- X to cut

- C to copy

- V to paste

The IBM Common User Access (CUA) standard also uses combinations of the Insert, Del, Shift and Control keys. Early versions of Windows used the IBM standard. Microsoft later also adopted the Apple key combinations with the introduction of Windows, using the control key as modifier key.

Similar patterns of key combinations, later borrowed by others, remain widely available today in most GUI text editors, word processors, and file system browsers.

Cut and Paste

Computer-based editing can involve very frequent use of cut-and-paste operations. Most software-suppliers provide several methods for performing such tasks, and this can involve (for example) key combinations, pulldown menus, pop-up menus, or toolbar buttons.

1. The user selects or "highlights" the text or file for moving by some method, typically by dragging over the text or file name with the pointing-device or holding down the Shift key while using the arrow keys to move the text cursor

2. The user performs a "cut" operation via key combination Ctrl+x (⌘+x for Macintosh users), menu, or other means

3. Visibly, "cut" text immediately disappears from its location. "Cut" files typically change color to indicate that they will be moved.

4. Conceptually, the text has now moved to a location often called the clipboard. The clipboard typically remains invisible. On most systems only one clipboard location exists, hence another cut or copy operation overwrites the previously stored information. Many UNIX text-editors provide multiple clipboard entries, as do some Macintosh programs such as Clipboard Master, and Windows clipboard-manager programs such as the one in Microsoft Office.

5. The user selects a location for insertion by some method, typically by clicking at the desired insertion point

6. A *paste* operation takes place which visibly inserts the clipboard text at the insertion point. (The paste operation does not typically destroy the clipboard text: it remains available in the clipboard and the user can insert additional copies at other points)

Whereas cut-and-paste often takes place with a mouse-equivalent in Windows-like GUI environments, it may also occur entirely from the keyboard, especially in UNIX text editors, such as Pico or vi. Cutting and pasting without a mouse can involve a selection (for which Ctrl+x is pressed in most graphical systems) or the entire current line, but it may also involve text after the cursor until the end of the line and other more sophisticated operations.

When a software environment provides *cut* and *paste* functionality, a nondestructive operation called *copy* usually accompanies them; *copy* places a copy of the selected text in the clipboard without removing it from its original location.

The clipboard usually stays invisible, because the operations of cutting and pasting, while actually independent, usually take place in quick succession, and the user (usually) needs no assistance in understanding the operation or maintaining mental context. Some application programs provide a means of viewing, or sometimes even editing, the data on the clipboard.

Copy and Paste

The term "copy-and-paste" refers to the popular, simple method of reproducing text or other data from a source to a destination. It differs from cut and paste in that the original source text or data does not get deleted or removed. The popularity of this method stems from its simplicity and the ease with which users can move data between various applications visually - without resorting to permanent storage.

Once one has copied data into the clipboard, one may paste the contents of the clipboard into a destination document.

The X Window System maintains an additional clipboard containing the most recently selected text; middle-clicking pastes the content of this "selection" clipboard into whatever the pointer is on at that time.

Most terminal emulators and some other applications support the key combinations Ctrl-Insert to copy and Shift-Insert to paste. This is in accordance with the IBM Common User Access (CUA) standard.

Find and Go

The NeXTStep operating system extended the concept of having a single copy buffer by adding a second system-wide Find buffer used for searching. The Find buffer is also available in Mac OS X.

Text can be placed in the Find buffer by either using the Find panel or by selecting text and hitting ⌘E.

The text can then be searched with Find Next ⌘G and Find Previous ⌘D

The functionality comes in handy when for example editing source code. To find the occurrence of a variable or function name elsewhere in the file, simply select the name by double clicking, hit ⌘E and then jump to the next or previous occurrence with ⌘G / ⌘D

Note that this does *not* destroy your copy buffer as with other UIs like Windows or X-Windows.

Together with copy and paste this can be used for quick and easy replacement of repeated text:

- select the text that you want to replace (i.e. by double clicking)
- put the text in the Find buffer with ⌘E
- overwrite the selected text with your replacement text
- select the replacement text (try ⌥⇧← to avoid lifting your hands from the keyboard)
- copy the replacement text ⌘C
- find the next or previous occurrence ⌘G / ⌘D

- paste the replacement text ⌘V

- repeat the last two steps as often as needed

or in short:

- select ⌘ E replstr ⌫⇧← ⌘C ⌘G⌘V ⌘G⌘V ...

While this might sound a bit complicated at first, it is often *much* faster than using the find panel, especial when only a few occurrences shall be replaced or when only some of the occurrences shall be replaced. When a text shall not be replaced, simply hit ⌘G again to skip to the next occurrence.

The find buffer is system wide. That is, if you enter a text in the find panel (or with ⌘E) in one application and then switch to another application you can immediately start searching without having to enter the search text again.

Common Keyboard Shortcuts

	Cut	Copy	Paste
Apple	Command+X	Command-C	Command-V
Windows/ GNOME/KDE	Control-X / Shift-Delete	Control-C / Control-Insert	Control-V / Shift-Insert
GNOME/KDE terminal emulators		Shift-Control-C / Control-Insert	Shift-Control-V / Shift-Control-Insert (Shift-Insert for pasting selected text)
BeOS	Alt-X	Alt-C	Alt-V
Common User Access	Shift+Delete	Control+Insert	Shift+Insert
Emacs	Control-W (to mark) Control-K (to end of line)	meta-W (to mark)	Control-Y
vi	d (delete)	y (yank)	p (put)
X Window System		click-and-drag to highlight	middle mouse button

Copy and Paste Automation

Copying data one by one from one application to another, such as from Excel to a web form, might involve a lot of manual work. Copy and paste can be automated with the help of a program that would iterate through the values list and paste them to the active application window. Such programs might come in the form of macros or dedicated programs which involve more or less scripting. Alternatively, applications supporting simultaneous editing may be used to copy or move collections of items.

Additional Differences between Moving and Copying

In a spreadsheet, moving (cut and paste) need not equate to copying (copy and paste) and then deleting the original: when moving, references to the moved cells may move accordingly.

Windows Explorer also differentiates moving from merely copy-and-delete: a "cut" file will not actually disappear until pasted elsewhere and cannot be pasted more than once. The icon fades to show the transient "cut" state until it is pasted somewhere. Cutting a second file while the first one is cut will release the first from the "cut" state and leave it unchanged. Shift+Delete cannot be used to cut files; instead it deletes them without using the Recycle bin.

Multiple Clipboards

Several editors allow copying text into or pasting text from specific clipboards, typically using a special keystroke-sequence to specify a particular clipboard-number.

Clipboard managers can be very convenient productivity-enhancers by providing many more features than system-native clipboards. Thousands of clips from the clip history are available for future pasting, and can be searched, edited, or deleted. Favorite clips that a user frequently pastes (for example, the current date, or the various fields of a user's contact info) can be kept standing ready to be pasted with a few clicks or keystrokes.

Similarly, a kill ring provides a LIFO stack used for cut-and-paste operations as a type of clipboard capable of storing multiple pieces of data. For example, the GNU Emacs text editor provides a kill ring. Each time a user performs a cut or copy operation, the system adds the affected text to the ring. The user can then access the contents of a specific (relatively numbered) buffer in the ring when performing a subsequent paste-operation. One can also give kill-buffers individual names, thus providing another form of multiple-clipboard functionality.

Use in Healthcare

Concerns have been raised over the use of copy and paste functions in healthcare documentation and electronic health records. There is potential for the introduction of errors, information overload, and fraud.

Use in Software Development

Copy and paste programming is an antipattern arising from the blind pasting of pre-existing code into another source code file.

Drag and Drop

An image is dragged onto a web browser icon, which opens the image in the web browser.

In computer graphical user interfaces, drag and drop is a pointing device gesture in which the user selects a virtual object by "grabbing" it and dragging it to a different location or onto another virtual object. In general, it can be used to invoke many kinds of actions, or create various types of associations between two abstract objects.

As a feature, drag-and-drop support is not found in all software, though it is sometimes a fast and easy-to-learn technique. However, it is not always clear to users that an item can be dragged and dropped, or what is the command performed by the drag and drop, which can decrease usability.

Actions

The basic sequence involved in drag and drop is:

- Move the pointer to the object

- Press, and hold down, the button on the mouse or other pointing device, to "grab" the object

- "Drag" the object to the desired location by moving the pointer to this one

- "Drop" the object by releasing the button

Dragging requires more physical effort than moving the same pointing device without holding down any buttons. Because of this, a user cannot move as quickly and precisely while dragging (see Fitts' law). However, drag-and-drop operations have the advantage of thoughtfully chunking together two operands (the object to drag, and the drop location) into a single action. Extended dragging and dropping (as in graphic design) can stress the mousing hand.

A design problem appears when the same button selects and drags items. Imprecise movement can cause a dragging when the user just wants to select.

Another problem is that the target of the dropping can be hidden under other objects.

The user would have to stop the dragging, make both the source and the target visible and start again. In classic Mac OS the top-of-screen menu bar served as a universal "drag cancel" target. This issue has been dealt with in Mac OS X with the introduction of Exposé.

In Mac OS

Drag and drop, called click and drag at the time, was used in the original Macintosh to manipulate files (for example, copying them between disks or folders.). System 7 added the ability to open a document in an application by dropping the document icon onto the application's icon.

In System 7.5, drag and drop was extended to common clipboard operations like copying or moving textual content within a document. Content could also be dragged into the filesystem to create a "clipping file" which could then be stored and reused.

For most of its history Mac OS has used a single button mouse with the button covering a large portion of the top surface of the mouse. This may mitigate the ergonomic concerns of keeping the button pressed while dragging.

In OS/2

The Workplace Shell of OS/2 uses dragging and dropping extensively with the secondary mouse button, leaving the primary one for selection and clicking. Its use like that of other advanced Common User Access features distinguished native OS/2 applications from platform-independent ports.

In HTML

The HTML5 working draft specification includes support for drag & drop. HTML5 supports different kinds of dragging and dropping features including:

- Drag and Drop texts and HTML codes

- Drag and Drop HTML elements

- Drag and Drop files

Based on needed action, one of the above types can be used. Note that when an HTML element is dragged for moving its current position, its ID is sent to the destination parent element; so it sends a text and can be considered as the first group.

Google's web-based e-mail application Gmail supports drag-and-drop of images and attachments in the latest Google Chrome browser and Apple's Safari (5.x). And Google Image search supports drag & drop.

On a Touch Screen

Touch screen interfaces also include drag and drop, or more precisely, long press, and then drag, e.g. on the iPhone or Android home screens.

In end-user Programming

Drag and drop is considered an important program construction approach in many end-user development systems. In contrast to more traditional, text-based programming languages, many end-user programming languages are based on visual components such as tiles or icons that are manipulated by end users through drag-and-drop interfaces. Drag and drop is also featured in many shader editing programs for graphics tools, such as Blender. Drag and drop also features in some video game engines, including Unreal Engine, GameMaker: Studio, Construct 2 and, with expansion, Unity (game engine).

Point and Click

Point and click are the actions of a computer user moving a pointer to a certain location on a screen (*pointing*) and then pressing a button on a mouse, usually the left button (*click*), or other pointing device. An example of point and click is in hypermedia, where users click on hyperlinks to navigate from document to document.

Point and click can be used with any number of input devices varying from mouses, touch pads, trackpoint, joysticks, scroll buttons, and roller balls.

User interfaces, for example graphical user interfaces, are sometimes described as "point-and-click interfaces", often to suggest that they are very easy to use, requiring that the user simply point to indicate their wishes. These interfaces are sometimes referred to condescendingly (e.g., by Unix users) as "click-and-drool interfaces".

The use of this phrase to describe software implies that the interface can be controlled solely through the mouse (or some other means such as a stylus), with little or no input from the keyboard, as with many graphical user interfaces.

Hovering and Tooltips

Demonstrations of tooltip usage are prevalent on Web pages. Many graphical Web browsers display the title attribute of an HTML element as a tooltip when a user hovers the mouse cursor over that element, in such a Hypertext Markup Language over Wikipedia images and hyperlinks and see a tooltip appear.

A web browser tooltip displayed for a hyperlink.

In some systems, such as Internet Explorer, moving the pointer over a link (or other GUI control) and waiting for a split-second can cause a tooltip to be displayed.

Single Click

A single click or click is the act of pressing a computer mouse button once without moving the mouse. Single clicking is usually a primary action of the mouse. Single clicking, by default in many operating systems, selects (or highlights) an object while double-clicking executes or opens the object. The single click has many advantages over double click due the reduced time needed to complete the action. The single-click or one-click phrase has also been used to apply to the commercial field as a competitive advantage. The slogan "single click" or "one click" has become very common to show clients the ease of use of their services.

On Icons

By default on most computer systems, for a person to select a certain software function, he or she will have to click on the left button. An example of this can be a person clicking on an icon. Similarly, clicking on the right button will present the user with a text menu to select more actions. These actions can range from open, explore, properties, etc. In terms of entertainment software, point-and-click interfaces are common input methods, usually offering a 'menu' or 'icon bar' interface that functions in the expected manner. In other games, the character explores different areas within the game world. To move to another area, the player will move the cursor to one point of the screen, where the cursor will turn into an arrow. Clicking will then move the player to that area.

On Text

In many text processing programs, such as web browsers or word processors, clicking on text moves the cursor to that location. Clicking and holding the left button will allow users to highlight the selected text enabling the user with more options to edit or use the text.

Double Click

Double click is most commonly used with a computer mouse when the pointer is placed over an icon or object and the button is quickly pressed twice. This action, when performed without moving the location of the mouse, will produce a double click.

Context Clicks

Fitts's Law

Fitts's law can be used to quantify the time required to perform a point-and-click action.

$$T = a + b \log_2(1 + \frac{D}{W}) \text{ where:}$$

- *T* is the average time taken to complete the movement.

- *a* represents the start/stop time of the device and *b* stands for the inherent speed of the device. These constants can be determined experimentally by fitting a straight line to measured data.

- *D* is the distance from the starting point to the center of the target.

- *W* is the width of the target measured along the axis of motion. *W* can also be thought of as the allowed error tolerance in the final position, since the final point of the motion must fall within $\pm \dfrac{W}{2}$ of the target's centre.

References

- Chalil Madathil, Kapil; Joel S. Greenstein (May 2011). "Synchronous remote usability testing: a new approach facilitated by virtual worlds". Proceedings of the 2011 annual conference on Human factors in computing systems. CHI '11: 2225–2234. doi:10.1145/1978942.1979267. ISBN 9781450302289.

- Nielsen, Jakob (1994). Usability Engineering. San Diego: Academic Press. pp. 115–148. ISBN 0-12-518406-9.

- Dennis G. Jerz (July 19, 2000). "Usability Testing: What Is It?". Jerz's Literacy Weblog. Retrieved June 29, 2016.

- Breuch, Lee-Ann; Mark Zachry; Clay Spinuzzi (April 2001). "Usability Instruction in Technical Communication Programs" (PDF). Journal of Business and Technical Communication. 15 (2): 223–240. doi:10.1177/105065190101500204. Retrieved 3 March 2014.

- Laubach, Lori; Wakefield, Catherine (June 8, 2012). "Cloning and Other Compliance Risks in Electronic Medical Records" (PDF). Moss Adams LLP, MultiCare. Retrieved April 23, 2014.

- "Appropriate Use of the Copy and Paste Functionality in Electronic Health Records" (PDF). American Health Information Management Association. March 17, 2014. Retrieved April 23, 2014.

Models and laws Related to Human-computer Interaction

The study of the time it takes for a professional to complete a task without errors using a computer system is known as the keystroke level model. Human processor models are used to calculate the time it takes to perform a particular task. This chapter helps the reader in understanding all the models and laws related to human-computer interactions.

GOMS

GOMS is a specialized human information processor model for human-computer interaction observation that describes a user's cognitive structure on four components. In the book *The Psychology of Human Computer Interaction.* written in 1983 by Stuart K. Card, Thomas P. Moran and Allen Newell, the authors introduce: "a set of Goals, a set of Operators, a set of Methods for achieving the goals, and a set of Selections rules for choosing among competing methods for goals." GOMS is a widely used method by usability specialists for computer system designers because it produces quantitative and qualitative predictions of how people will use a proposed system.

Overview

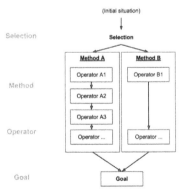

The concepts behind a GOMS model and their relationships

A GOMS model is composed of methods that are used to achieve specific goals. These methods are then composed of operators at the lowest level. The operators are specific steps that a user performs and are assigned a specific execution time. If a goal can be achieved by more than one method, then selection rules are used to determine the proper Method.

- Goals are symbolic structures that define a state of affairs to be achieved and determinate a set of possible methods by which it may be accomplished

- Operators are elementary perceptual, motor or cognitive acts, whose execution is necessary to change any aspect of the user's mental state or to affect the task environment

- Methods describe a procedure for accomplishing a goal

- Control Structure: Selection Rules are needed when a goal is attempted, there may be more than one method available to the user to accomplish it.

There are several different GOMS variations which allow for different aspects of an interface to be accurately studied and predicted. For all of the variants, the definitions of the major concepts are the same. There is some flexibility for the designer's/analyst's definition of all of the entities. For instance, an operator in one method may be a goal in a different method. The level of granularity is adjusted to capture what the particular evaluator is examining. For a simple applied example see CMN-GOMS.

Qualification

Advantages

The GOMS approach to user modeling has strengths and weaknesses. This method is not necessarily the most accurate method to measure human-computer interface interaction but it certainly has its advantages, like the visibility of all procedural knowledge. With GOMS an analyst can easily estimate a particular interaction and can calculate it with little effort in a short amount of time and at little cost. This is only possible if the average Methods-Time Measurement data for each specific task has previously been measured experimentally to a high degree of accuracy.

Disadvantages

GOMS only applies to skilled users. It does not work for beginners or intermediates for errors may occur which can alter the data. Also the model doesn't apply to learning the system or a user using the system after a longer time of not using it. Another big disadvantage is the lack of account for errors, even skilled users make errors but GOMS does not account for errors. Mental workload is not addressed in the model, making this an unpredictable variable. The same applies to fatigue. GOMS only addresses the usability of a task on a system, it does not address its functionality. User personalities, habits or physical restrictions (for example disabilities) are not accounted for in any of the GOMS models. All users are assumed to be exactly the same.

Recently some extensions of GOMS were developed, that allow to formulate GOMS models describing the interaction behavior of disabled users.

Variations

Basically there are four different GOMS models: the Keystroke-Level Model , CMN-GOMS, NGOMSL and CPM-GOMS. Each model has a different complexity and varies in activities.

KLM

The Keystroke-Level Model (KLM) is the first and simplest GOMS technique Stuart Card, Thomas P. Moran and Allen Newell created. Estimating an execution time for a task is done by listing the sequence of operators and then totaling the execution times for the individual operators. With KLM the analyst must specify the method used to accomplish each particular task instance. Furthermore, the specified methods are limited to being in sequence form and containing only keystroke-level primitive operators.

KLM's execution part is described in four physical-motor operators:

- K keystroking/ keypressing

- P pointing with a mouse to a target

- H homing the hand on the keyboard

- D drawing a line segment on a grid

One mental operator M that stands for the time a user has to mentally prepare himself to do an action, and a system response operator R in with the user has to wait for the system. Execution time is the sum of the times spent executing the different operator types:

$$T\text{execute} = T\text{K} + T\text{P} + T\text{H} + T\text{D} + T\text{M} + T\text{R}.$$

Each of these operators has an estimate of execution time, either a single value, a parameterized estimate.

Touch Level Model (TLM)

GOMS and it variants were designed for keyboard interfaces, nowadays a new type of interface is omnipresent. This addition to the GOMS family, together with updates to the existing KLM operators, is called the Touch Level Model (TLM). Andrew D. Rice and Jonathan W. Lartigue propose this model for the used to model human task performance on a constrained input touchscreen device and, with proper benchmarking, accurately predict actual user performance.

The goal is to provide an instrument for quantitative analysis of touchscreen interfaces. A number of operators are added for touchscreen interactions:

- Distraction (X) a multiplicative operator that is applied to other operators to model real world distractions

- Gesture (G) gestures are conceptualized as specialized combinations of finger movements across the device's screen

- Pinch (P) refers to the common two-finger gesture

- Zoom (Z) the reverse application of the Pinch operator. value in MS = 200 Ms

- Initial Act (I) KLM assumed the user is prepared to begin an action, touchscreen devices require users to prepare them for use (home button or password)

- Tap (T) operator refers to the physical action of tapping an area on the touchscreen device in order to initiate some change or action

- Swipe (S) usually a horizontally or vertically swipe like changing the page in a book. value in MS = 70 Ms

- Tilt (L(d)) used with an interacting with a devices equipped with accelerometers.

- Rotate (O(d)) gesture in which two or more fingers are placed on the screen and then rotated about a central point

- Drag (D) similar to Swipe, Drag also involves tapping a location on the screen and then moving one or more fingers in specific direction

CMN-GOMS

CMN-GOMS is the original GOMS model proposed by Stuart Card, Thomas P. Moran and Allen Newell. CMN stands for Card, Moran and Newell and it takes the KLM as its basic and adds subgoals and selection rules. This model can predict operator sequence as well as execution time. A CMN-GOMS model can be represented in program form, making it amenable to analysis as well as execution. CMN-GOMS has been used to model word processors and CAD systems for ergonomic design. The CMN method can predict the operator sequence and the execution time of a task on a quantitative level and can focus its attention on methods to accomplish goals on a qualitative level. In the example by Bonnie E. John and David E. Kieras a simple CMN-GOMS on editing a manuscript is shown.

GOAL: EDIT-MANUSCRIPT

GOAL: EDIT-UNIT-TASK ...repeat until no more unit tasks

GOAL: ACQUIRE UNIT-TASK ...if task not remembered

```
GOAL: TURN PAGE ...if at end of manuscript

GOAL: GET-FROM-MANUSCRIPT

GOAL: EXECUTE-UNIT-TASK ...if a unit task was found

GOAL: MODIFY-TEXT

select: GOAL: MOVE-TEXT* ...if test is to be moved

GOAL: DELETE-PHRASE ...if a phrase is to be deleted

GOAL: INSERT-WORD ... if a word is to be inserted

VERIFY-EDIT
```

NGOMSL

NGOMSL is a structured natural language notation for representing GOMS models and a procedure for constructing them. This program form provides predictions of operator sequences, execution time and time to learn methods. An analyst constructs an NGOMSL model by performing a top-down, breadth-first expansion of the user's top-level goals into methods, until the methods contain only primitive operators, typically keystroke-level operators. This model explicitly represents the goal structure just like the CMN-GOMS and can so represent high-level goals. Shown below is a simple example.

```
NGOMSL Statements

METHOD for GOAL: MOVE TEXT

STEP 1: ACCOMPLISH GOAL: CUT TEXT

STEP 2: ACCOMPLISH GOAL: PASTE TEXT

STEP 3: RETURN WITH GOAL ACCOMPLISHED

METHOD for GOAL: CUT TEXT

STEP 1: ACCOMPLISH GOAL: HIGHLIGHT TEXT

STEP 2: RETAIN THAT COMMAND IS CUT, AND

ACCOMPLISH GOAL: ISSUE A COMMAND

STEP 3: RETURN WITH GOAL ACCOMPLISHED etc.
```

CPM-GOMS

Bonnie E. John and David Kieras describe four different types of GOMS. CMN-GOMS, KLM and NGOMSL assume that all of the operators occur in sequence and do not contain operators that are below the activity level. CPM-GOMS being the fourth method uses operators at the level of Model Human Processor which assumes that operators of the cognitive processor, perceptual processor, and the motor processor can work in parallel to each other. The most important point of CPM-GOMS is the ability to predict skilled behavior from its ability to model overlapping actions.

Shown below is a simple copy and paste example.

```
GOAL COPY-AND-PASTE-TEXT

GOAL COPY-TEXT

GOAL HIGHLIGH-TEXT

Operator MOVE-CURSOR-TO-BEGINNING

Operator CLICK-MOUSE-BUTTON

Operator MOVE-CURSOR-TO-END

Operator SHIFT-CLICK-MOUSE-BUTTON

Operator VERIFY-HIGHLIGHT

GOAL ISSUE-COPY-COMMAND

Select*:

GOAL USE-MOUSE

Operator MOVE-CURSOR-TO-EDIT-MENU

Operator PRESS-MOUSE-BUTTON

Operator MOVE-CURSOR-TO-COPY-ITEM

Operator VERIFY-HIGHLIGHT

Operator RELEASE-MOUSE-BUTTON

GOAL USE-KEYBOARD

Operator PRESS-KEY-STRG

Operator PRESS-KEY-C

Operator RELEASE-KEYS

GOAL PASTE-TEXT[...]

*Selection rule for GOAL ISSUE-COPY-COMMAND if HANDS-ARE-ON-KEYBOARD then

select GOAL USE-KEYBOARD

else

select GOAL USE-MOUSE
```

GOMS and KLM

The biggest difference between GOMS and KLM is how time is assigned to cognitive and perceptual operators when it comes to execution time predictions. Another major difference is that the goal-hierarchy is explicit in GOMS while it was implicit in the KLM. The nature of unobservable operators is another important difference. KLM has a single M operator that precedes each cognitive unit of action. In contrast, GOMS assigns no time to such cognitive overhead. But both models include M-like operators for substantial time-consuming mental actions such as locating information on the screen and verifying entries. Both methods assign roughly the same time to unobservable perceptual and cognitive activities. Also they make different assumptions about unobservable cognitive and perceptual operators and so distribute the time in different ways.

Assumptions and Errors

Importance of Assumptions in GOMS Analysis

Accurate assumptions are vital in GOMS analysis. Before applying the average times for detailed functions, it is very important that an experimenter make sure he or she has accounted for as many variables as possible by using assumptions. Experimenters should design their GOMS analysis for the users who will most likely be using the system which is being analyzed. Consider, for example, an experimenter wishes to determine how long it will take an F22 Raptor pilot to interact with an interface he or she has used for years. It can probably be assumed that the pilot has outstanding vision and is in good physical health. In addition, it can be assumed that the pilot can interact with the interface quickly because of the vast hours of simulation and previous use he or she has endured. All things considered, it is fair to use fastman times in this situation. Contrarily, consider an 80-year-old person with no flight experience attempting to interact with the same F22 Raptor interface. It is fair to say that the two people would have much different skill sets and those skill sets should be accounted for subjectively.

Accounting for Errors

The only way to account for errors in GOMS analysis is to predict where the errors are most likely to occur and measure the time it would take to correct the predicted errors. For example, assume an experimenter thought that in typing the word "the" it was likely that a subject would instead incorrectly type "teh." The experimenter would calculate the time it takes to type the incorrect word, the time it takes to recognize that a mistake has been made, and the time it takes to correct the recognized error.

Applications of GOMS

A successful implementation of CPM-GOMS was in *Project Ernestine* held by New England Telephone. New ergonomically designed workstations were compared to old workstations in terms of improvement in telephone operators' performance. CPM-GOMS analysis estimated a 3% decrease in productivity. Over the four-month trial 78,240 calls were analysed and it was concluded that the new workstations produced an actual 4% decrease in productivity. As the proposed workstation required less keystrokes than the original it was not clear from the time trials why the decrease occurred. However CPM-GOMS analysis made it apparent that the problem was that the new workstations did not utilize the workers' slack time. Not only did CPM-GOMS give a close estimate, but it provided more information of the situation.

CAD

GOMS models were employed in the redesign of a CAD (computer-aided design) system for industrial ergonomics. An applied GOMS model shows where the interface needs to be redesigned, as well as provides an evaluation of design concepts and ideas. In Richard Gong's example, when GOMS revealed a frequent goal supported by a very inefficient method, he changed the method to a more efficient one. If GOMS showed that there were goals not supported by any method at all, then new methods were added. GOMS also revealed where similar goals are supported by inconsistent methods, a situation in which users are likely to have problems remembering what to do, and showed how to make the methods consistent.

Software Tools

There exist various tools for the creation and analysis of Goms-Models. A selection is listed in the following:

- QGoms (Quick-Goms)
- CogTool KLM-based modelling tool
- Cogulator Cognitive calculator for GOMS modeling

Keystroke-level Model

In human–computer interaction, the keystroke-level model (KLM) predicts how long it will take an expert user to accomplish a routine task without errors using an interactive computer system. It was proposed by Stuart K. Card, Thomas P. Moran and Allen Newell in 1980 in the *Communications of the ACM* and published in their book *The Psychology of Human-Computer Interaction* in 1983, which is considered as a classic in the HCI field. The foundations were laid in 1974, when Card and Moran joined the Palo Alto Research Center (PARC) and created a group named Applied Information-Processing Psychology Project (AIP) with Newell as a consultant aiming to create an applied psychology of human-computer interaction. The keystroke-level model is still relevant today, which is shown by the recent research about mobile phones and touchscreens.

Structure of the Keystroke-level Model

The keystroke-level model consists of six operators: the first four are physical motor operators followed by one mental operator and one system response operator:

- K (keystroke or button press): it is the most frequent operator and means keys and not characters (so e.g. pressing SHIFT is a separate K operation). The time for this operator depends on the motor skills of the user and is determined by one-minute typing tests, where the total test time is divided by the total number of non-error keystrokes.

- P (pointing to a target on a display with a mouse): this time differs depending on the distance to the target and the size of the target, but is held constant. A mouse click is not contained and counts as a separate K operation.

- H (homing the hand(s) on the keyboard or other device): This includes movement between any two devices as well as the fine positioning of the hand.

- D (drawing (manually) n_D straight-line segments with a total length of $D(n_D, l_D)$ cm): where n_D is the number of the line segments drawn and l_D is the total length of the line segments. This operator is very specialized because it is restricted to the mouse and the drawing system has to constrain the cursor to a .56 cm grid.

- M (mentally preparing for executing physical actions): denotes the time a user needs for thinking or decision making. The number of Ms in a method depends on the knowledge and skill of the user. Heuristics are given to help decide where an M should be placed in a method. For example, when pointing with the mouse a button press is usually fully anticipated and no M is needed between both operators. The following table shows the heuristics for placing the M operator:

Begin with a method encoding that includes all physical operators and response operations. Use Rule 0 to place candidate Ms, and then cycle through Rules 1 to 4 for each M to see whether it should be deleted.	
Rule 0	Insert Ms in front of all Ks that are not part of argument strings proper (e.g., text strings or numbers). Place Ms in front of all Ps that select commands (not arguments).
Rule 1	If an operator following an M is fully anticipated in the operator just previous to M, then delete the M (e.g., PMK -> PK).
Rule 2	If a string of MKs belong to a cognitive unit (e.g., the name of a command), then delete all Ms but the first.

Rule 3	If a K is a redundant terminator (e.g., the terminator of a command immediately following the terminator of its argument), then delete the M in front of the K.
Rule 4	If a K terminates a constant string (e.g., a command name), then delete the M in front of the K; but if the K terminates a variable string (e.g., an argument string) then keep the M.

R (response time of the system): the response time depends on the system, the command and the context of the command. It only used when the user actually has to wait for the system. For instance, when the user mentally prepares (M) for executing his next physical action only the non-overlapping part of the response time is needed for R because the user uses the response time for the M operation (e.g. R of 2 seconds – M of 1.35 seconds = R of .65 seconds). To make things clearer, Kieras suggests the naming waiting time (W) instead of response time (R) to avoid confusion. Sauro suggests taking a sample of the system response time.

The following table shows an overview of the times for the mentioned operators as well as the times for suggested operators:

operator	time (sec)	
K	total typing test time/total number of non-error	keystrokes
Guidelines:		
	.08 (135 wpm: best typist)	
	.12 (90 wpm: good typist)	
	.20 (55 wpm: average skilled typist)	
	.28 (40 wpm: average non-secretary typist)	
	.50 (typing random letters)	
	.75 (typing complex codes)	
	1.20 (worst typist and unfamiliar with the key	board)
P	1.1	
H	0.4	
D	$.9n_D +. 16 l_D$	
M	1.35	
R	system dependent	
suggested operators		
B (mouse button press or release)	0.1	

Click a Link/ Button	3.73	
Pull-Down List (No Page Load)	3.04	
Pull-Down List (Page Load)	3.96	
Date-Picker	6.81	
Cut & Paste (Keyboard)	4.51	
Typing Text in a Text Field	2.32	
Scrolling	3.96	

Comparison with GOMS

The KLM is based on the keystroke level, which belongs to the family of GOMS models. The KLM and the GOMS models have in common that they only predict behaviour of experts without errors, but in contrast the KLM needs a specified method to predict the time because it does not predict the method like GOMS. Therefore, the KLM has no goals and method selection rules, which in turn makes it easier to use. The KLM resembles the model K1 from the family of GOMS models the most because both are at the keystroke level and possess a generic M operator. The difference is that the M operator of the KLM is more aggregated and thus larger (1.35 seconds vs. 0.62 seconds), which makes its mental operator more similar to the CHOOSE operations of the model K2. All in all, the KLM represents the practical use of the GOMS keystroke level.

Advantages

The KLM was designed to be a quick and easy to use system design tool, which means that no deep knowledge about psychology is required for its usage. Also, task times can be predicted (given the limitations) without having to build a prototype, recruit and test users, which saves time and money. See the example for a practical use of the KLM as a system design tool.

Limitations

The keystroke-level model has several restrictions:

- It measures only one aspect of performance: time, which means execution time and not the time to acquire or learn a task

- It considers only expert users. Generally, users differ regarding their knowledge and experience of different systems and tasks, motor skills and technical ability

- It considers only routine unit tasks

- The method has to be specified step by step

- The execution of the method has to be error-free

- The mental operator aggregates different mental operations and therefore cannot model a deeper representation of the user's mental operations. If this is crucial, a GOMS model has to be used (e.g. model K2)

Also, one should keep in mind when assessing a computer system that other aspects of performance (errors, learning, functionality, recall, concentration, fatigue, and acceptability), types of users (novice, casual) and non-routine tasks have to be considered as well.

Furthermore, tasks which take more than a few minutes take several hours to model and a source of errors is forgetting operations. This implies that the KLM is best suited for short tasks with few operators. In addition, the KLM can not make a perfect prediction and has a root-mean-square error of 21%.

Example

The following example slightly modified to be more compact from Kieras shows the practical use of the KLM by comparing two different ways to delete a file for an average skilled typist. Note that M is 1.35 seconds as stated in the KLM instead of 1.2 seconds used by Kieras. The difference between the two designs would remain the same either way for this example.

Design A: drag the file into the trash can	Design B: use the short cut "control + T"
method encoding (operator sequence)	method encoding (operator sequence)
	1. initiate the deletion (M)
1. initiate the deletion (M)	2. find the icon for the to-be-deleted file (M)
2. find the file icon (M)	3. point to file icon (P)
3. point to file icon (P) 4. press and hold mouse button (B) 5. drag file icon to trash can icon (P) 6. release mouse button (B) 7. point to original window (P)	4. press mouse button (B) 5. release mouse button (B) 6. move hand to keyboard (H) 7. press control key (K) 8. press T key (K) 9. move hand back to mouse (H)
Total time	Total time
3P + 2B + 2M = 3*1.1 sec + 2*.1 sec+ 2*1.35 sec = 6.2 sec	P + 2B + 2H + 2K + 2M = 1.1 sec + 2*.1 sec + 2*.4 sec + 2*.2 sec + 2*1.35 sec = 5.2 sec

This shows that Design B is 1 second faster than Design A, although it contains more operations.

Adaptions

The six operators of the KLM can be reduced, but this decreases the accuracy of the model. If this low of an accuracy makes sense (e.g. "back-of-the-envelope" calculations) such a simplification can be sufficient.

While the existing KLM applies to desktop applications, the model might not fulfill the range of mobile tasks, or as Dunlop and Cross declaimed KLM is no longer precise for mobile devices. There are various efforts to extend the KLM regarding the use for mobile phones or touch devices. One of the significant contributions to this field is done by Holleis, who retained existing operators while revisiting the timing specifications. Furthermore, he introduced new operators: Distraction (X), Gesture (G), Initial Act (I). While Li and Holleis both agree that the KLM model can be applied to predict task times on mobile devices, Li suggests further modifications to the model, by introducing a new concept called operator blocks. These are defined as "the sequence of operators that can be used with high repeatability by analyst of the extended KLM.". He also discards old operators and defines 5 new mental operators and 9 new physical operators, while 4 of the physical operators focus on pen-based operations. Rice and Lartigue suggest numerous operators for touch devices together with updating existing operators naming the model TLM (Touch Level Model). They retain the operators Keystroke (K/B), Homing (H), Mental (M) and Response Time (R(t)) and suggest new touch specific operators partly based on Holleis' suggested operators:

- Distraction. A multiplicative operator that adds time to other operators.

- Pinch. A 2+ finger gesture commonly used to zoom out

- Zoom. A 2+ finger gesture commonly used to zoom in

- Initial Act. The action or actions necessary to prepare the system for use (e.g. unlocking device, tapping an icon, entering a password).

- Tap. Tapping some area of the screen to effect a change or initiate an action.

- Swipe. A 1+ finger gesture in which a finger or fingers are placed on the screen and subsequently moved in a single direction for a specified amount of time.

- Tilt. The tilting — or full rotation of — the entire device d degrees (or radians).

- Rotate. A 2+ finger gesture in which fingers are placed on the screen and then rotated d degrees (or radians) about a central axis.

- Drag. A 1+ finger gesture in which fingers are placed on the screen and then moved — usually in a straight line — to another location.

Human Processor Model

Human processor model or MHP (Model Human Processor) is a cognitive modeling method used to calculate how long it takes to perform a certain task. Other cognitive modeling methods include parallel design, GOMS, and KLM (human-computer interaction).

Overview

Cognitive modeling methods are one way to evaluate the usability of a product. This method uses experimental times to calculate cognitive and motor processing time. The value of the human processor model is that it allows a system designer to predict the performance with respect to time it takes a person to complete a task without performing experiments. Other modeling methods include inspection methods, inquiry methods, prototyping methods, and testing methods.

The standard definition for MHP is: The MHP draws an analogy between the processing and storage areas of a computer, with the perceptual, motor, cognitive and memory areas of the computer user.

The human processor model uses the cognitive, perceptual, and motor processors along with the visual image, working memory, and long term memory storages. A diagram is shown below. Each processor has a cycle time and each memory has a decay time. These values are also included below. By following the connections diagrammed below, along with the associated cycle or decay times, the time it takes a user to perform a certain task can be calculated. Studies into this field were initially done by Stuart K. Card, Thomas P. Moran, & Allen Newell in 1983. Current studies in the field include work to distinguish process times in older adults by Tiffany Jastrembski and Neil Charness (2007).

How To Calculate

The calculations depend on the ability to break down every step of a task into the basic process level. The more detailed the analysis the more accurate the model will be to predict human performance. The method for determining processes can be broken down into the following steps.

- Write out main steps based on: a working prototype, simulation, step by step walk-through of all steps

- Clearly identify the specific task and method to accomplish that task

- For each final step identify sub-levels down to a basic process (in the diagram or chart below)

- Convert into pseudo code (writing out methods for each step)

- List all assumptions (will be helpful as multiple iterations are completed)

- Determine time of each operation (based on the table below)

- Determine if operation times should be adjusted (slower for elderly, disability, unfamiliarity, etc.)

- Sum up execution times

- Iterate as needed and check with prototyping if possible

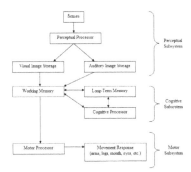

Parameter	Mean	Range
Eye movement time	230 ms	70-700 ms
Decay half-life of visual image storage	200 ms	90-1000 ms
Visual Capacity	17 letters	7-17 letters
Decay half-life of auditory storage	1500 ms	90-3500 ms
Auditory Capacity	5 letters	4.4-6.2 letters
Perceptual processor cycle time	100 ms	50-200 ms
Cognitive processor cycle time	70 ms	25-170 ms
Motor processor cycle time	70 ms	30-100 ms
Effective working memory capacity	7 chunks	5-9 chunks
Pure working memory capacity	3 chunks	2.5-4.2 chunks
Decay half-life of working memory	7 sec	5-226 sec
Decay half-life of 1 chunk working memory	73 sec	73-226 sec
Decay half-life of 3 chunks working memory	7 sec	5-34 sec

Potential Uses

Once complete, the calculations can then be used to determine the probability of a user remembering an item that may have been encountered in the process. The following formula can be used to find the probability: $P = e^{-K*t}$ where K is the decay constant for the respective memory in question (working or long term) and t is the amount of time elapsed (with units corresponding to that of K). The probability could then be used to determine whether or not a user would be likely to recall an important piece of information they were presented with while doing an activity.

It is important to deduce beforehand whether the user would be able to repeat the vital information throughout time t, as this has a negative impact on the working memory if they cannot. For example, if a user is reading lines of text and is presented with an important phone number in that text, they may not be able to repeat the number if they have to continue to read. This would cause the user's working memory's decay time to be smaller, thus reducing their probability of recall.

Fitts's Law

Fitts's law (often cited as Fitts' law) is a descriptive model of human movement primarily used in human–computer interaction and ergonomics. This scientific law predicts that the time required to rapidly move to a target area is a function of the ratio between the distance to the target and the width of the target. Fitts's law is used to model the act of *pointing*, either by physically touching an object with a hand or finger, or virtually, by pointing to an object on a computer monitor using a pointing device.

Fitts's law has been shown to apply under a variety of conditions, with many different limbs (hands, feet, the lower lip, head-mounted sights, eye gaze), manipulanda (input devices), physical environments (including underwater), and user populations (young, old, special educational needs, and drugged participants).

Original Model Formulation

The original 1954 paper by Paul Fitts proposed a metric to quantify the difficulty of a target selection task. The metric was based on an information analogy, where the distance to the target (D) is like a signal and the tolerance or width of the target (W) is like noise. The metric is Fitts's *index of difficulty* (*ID*, in bits):

$$\text{ID} = \log_2\left(\frac{2D}{W}\right)$$

Fitts also proposed an *index of performance* (*IP*, in bits per second) as a measure of human performance. The metric combines a task's index of difficulty (*ID*) with the movement time (*MT*, in seconds) in selecting the target. In Fitts's words, "The average rate of information generated by a series of movements is the average information per movement divided by the time per movement" (1954, p. 390). Thus,

$$IP = \left(\frac{ID}{MT}\right)$$

Today, *IP* is more commonly called *throughput* (*TP*). It is also common to include an adjustment for accuracy in the calculation.

Researchers after Fitts began the practice of building linear regression equations and examining the correlation (*r*) for goodness of fit. The equation expresses the relationship between *MT* and the *D* and *W* task parameters:

$$MT = a + b \cdot ID = a + b \cdot \log_2\left(\frac{2D}{W}\right)$$

where:

- *MT* is the average time to complete the movement.

- *a* and *b* are model parameters.

- *ID* is the index of difficulty.

- *D* is the distance from the starting point to the center of the target.

- *W* is the width of the target measured along the axis of motion. *W* can also be thought of as the allowed error tolerance in the final position, since the final point of the motion must fall within $\pm W/_2$ of the target's center.

Since shorter movement times are desirable for a given task, the value of the *b* parameter can be used as a metric when comparing computer pointing devices against one another. The first Human-Computer Interface application of Fitts's law was by Card, English, and Burr (1978), who used the index of performance (*IP*), interpreted as $1/_b$, to compare performance of different input devices, with the mouse coming out on top compared to the joystick or directional movement keys. This early work, according to Stuart Card's biography, "was a major factor leading to the mouse's commercial introduction by Xerox".

Many experiments testing Fitts's law apply the model to a dataset in which either distance or width, but not both, are varied. The model's predictive power deteriorates when both are varied over a significant range. Notice that because the *ID* term depends only on the *ratio* of distance to width, the model implies that a target distance and width combination can be re-scaled arbitrarily without affecting movement time, which is impossible. Despite its flaws, this form of the model does possess remarkable predictive power across a range of computer interface modalities and motor tasks, and has provided many insights into user interface design principles.

Bits Per Second: Model Innovations Driven by Information Theory

The formulation of Fitts's index of difficulty most frequently used in the Human-Computer Interaction community is called the Shannon formulation:

$$\text{ID} = \log_2\left(\frac{D}{W}+1\right)$$

This form was proposed by Scott MacKenzie, professor at York University, and named for its resemblance to the Shannon–Hartley theorem.

Using this form of the model, the difficulty of a pointing task was equated to a quantity of information transmitted (in units of bits) by performing the task. This was justified by the assertion that pointing reduces to an information processing task. Although no formal mathematical connection was established between Fitts's law and the Shannon-Hartley theorem it was inspired by, the Shannon form of the law has been used extensively, likely due to the appeal of quantifying motor actions using information theory. In 2002 the ISO 9241 was published, providing standards for human-computer interface testing, including the use of the Shannon form of Fitts's law. It has been shown that the information transmitted via serial keystrokes on a keyboard and the information implied by the *ID* for such a task are not consistent.

Adjustment for Accuracy: Use of the Effective Target Width

An important improvement to Fitts's law was proposed by Crossman in 1956 and used by Fitts in his 1964 paper with Peterson. With the adjustment, target width (W) is replaced by an effective target width (W_e). W_e is computed from the standard deviation in the selection coordinates gathered over a sequence of trials for a particular *D-W* condition. If the selections are logged as x coordinates along the axis of approach to the target, then

$$W_e = 4.133 \times SD_x$$

This yields

$$\text{ID}_e = \log_2\left(\frac{D}{W_e}+1\right)$$

and hence

$$\text{IP} = \left(\frac{ID_e}{MT}\right)$$

If the selection coordinates are normally distributed, W_e spans 96% of the distribution. If the observed error rate was 4% in the sequence of trials, then $W_e = W$. If the error rate was greater than 4%, $W_e > W$, and if the error rate was less than 4%, $W_e < W$. By using W_e, a Fitts' law model more closely reflects what users actually did, rather than what they were asked to do.

The main advantage in computing *IP* as above is that spatial variability, or accuracy, is included in the measurement. With the adjustment for accuracy, Fitts's law more truly encompasses the speed-accuracy tradeoff. The equations above appear in ISO 9241-9 as the recommended method of computing *throughput*.

Welford's Model: Innovations Driven by Predictive Power

Not long after the original model was proposed, a 2-factor variation was proposed under the intuition that target distance and width have separate effects on movement time. Welford's model, proposed in 1968, separated the influence of target distance and width into separate terms, and provided improved predictive power:

$$T = a + b_1 \log_2(D) + b_2 \log_2(W)$$

This model has an additional parameter, so its predictive accuracy cannot be directly compared with 1-factor forms of Fitts's law. However, a variation on Welford's model inspired by the Shannon formulation,

$$T = a + b_1 \log_2(D + W) + b_2 \log_2(W) = a + b \log_2\left(\frac{D + W}{W^k}\right)$$

reduces to the Shannon form when $k = 1$. Therefore, this model *can* be directly compared against the Shannon form of Fitts's law using the F-test of nested models. This comparison reveals that not only does the Shannon form of Welford's model better predict movement times, but it is also more robust when control-display gain (the ratio between e.g. hand movement and cursor movement) is varied. Consequently, although the Shannon model is slightly more complex and less intuitive, it is empirically the best model to use for virtual pointing tasks.

Extending the Model from 1D to 2D and Other Nuances

Extensions to two or More Dimensions

In its original form, Fitts's law is meant to apply only to one-dimensional tasks. However, the original experiments required subjects to move a stylus (in three dimensions) between two metal plates on a table, termed the reciprocal tapping task. The target width perpendicular to the direction of movement was very wide to avoid it having a significant influence on performance. A major application for Fitts's law is 2D virtual pointing tasks on computer screens, in which targets have bounded sizes in both dimensions.

Fitts's law has been extended to two-dimensional tasks in two different ways. For navigating e.g. hierarchical pull-down menus, the user must generate a trajectory with the pointing device that is constrained by the menu geometry; for this application the Accot-Zhai steering law was derived.

For simply pointing to targets in a two-dimensional space, the model generally holds as-is but requires adjustments to capture target geometry and quantify targeting errors in a logically consistent way.

Characterizing performance

Since the a and b parameters should capture movement times over a potentially wide range of task geometries, they can serve as a performance metric for a given interface. In doing so, it is necessary to separate variation between users from variation between interfaces. The a parameter is typically positive and close to zero, and sometimes ignored in characterizing average performance. Multiple methods exist for identifying parameters from experimental data, and the choice of method is the subject of heated debate, since method variation can result in parameter differences that overwhelm underlying performance differences.

An additional issue in characterizing performance is incorporating success rate: an aggressive user can achieve shorter movement times at the cost of experimental trials in which the target is missed. If the latter are not incorporated into the model, then average movement times can be artificially decreased.

Steering Law

The steering law in human–computer interaction and ergonomics is a predictive model of human movement that describes the time required to navigate, or *steer*, through a 2-dimensional tunnel. The tunnel can be thought of as a path or trajectory on a plane that has an associated thickness or width, where the width can vary along the tunnel. The goal of a steering task is to navigate from one end of the tunnel to the other as quickly as possible, without touching the boundaries of the tunnel. A real-world example that approximates this task is driving a car down a road that may have twists and turns, where the car must navigate the road as quickly as possible without touching the sides of the road. The steering law predicts both the instantaneous speed at which we may navigate the tunnel, and the total time required to navigate the entire tunnel.

The steering law has been independently discovered and studied three times (Rashevsky, 1959; Drury, 1971; Accot and Zhai, 1997). Its most recent discovery has been within the human–computer interaction community, which has resulted in the most general mathematical formulation of the law.

The steering Law in Human–computer Interaction

Within human–computer interaction, the law was rediscovered by Johnny Accot and Shumin Zhai, who mathematically derived it in a novel way from Fitts's law using integral calculus, experimentally verified it for a class of tasks, and developed the most general mathematical statement of it. Some researchers within this community have sometimes referred to the law as the Accot–Zhai steering law or Accot's law (Accot is pronounced *ah-cot* in English and *ah-koh* in French). In this context, the steering law is a predictive model of human movement, concerning the speed and total time with which a user may steer a pointing device (such as a mouse or stylus) through a 2D tunnel presented on a screen (i.e. with a bird's eye view of the tunnel), where the user must travel from one end of the path to the other as quickly as possible, while staying within the confines of the path. One potential practical application of this law is in modelling a user's performance in navigating a hierarchical cascading menu.

Many researchers in human–computer interaction, including Accot himself, find it surprising or even amazing that the steering law model predicts performance as well as it does, given the almost purely mathematical way in which it was derived. Some consider this a testament to the robustness of Fitts's law.

In its general form, the steering law can be expressed as

$$T = a + b \int_C \frac{ds}{W(s)}$$

where T is the average time to navigate through the path, C is the path parameterized by s, $W(s)$ is the width of the path at s, and a and b are experimentally fitted constants. In general, the path may have a complicated curvilinear shape (such as a spiral) with variable thickness $W(s)$.

Simpler paths allow for mathematical simplifications of the general form of the law. For example, if the path is a straight tunnel of constant width W, the equation reduces to

$$T = a + b \frac{A}{W}$$

where A is the length of the path. We see, especially in this simplified form, a *speed–accuracy* tradeoff, somewhat similar to that in Fitts's law.

We can also differentiate both sides of the integral equation with respect to s to obtain the local, or instantaneous, form of the law:

$$\frac{ds}{dT} = \frac{W(s)}{b}$$

which says that the instantaneous speed of the user is proportional to the width of the tunnel. This makes intuitive sense if we consider the analogous task of driving a car down a road: the wider the road, the faster we can drive and still stay on the road, even if there are curves in the road.

Derivation of the Model from Fitts's Law

This derivation is only meant as a high level sketch. It lacks the illustrations of, and may differ in detail from, the derivation given by Accot and Zhai (1997).

Assume that the time required for goal passing (i.e. passing a pointer through a goal at distance A and of width W, oriented perpendicular to the axis of motion) can be modeled with this form of Fitts's law:

$$T_{goal} = b \log_2 \left(\frac{A}{W} + 1 \right)$$

Then, a straight tunnel of length A and constant width W can be approximated as a sequence of N evenly spaced goals, each separated from its neighbours by a distance of A/N. We can let N grow arbitrarily large, making the distance between successive goals become infinitesimal. The total time to navigative through all the goals, and thus through the tunnel, is

$$T_{straight\ tunnel} = \lim_{N\to\infty} \sum_{i=1}^{N} b \log_2 \left(\frac{A/N}{W} + 1 \right)$$

$$= \lim_{N\to\infty} Nb \log_2 \left(\frac{A}{NW} + 1 \right)$$

$$= b \lim_{N\to\infty} \frac{\log_2 \left(\frac{A}{NW} + 1 \right)}{1/N} \qquad \text{(applying L'Hôpital's rule ...)}$$

$$= b \lim_{N\to\infty} \frac{\frac{1}{\left(\frac{A}{NW} + 1 \right)} \frac{A}{W} (-1/N^2)}{-1/N^2}$$

$$b \frac{A}{W} \lim_{N\to\infty} \frac{1}{\left(\frac{A}{NW} + 1 \right)}$$

$$= b\frac{A}{W}$$

Next, consider a curved tunnel of total length A, parameterized by s varying from 0 to A. Let $W(s)$ be the variable width of the tunnel. The tunnel can be approximated as a sequence of N straight tunnels, numbered 1 through N, each located at s_i where $i = 1$ to N, and each of length $s_{i+1} - s_i$ and of width $W(s_i)$. We can let N grow arbitrarily large, making the length of successive straight tunnels become infinitesimal. The total time to navigative through the curved tunnel is

$$T_{\text{curved tunnel}} = \lim_{N\to\infty} \sum_{i=1}^{N} b\frac{s_{i+1} - s_i}{W(s_i)}$$

$$= b\int_0^A \frac{ds}{W(s)} \qquad (\text{... by the definition of the definite integral})$$

yielding the general form of the steering law.

Modeling Steering in Layers

Steering law has been extended to predict movement time for steering in layers of thickness t (Kattinakere et al., 2007). The relation is givenby

$$T = a + b\sqrt{(A/W)^2 + (A/t)^2}.$$

References

- Card, Stuart; Thomas P. Moran; Allen Newell (1983). The Psychology of Human Computer Interaction. Lawrence Erlbaum Associates. ISBN 0-89859-859-1.

- Rogers, Yvonne; Helen Sharp; Jenny Preece (2002). Interaction Design. United States of America: John Wiley & Sons. p. 454. ISBN 0-471-49278-7.

- Card, Stuart; Thomas P. Moran; Allen Newell (1980). The keystroke-level model for user performance time with interactive systems. Lawrence Erlbaum Associates. doi:10.1145/358886.358895. ISBN 0-13-444910-X.

- Rice, Andrew D.; Jonathan W. Lartigue (2014). Touch-level model (TLM): evolving KLM-GOMS for touchscreen and mobile devices. ACM. doi:10.1145/2638404.2638532. ISBN 978-1-4503-2923-1.

- John, Bonnie E; Wayne D. Gray (1995). CPM-GOMS: an analysis method for tasks with parallel activities. ACM. ISBN 0-89791-755-3.

- Gray, Wayne D.; John,Bonnie E.; Atwood, Michael E. (1992). "The Precis of Project Ernestine or an overview of a validation of GOMS". Proceedings of the SIGCHI conference on Human factors in computing systems. doi:10.1145/142750.142821. ISBN 0897915135.

- Gong, Richard; David Kieras (1994). A Validation of the GOMS Model Methodology in the Development of a Specialized, Commercial Software Application. ACM. doi:10.1145/191666.191782. ISBN 0-89791-650-6.

- Card, Stuart K; Moran, Thomas P; Newell, Allen (1983). The Psychology of Human-Computer Interaction. Hillsdale: L. Erlbaum Associates Inc. pp. ix–x. ISBN 0898592437.

User Interface: A Comprehensive Study

The following text briefly explains the concept of user interface. User interface is the design of the human – machine interaction. The aim of this is to achieve an efficient interaction between machines and humans. This section is an overview of the subject matter incorporating all the major aspects of user interface.

User Interface

Example of a tangible user interface.

The user interface (UI), in the industrial design field of human–machine interaction, is the space where interactions between humans and machines occur. The goal of this interaction is to allow effective operation and control of the machine from the human end, whilst the machine simultaneously feeds back information that aids the operators' decision-making process. Examples of this broad concept of user interfaces include the interactive aspects of computer operating systems, hand tools, heavy machinery operator controls, and process controls. The design considerations applicable when creating user interfaces are related to or involve such disciplines as ergonomics and psychology.

Generally, the goal of user interface design is to produce a user interface which makes it easy (self-explanatory), efficient, and enjoyable (user-friendly) to operate a machine in the way which produces the desired result. This generally means that the operator needs to provide minimal input to achieve the desired output, and also that the machine minimizes undesired outputs to the human.

With the increased use of personal computers and the relative decline in societal awareness of heavy machinery, the term user interface is generally assumed to mean the graphical user interface, while industrial control panel and machinery control design discussions more commonly refer to human-machine interfaces.

Other terms for user interface include human–computer interface and man–machine interface (MMI).

Overview

A graphical user interface following the desktop metaphor.

The user interface or *human–machine interface* is the part of the machine that handles the human–machine interaction. Membrane switches, rubber keypads and touchscreens are examples of the physical part of the Human Machine Interface which we can see and touch.

In complex systems, the human–machine interface is typically computerized. The term *human–computer interface* refers to this kind of system. In the context of computing the term typically extends as well to the software dedicated to control the physical elements used for human-computer interaction.

The engineering of the human–machine interfaces is enhanced by considering ergonomics (human factors). The corresponding disciplines are human factors engineering (HFE) and usability engineering (UE), which is part of systems engineering.

Tools used for incorporating human factors in the interface design are developed based on knowledge of computer science, such as computer graphics, operating systems, programming languages. Nowadays, we use the expression graphical user interface for human–machine interface on computers, as nearly all of them are now using graphics.

Terminology

There is a difference between a user interface and an operator interface or a human–machine interface (HMI).

- 'The term "user interface" is often used in the context of (personal) computer systems and electronic devices

  o Where a network of equipment or computers are interlinked through an MES (Manufacturing Execution System)-or Host to display information.

  o An HMI is typically local to one machine or piece of equipment, and is the interface method between the human and the equipment/machine. An operator interface is the interface method by which multiple equipment that are linked by a host control system is accessed or controlled.

  o The system may expose several user interfaces to serve different kinds of users. For example, a computerized library database might provide two user interfaces, one for library patrons (limited set of functions, optimized for ease of use) and the other for library personnel (wide set of functions, optimized for efficiency).

- The user interface of a mechanical system, a vehicle or an industrial installation is sometimes referred to as the human–machine interface (HMI). HMI is a modification of the original term MMI (man-machine interface). In practice, the abbreviation MMI is still frequently used although some may claim that MMI stands for something different now. Another abbreviation is HCI, but is more commonly used for human–computer interaction. Other terms used are operator interface console (OIC) and operator interface terminal (OIT). However it is abbreviated, the terms refer to the 'layer' that separates a human that is operating a machine from the machine itself. Without a clean and usable interface, humans would not be able to interact with information systems.

In science fiction, HMI is sometimes used to refer to what is better described as direct neural interface. However, this latter usage is seeing increasing application in the real-life use of (medical) prostheses—the artificial extension that replaces a missing body part (e.g., cochlear implants).

In some circumstances, computers might observe the user and react according to their actions without specific commands. A means of tracking parts of the body is required, and sensors noting the position of the head, direction of gaze and so on have been used experimentally. This is particularly relevant to immersive interfaces.

History

The history of user interfaces can be divided into the following phases according to the dominant type of user interface:

1945–1968: Batch Interface

In the batch era, computing power was extremely scarce and expensive. User interfaces were rudimentary. Users had to accommodate computers rather than the other way around; user interfaces were considered overhead, and software was designed to keep the processor at maximum utilization with as little overhead as possible.

IBM 029

The input side of the user interfaces for batch machines were mainly punched cards or equivalent media like paper tape. The output side added line printers to these media. With the limited exception of the system operator's console, human beings did not interact with batch machines in real time at all.

Submitting a job to a batch machine involved, first, preparing a deck of punched cards describing a program and a dataset. Punching the program cards wasn't done on the computer itself, but on specialized typewriter-like machines that were notoriously balky, unforgiving, and prone to mechanical failure. The software interface was similarly unforgiving, with very strict syntaxes meant to be parsed by the smallest possible compilers and interpreters.

Once the cards were punched, one would drop them in a job queue and wait. Eventually. operators would feed the deck to the computer, perhaps mounting magnetic tapes to supply another dataset or helper software. The job would generate a printout, containing final results or (all too often) an abort notice with an attached error log. Successful runs might also write a result on magnetic tape or generate some data cards to be used in later computation.

Holes are punched in the card according to a prearranged code transferring the facts from the census questionnaire into statistics

The turnaround time for a single job often spanned entire days. If one were very lucky, it might be hours; real-time response was unheard of. But there were worse fates than the card queue; some computers actually required an even more tedious and error-prone process of toggling in programs in binary code using console switches. The very earliest machines actually had to be partly rewired to incorporate program logic into themselves, using devices known as plugboards.

Early batch systems gave the currently running job the entire computer; program decks and tapes had to include what we would now think of as operating-system code to talk to I/O devices and do whatever other housekeeping was needed. Midway through the batch period, after 1957, various groups began to experiment with so-called "load-and-go" systems. These used a monitor program which was always resident on the computer. Programs could call the monitor for services. Another function of the monitor was to do better error checking on submitted jobs, catching errors earlier and more intelligently and generating more useful feedback to the users. Thus, monitors represented a first step towards both operating systems and explicitly designed user interfaces.

1969–present: Command-line User Interface

Teletype Model 33 ASR

Command-line interfaces (CLIs) evolved from batch monitors connected to the system console. Their interaction model was a series of request-response transactions, with requests expressed as textual commands in a specialized vocabulary. Latency was far lower than for batch systems, dropping from days or hours to seconds. Accordingly, command-line systems allowed the user to change his or her mind about later stages of the transaction in response to real-time or near-real-time feedback on earlier results. Software could be exploratory and interactive in ways not possible before. But these interfaces still placed a relatively heavy mnemonic load on the user, requiring a serious investment of effort and learning time to master.

The earliest command-line systems combined teleprinters with computers, adapting a mature technology that had proven effective for mediating the transfer of information over wires between human beings. Teleprinters had originally been invented as devices for automatic telegraph transmission and reception; they had a history going back to 1902 and had already become well-established in newsrooms and elsewhere by 1920. In reusing them, economy was certainly a consideration, but psychology and the Rule of Least Surprise mattered as well; teleprinters provided a point of interface with the system that was familiar to many engineers and users.

DEC VT100 terminal

The widespread adoption of video-display terminals (VDTs) in the mid-1970s ushered in the second phase of command-line systems. These cut latency further, because characters could be thrown on the phosphor dots of a screen more quickly than a printer head or carriage can move. They helped quell conservative resistance to interactive programming by cutting ink and paper consumables out of the cost picture, and were to the first TV generation of the late 1950s and 60s even more iconic and comfortable than teleprinters had been to the computer pioneers of the 1940s.

Just as importantly, the existence of an accessible screen — a two-dimensional display of text that could be rapidly and reversibly modified — made it economical for software designers to deploy interfaces that could be described as visual rather than textual. The pioneering applications of this kind were computer games and text editors; close descendants of some of the earliest specimens, such as rogue(6), and vi(1), are still a live part of Unix tradition.

1985: SAA User Interface or Text-Based User Interface

In 1985, with the beginning of Microsoft Windows and other graphical user interfaces, IBM created what is called the Systems Application Architecture (SAA) standard which include the Common User Access (CUA) derivative. CUA successfully created what we know and use today in Windows, and most of the more recent DOS or Windows Console Applications will use that standard as well.

This defined that a pulldown menu system should be at the top of the screen, status bar at the bottom, shortcut keys should stay the same for all common functionality (F2 to Open for example would work in all applications that followed the SAA standard). This greatly helped the speed at which users could learn an application so it caught on quick and became an industry standard.

1968–present: Graphical User Interface

WYSIWYG 2000 –
interaktive Gestaltung von
professionellem Satz.   Linotype

AMX Desk made a basic WIMP GUI   Linotype WYSIWYG 2000, 1989

- 1968 – Doug Engelbart demonstrated NLS, a system which uses a mouse, pointers, hypertext, and multiple windows.

- 1970 – Researchers at Xerox Palo Alto Research Center (many from SRI) develop WIMP paradigm (Windows, Icons, Menus, Pointers)

- 1973 – Xerox Alto: commercial failure due to expense, poor user interface, and lack of programs

- 1979 – Steve Jobs and other Apple engineers visit Xerox. Pirates of Silicon Valley dramatizes the events, but Apple had already been working on the GUI before the visit

- 1981 – Xerox Star: focus on WYSIWYG. Commercial failure (25K sold) due to expense ($16K each), performance (minutes to save a file, couple of hours to recover from crash), and poor marketing

- 1984 – Apple Macintosh popularizes the GUI. Super Bowl commercial shown once, most expensive ever made at that time

- 1984 – MIT's X Window System: hardware- independent platform and networking protocol for developing GUIs on UNIX-like systems

- 1985 – Windows 1.0 – provided GUI interface to MS-DOS. No overlapping windows (tiled instead).

- 1985 – Microsoft and IBM start work on OS/2 meant to eventually replace MS-DOS and Windows

- 1986 – Apple threatens to sue Digital Research because their GUI desktop looked too much like Apple's Mac.

- 1987 – Windows 2.0 – Overlapping and resizable windows, keyboard and mouse enhancements

- 1987 – Macintosh II: first full-color Mac

- 1988 – OS/2 1.10 Standard Edition (SE) has GUI written by Microsoft, looks a lot like Windows 2

Interface Design

Primary methods used in the interface design include prototyping and simulation.

Typical human–machine interface design consists of the following stages: interaction specification, interface software specification and prototyping:

- Common practices for interaction specification include user-centered design, persona, activity-oriented design, scenario-based design, resiliency design.

- Common practices for interface software specification include use cases, constrain enforcement by interaction protocols (intended to avoid use errors).

- Common practices for prototyping are based on interactive design based on libraries of interface elements (controls, decoration, etc.).

Quality

All great interfaces share eight qualities or characteristics:

1. Clarity The interface avoids ambiguity by making everything clear through language, flow, hierarchy and metaphors for visual elements.

2. Concision It's easy to make the interface clear by over-clarifying and labeling everything, but this leads to interface bloat, where there is just too much stuff on the screen at the same time. If too many things are on the screen, finding what you're looking for is difficult, and so the interface becomes tedious to use. The real challenge in making a great interface is to make it concise and clear at the same time.

3. Familiarity Even if someone uses an interface for the first time, certain elements can still be familiar. Real-life metaphors can be used to communicate meaning.

4. Responsiveness A good interface should not feel sluggish. This means that the interface should provide good feedback to the user about what's happening and whether the user's input is being successfully processed.

5. Consistency Keeping your interface consistent across your application is important because it allows users to recognize usage patterns.

6. Aesthetics While you don't need to make an interface attractive for it to do its job, making something look good will make the time your users spend using your application more enjoyable; and happier users can only be a good thing.

7. Efficiency Time is money, and a great interface should make the user more productive through shortcuts and good design.

8. Forgiveness A good interface should not punish users for their mistakes but should instead provide the means to remedy them.

Principle of Least Astonishment

The principle of least astonishment (POLA) is a general principle in the design of all kinds of interfaces. It is based on the idea that human beings can only pay full attention to one thing at one time, leading to the conclusion that novelty should be minimized.

Types

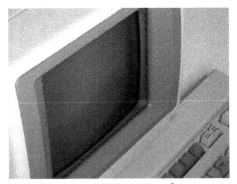

HP Series 100 HP-150 Touchscreen

- Direct manipulation interface is the name of a general class of user interfaces that allow users to manipulate objects presented to them, using actions that correspond at least loosely to the physical world.

- Graphical user interfaces (GUI) accept input via devices such as a computer keyboard and mouse and provide articulated graphical output on the computer monitor. There are at least two different principles widely used in GUI design: Object-oriented user interfaces (OOUIs) and application oriented interfaces.

- Web-based user interfaces or web user interfaces (WUI) that accept input and provide output by generating web pages which are transmitted via the Internet and viewed by the user using a web browser program. Newer implementations utilize PHP, Java, JavaScript, AJAX, Apache Flex, .NET Framework, or similar technologies to provide real-time control in a separate program, eliminating the need to refresh a traditional HTML based web browser. Administrative web interfaces for web-servers, servers and networked computers are often called control panels.

- Touchscreens are displays that accept input by touch of fingers or a stylus. Used in a growing amount of mobile devices and many types of point of sale, industrial processes and machines, self-service machines etc.

- Command line interfaces, where the user provides the input by typing a command string with the computer keyboard and the system provides output by printing text on the computer monitor. Used by programmers and system administrators, in engineering and scientific environments, and by technically advanced personal computer users.

- Touch user interface are graphical user interfaces using a touchpad or touchscreen display as a combined input and output device. They supplement or replace other forms of output with haptic feedback methods. Used in computerized simulators etc.

- Hardware interfaces are the physical, spatial interfaces found on products in the real world from toasters, to car dashboards, to airplane cockpits. They are generally a mixture of knobs, buttons, sliders, switches, and touchscreens.

- Attentive user interfaces manage the user attention deciding when to interrupt the user, the kind of warnings, and the level of detail of the messages presented to the user.

- Batch interfaces are non-interactive user interfaces, where the user specifies all the details of the *batch job* in advance to batch processing, and receives the output when all the processing is done. The computer does not prompt for further input after the processing has started.

- Conversational interfaces enable users to command the computer with plain text English (e.g., via text messages, or chatbots) or voice commands, instead of graphic elements. These interfaces often emulate human-to-human conversations.

- Conversational interface agents attempt to personify the computer interface in the form of an animated person, robot, or other character (such as Microsoft's Clippy the paperclip), and present interactions in a conversational form.

- Crossing-based interfaces are graphical user interfaces in which the primary task consists in crossing boundaries instead of pointing.

- Gesture interfaces are graphical user interfaces which accept input in a form of hand gestures, or mouse gestures sketched with a computer mouse or a stylus.

- Holographic user interfaces provide input to electronic or electro-mechanical devices by passing a finger through reproduced holographic images of what would otherwise be tactile controls of those devices, floating freely in the air, detected by a wave source and without tactile interaction.

- Intelligent user interfaces are human-machine interfaces that aim to improve the efficiency, effectiveness, and naturalness of human-machine interaction by representing, reasoning, and acting on models of the user, domain, task, discourse, and media (e.g., graphics, natural language, gesture).

- Motion tracking interfaces monitor the user's body motions and translate them into commands, currently being developed by Apple.

- Multi-screen interfaces, employ multiple displays to provide a more flexible interaction. This is often employed in computer game interaction in both the commercial arcades and more recently the handheld markets.

- Non-command user interfaces, which observe the user to infer his / her needs and intentions, without requiring that he / she formulate explicit commands.

- Object-oriented user interfaces (OOUI) are based on object-oriented programming metaphors, allowing users to manipulate simulated objects and their properties.

- Reflexive user interfaces where the users control and redefine the entire system via the user interface alone, for instance to change its command verbs. Typically this is only possible with very rich graphic user interfaces.

- Search interface is how the search box of a site is displayed, as well as the visual representation of the search results.

- Tangible user interfaces, which place a greater emphasis on touch and physical environment or its element.

- Task-focused interfaces are user interfaces which address the information overload problem of the desktop metaphor by making tasks, not files, the primary unit of interaction.

- Text-based user interfaces are user interfaces which output a text. TUIs can either contain a command-line interface or a text-based WIMP environment.

- Voice user interfaces, which accept input and provide output by generating voice prompts. The user input is made by pressing keys or buttons, or responding verbally to the interface.

- Natural-language interfaces – Used for search engines and on webpages. User types in a question and waits for a response.

- Zero-input interfaces get inputs from a set of sensors instead of querying the user with input dialogs.

- Zooming user interfaces are graphical user interfaces in which information objects are represented at different levels of scale and detail, and where the user can change the scale of the viewed area in order to show more detail.

Object-oriented User Interface

In computing, an object-oriented user interface (OOUI) is a type of user interface based on an object-oriented programming metaphor. In an OOUI, the user interacts explicitly with objects that represent entities in the domain that the application is concerned with. Many vector drawing applications, for example, have an OOUI – the objects being lines, circles and canvases. The user may explicitly select an object, alter its properties (such as size or colour), or invoke other actions upon it (such as to move, copy, or re-align it). If a business application has any OOUI, the user may be selecting and/or invoking actions on objects representing entities in the business domain such as customers, products or orders.

Jakob Nielsen defines the OOUI in contrast to function-oriented interfaces: "Object-oriented interfaces are sometimes described as turning the application inside-out as compared to function-oriented interfaces. The main focus of the interaction changes to become the users' data and other information objects that are typically represented graphically on the screen as icons or in windows."

Dave Collins defines an OOUI as demonstrating three characteristics:

- Users perceive and act on objects

- Users can classify objects based on how they behave

- In the context of what users are trying to do, all the user interface objects fit together into a coherent overall representation.

Jef Raskin suggests that the most important characteristic of an OOUI is that it adopts a 'noun-verb', rather than a 'verb-noun' style of interaction, and that this has several advantages in terms of usability.

Relationship to Other User Interface Ideas

There is a great deal of potential synergy between the OOUI concept and other important ideas in user interface design including:

- graphical user interface (GUI).

- direct manipulation interface

- interface metaphor

Many futuristic imaginings of user interfaces rely heavily on OOUI and especially OOGUI concepts. However there are many examples of user interfaces that implement one or more of those other ideas, but which are not in fact OOUIs - though they are often wrongly labelled as OOUIs. Conversely, there are examples of OOUIs that are neither graphical, nor employ direct manipulation techniques, nor employ strong metaphors. For example, the earliest versions of the Smalltalk programming language had a command line interface that was nonetheless also clearly an OOUI, though it subsequently became better known for its pioneering role in the development of GUIs, direct manipulation and visual metaphors.

Relationship to Object-oriented Programming

Although there are many conceptual parallels between OOUIs and object-oriented programming, it does not follow that an OOUI has to be implemented using an object-oriented programming language.

The guidelines for IBM's Common User Access (CUA), (possibly the most comprehensive attempt at defining a standard for OOUI design) stated that 'while object-oriented programming can facilitate the development of an object-oriented user interface, it is not a pre-requisite. An object-oriented user interface can be developed with more traditional programming languages and tools.'

However, there are strong synergies. Larry Tesler, who left Xerox PARC in 1980 to join Apple underlined the relationship:

Many observers have hypothesized that [the] Smalltalk user interface and the Smalltalk language are separable innovations. Consequently, most systems influenced by the Smalltalk user interface have been engineered without resorting to Smalltalk's implementation approach. At Apple, after using Pascal to implement six initial applications for Lisa, we discovered compelling reasons to change our programming language to incorporate more ideas from Smalltalk. Lisa applications are now written in the language Clascal, an extension of Pascal featuring objects, classes, subclasses, and procedure invocation by message-passing.

Relationship to Domain Object Modelling

There is also an obvious synergy between the concept of an OOUI and the idea of constructing software from domain objects. However, it does not follow that the objects that a user sees and interacts with in an OOUI have to correspond to the domain objects on which the application is built.

The CUA guidelines stated that 'In an object-oriented user interface, the objects that a user works with do not necessarily correspond to the objects, or modules of code, that a programmer used to create the product.' The basic design methods described in CUA were refined further into the OVID method which used UML to model the interface.

Mark van Harmelen states that 'Object-oriented user interface design does not require designers to take an object-oriented view of the problem from the beginning of the project. Furthermore, even if designers take an object-oriented perspective throughout, they will benefit from focusing separately on the object model and the object-oriented user interface design.'

By contrast, the naked objects pattern is an approach to the design of applications that, at least in its naive application, enforces a direct correspondence between the objects represented in the OOUI and the underlying domain objects, auto-generating the former from the latter.

Tangible User Interface

A tangible user interface (TUI) is a user interface in which a person interacts with digital information through the physical environment. The initial name was Graspable User Interface, which is no longer used. The purpose of TUI development is to empower collaboration, learning, and design by giving physical forms to digital information, thus taking advantage of human abilities of grasp and manipulate physical objects and materials.

One of the pioneers in tangible user interfaces is Hiroshi Ishii, a professor in the MIT Media Laboratory who heads the Tangible Media Group. His particular vision for tangible UIs, called *Tangible Bits*, is to give physical form to digital information, making bits directly manipulable and perceptible. Tangible bits pursues the seamless coupling between physical objects and virtual data.

Characteristics of Tangible User Interfaces

1. Physical representations are computationally coupled to underlying digital information.

2. Physical representations embody mechanisms for interactive control.

3. Physical representations are perceptually coupled to actively mediated digital representations.

4. Physical state of tangibles embodies key aspects of the digital state of a system

According to, five basic defining properties of tangible user interfaces are as follows:

1. space-multiplex both input and output;

2. concurrent access and manipulation of interface components;

3. strong specific devices;

4. spatially aware computational devices;

5. spatial re-configurability of devices.

Examples

A simple example of tangible UI is the computer mouse. Dragging the mouse over a flat surface and having a pointer moving on the screen accordingly. There is a very clear relationship about the behaviors shown by a system with the movements of a mouse.

Another example of a tangible UI is the *Marble Answering Machine* by Durrell Bishop (1992). A marble represents a single message left on the answering machine. Dropping a marble into a dish plays back the associated message or calls back the caller.

Another example is the *Topobo* system. The blocks in Topobo are like LEGO blocks which can be snapped together, but can also move by themselves using motorized components. A person can push, pull, and twist these blocks, and the blocks can memorize these movements and replay them.

Another implementation allows the user to sketch a picture on the system's table top with a real tangible pen. Using hand gestures, the user can clone the image and stretch it in the X and Y axes just as one would in a paint program. This system would integrate a video camera with a gesture recognition system.

Another example is jive. The implementation of a TUI helped make this product more accessible to elderly users of the product. The 'friend' passes can also be used to activate different interactions with the product.

Several approaches have been made to establish a generic middleware for TUIs. They target toward the independence of application domains as well as flexibility in terms of the deployed sensor technology. For example, Siftables provides an application platform in which small gesture sensitive displays act together to form a human-computer interface.

For collaboration support TUIs have to allow the spatial distribution, asynchronous activities, and the dynamic modification of the TUI infrastructure, to name the most prominent ones. This approach presents a framework based on the LINDA tuple space concept to meet these requirements. The implemented TUIpist framework deploys arbitrary sensor technology for any type of application and actuators in distributed environments.

A further example of a type of TUI is a projection augmented model.

State of the Art

Interest in tangible user interfaces (TUIs) has grown constantly since the 1990s and with every year, more tangible systems are showing up. In 1999, Gary Zalewski patented a system of moveable children's blocks containing sensors and displays for teaching spelling and sentence composition. A similar system is being marketed as "Siftables".

The MIT Tangible Media Group, headed by Hiroshi Ishi is continuously developing and experimenting with TUIs including many tabletop applications.

The Urp and the more advanced Augmented Urban Planning Workbench allows digital simulations of air flow, shadows, reflections, and other data based on the positions and orientations of physical models of buildings, on the table surface.

Newer developments go even one step further and incorporate the third dimension by allowing a user to form landscapes with clay (Illuminating Clay) or sand (Sand Scape). Again different simulations allow the analysis of shadows, height maps, slopes and other characteristics of the interactively formable landmasses.

InfrActables is a back projection collaborative table that allows interaction by using TUIs that incorporate state recognition. Adding different buttons to the TUIs enables additional functions associated to the TUIs. Newer versions of the technology can even be integrated into LC-displays by using infrared sensors behind the LC matrix.

The Tangible Disaster allows the user to analyze disaster measures and simulate different kinds of disasters (fire, flood, tsunami,.) and evacuation scenarios during collaborative planning sessions. Physical objects allow positioning disasters by placing them on the interactive map and additionally tuning parameters (i.e. scale) using dials attached to them.

Apparently, the commercial potential of TUIs has been identified recently. The repeatedly awarded Reactable, an interactive tangible tabletop instrument, is now distributed commercially by Reactable Systems, a spinoff company of the Pompeu Fabra University, where it was developed. With the Reactable users can set up their own instrument interactively, by physically placing different objects (representing oscillators, filters, modulators...) and parametrise them by rotating and using touch-input.

Microsoft is distributing its novel Windows-based platform Microsoft Surface (now Microsoft PixelSense) since 2009. Beside multi-touch tracking of fingers, the platform supports the recognition of physical objects by their footprints. Several applications, mainly for the use in commercial space, have been presented. Examples range from designing an own individual graphical layout for a snowboard or skateboard to studying the details of a wine in a restaurant by placing it on the table and navigating through menus via touch input. Interactions such as the collaborative browsing of photographs from a handycam or cell phone that connects seamlessly once placed on the table are also supported.

Another notable interactive installation is instant city that combines gaming, music, architecture and collaborative aspects. It allows the user to build three-dimensional structures and set up a city with rectangular building blocks, which simultaneously results in the interactive assembly of musical fragments of different composers.

The development of the Reactable and the subsequent release of its tracking technology reacTIVision under the GNU/GPL as well as the open specifications of the TUIO protocol have triggered an enormous amount of developments based on this technology.

In the last few years, many amateur and semi-professional projects outside of academia and commerce have been started. Due to open source tracking technologies (reacTIVision) and the ever-increasing computational power available to end-consumers, the required infrastructure is now accessible to almost everyone. A standard PC, webcam, and some handicraft work allows individuals to set up tangible systems with a minimal programming and material effort. This opens doors to novel ways of perceiving human-computer interaction and allows for new forms of creativity for the public to experiment with.

It is difficult to keep track and overlook the rapidly growing number of all these systems and tools, but while many of them seem only to utilize the available technologies and are limited to initial experiments and tests with some basic ideas or just reproduce existing systems, a few of them open out into novel interfaces and interactions and are deployed in public space or embedded in art installations.

The Tangible Factory Planning is a tangible table based on reacTIVision that allows to collaboratively plan and visualize production processes in combination with plans of new factory buildings and was developed within a diploma thesis.

Another example of the many reacTIVision-based tabletops is ImpulsBauhaus-Interactive Table and was on exhibition at the Bauhaus-University in Weimar marking the 90th anniversary of the establishment of Bauhaus. Visitors could browse and explore the biographies, complex relations and social networks between members of the movement.

Using principles derived from embodied cognition, cognitive load theory, and embodied design TUIs have been shown to increase learning performance by offering multimodal feedback. However, these benefits for learning require forms of interaction design that leave as much cognitive capacity as possible for learning.

Organic User Interface

PaperPhone (2011) was the first flexible smartphone prototype and the first OUI with bend interactions on a real flexible display.

In human–computer interaction, an organic user interface (OUI) is defined as a user interface with a non-flat display. After Engelbart and Sutherland's graphical user interface (GUI), which was based on the cathode ray tube (CRT), and Kay and Weiser's ubiquitous computing, which is based on the flat panel liquid-crystal display (LCD), OUI represents the third wave of display interaction paradigms, pertaining to multi-shaped and flexible displays. In an OUI, the display surface is always the locus of interaction, and may actively or passively change shape upon analog (i.e., as close to non-quantized as possible) inputs. These inputs are provided through direct physical gestures, rather than through indirect point-and-click control. Note that the term "Organic" in OUI was derived from organic architecture, referring to the adoption of natural form to design a better fit with human ecology. The term also alludes to the use of organic electronics for this purpose.

Organic user interfaces were first introduced in a special issue of the *Communications of the ACM* in 2008. The first International Workshop on Organic User Interfaces took place at CHI 2009 in Boston, Massachusetts. The second workshop took place at TEI 2011 in Madeira, Portugal. The third workshop was held at MobileHCI 2012 in Monterey, California, and the fourth workshop at CHI 2013 in Paris, France.

Types of Organic User Interface

According to Vertegaal and Poupyrev, there are three general types of organic user interface:

Flexible (or deformable) user interfaces: When flexible displays are deployed, shape deformation, e.g., through bends, is a key form of input for OUI. Flexible display technologies include flexible OLED (FOLED) and flexible E Ink, or can be simulated through 3D active projection mapping.

Shaped user interfaces: Displays with a static non-flat display. The physical shape is chosen so as to better support the main function of the interface. Shapes may include spheres, cylinders or take the form of everyday objects.

Actuated (or kinetic) user interfaces: Displays with a programmable shape controlled by a computer algorithm. Here, display shapes can actively adapt to the physical context of the user, the form of the data, or the function of the interface. An extreme example is that of Claytronics: fully physical 3D voxels that dynamically constitute physical 3D images.

Organic Design Principles

Holman and Vertegaal present three design principles that underlie OUI:

Input equals output: In traditional GUIs, input and output are physically separated: Output is generated graphically on the screen on the basis of input provided by a control device such as a mouse. A key feature of OUI is that the display surface, and its physical deformations are always the locus of user interaction.

Function equals form: Coined by Frank Lloyd Wright, this means the shape of an interface determines its physical functionality, and vice versa. Shapes should be chosen such that they best support the functionality of the interface. An example is a spherical multitouch interface, which is particularly suited to geographic information interfaces, which were previously limited to distorted flat projections of spherical earth data.

Form follows flow: OUIs physically adapt to the context of a user's multiple activities, e.g., by taking on multiple shapes. An example of this is the "clamshell" phone, where the physical metaphor of altering the phone's shape (by opening it) alters the state of the user interface (to open communications). Another example is folding a thin-film tablet PC into a smaller, pocket-sized smartphone for mobility.

Example Implementations

Early examples of OUIs include Gummi, a rigid prototype of a flexible credit card display, PaperWindows, featuring active projection-mapped pieces of paper, the Microsoft Sphere, one of the first spherical multitouch computers, and DisplayObjects (rigid objects with displays wrapped around them). PaperPhone was one of the first OUIs to introduce bend gestures on a real flexible screen. It featured a flexible electrophoretic display and an array of 5 bend sensors that allowed for user navigation of content. Examples of actuated OUIs include shape changing prototypes like MorePhone and Morphees. The Nokia Kinetic, a flexible smartphone that allows input techniques such as bend, twist and squeeze, and the Samsung Youm, are early commercial prototypes of OUIs. It is widely expected that OUIs will be introduced on the market by the year 2018.

Note that OUIs differ from a natural user interface (NUI) in that NUIs are limited to touch or remote gestural interactions with a flat display only. Although remote gestural interaction violates the principle of *Input Equals Output*, OUIs generally subsume NUIs. Also note that OUI is a successor to and form of Tangible User Interface that always features a bitmapped display skin around its multi-shaped body. Finally, note that all OUIs are examples of haptic technologies, as their physical shapes, like real objects, provide passive tactile-kinaesthetic feedback even in non-actuated cases.

Brain–computer Interface

A brain–computer interface (BCI), sometimes called a mind-machine interface (MMI), direct neural interface (DNI), or brain–machine interface (BMI), is a direct communication pathway between an enhanced or wired brain and an external device. BCIs are often directed at researching, mapping, assisting, augmenting, or repairing human cognitive or sensory-motor functions.

Research on BCIs began in the 1970s at the University of California, Los Angeles (UCLA) under a grant from the National Science Foundation, followed by a contract from DARPA. The papers published after this research also mark the first appearance of the expression *brain–computer interface* in scientific literature.

The field of BCI research and development has since focused primarily on neuro-prosthetics applications that aim at restoring damaged hearing, sight and movement. Thanks to the remarkable cortical plasticity of the brain, signals from implanted prostheses can, after adaptation, be handled by the brain like natural sensor or effector channels. Following years of animal experimentation, the first neuroprosthetic devices implanted in humans appeared in the mid-1990s.

History

The history of brain–computer interfaces (BCIs) starts with Hans Berger's discovery of the electrical activity of the human brain and the development of electroencephalography (EEG). In 1924 Berger was the first to record human brain activity by means of EEG. Berger was able to identify oscillatory activity, such as Berger's wave or the alpha wave (8–13 Hz), by analyzing EEG traces.

Berger's first recording device was very rudimentary. He inserted silver wires under the scalps of his patients. These were later replaced by silver foils attached to the patients' head by rubber bandages. Berger connected these sensors to a Lippmann capillary electrometer, with disappointing results. However, more sophisticated measuring devices, such as the Siemens double-coil recording galvanometer, which displayed electric voltages as small as one ten thousandth of a volt, led to success.

Berger analyzed the interrelation of alternations in his EEG wave diagrams with brain diseases. EEGs permitted completely new possibilities for the research of human brain activities.

Jacques Vidal coined the term "BCI" and produced the first peer-reviewed publications on this topic. Vidal is widely recognized as the inventor of BCIs in the BCI community, as reflected in numerous peer-reviewed articles reviewing and discussing the field (e.g.,).

Vidal's first BCI relied on visual evoked potentials to allow users to control cursor direction, and visual evoked potentials are still widely used in BCIs (Allison et al., 2010, 2012; Bin et al., 2011; Guger et al., 2012; Kaufmann et al., 2012; Jin et al., 2014; Kapeller et al., 2015).

After his early contributions, Vidal was not active in BCI research, nor BCI events such as conferences, for many years. In 2011, however, he gave a lecture in Graz, Austria, supported by the Future BNCI project, presenting the first BCI, which earned a standing ovation. Vidal was joined by his wife, Laryce Vidal, who previously worked with him at UCLA on his first BCI project. Prof. Vidal will also present a lecture on his early BCI work at the Sixth Annual BCI Meeting, scheduled for May–June 2016 at Asilomar, California.

Versus Neuroprosthetics

Neuroprosthetics is an area of neuroscience concerned with neural prostheses, that is, using artificial devices to replace the function of impaired nervous systems and brain related problems, or of sensory organs. The most widely used neuroprosthetic device is the cochlear implant which, as of December 2010, had been implanted in approximately 220,000 people worldwide. There are also several neuroprosthetic devices that aim to restore vision, including retinal implants.

The difference between BCIs and neuroprosthetics is mostly in how the terms are used: neuroprosthetics typically connect the nervous system to a device, whereas BCIs usually connect the brain (or nervous system) with a computer system. Practical neuroprosthetics can be linked to any part of the nervous system—for example, peripheral nerves—while the term "BCI" usually designates a narrower class of systems which interface with the central nervous system.

The terms are sometimes, however, used interchangeably. Neuroprosthetics and BCIs seek to achieve the same aims, such as restoring sight, hearing, movement, ability to communicate, and even cognitive function. Both use similar experimental methods and surgical techniques.

Animal BCI Research

Several laboratories have managed to record signals from monkey and rat cerebral cortices to operate BCIs to produce movement. Monkeys have navigated computer cursors on screen and commanded robotic arms to perform simple tasks simply by thinking about the task and seeing the visual feedback, but without any motor output. In May 2008 photographs that showed a monkey at the University of Pittsburgh Medical Center operating a robotic arm by thinking were published in a number of well known science journals and magazines. Other research on cats has decoded their neural visual signals.

Early Work

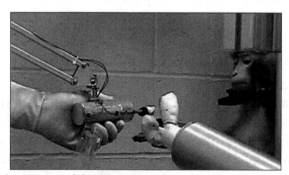

Monkey operating a robotic arm with brain–computer interfacing (Schwartz lab, University of Pittsburgh)

In 1969 the operant conditioning studies of Fetz and colleagues, at the Regional Primate Research Center and Department of Physiology and Biophysics, University of Washington School of Medicine in Seattle, showed for the first time that monkeys could learn to control the deflection of a biofeedback meter arm with neural activity. Similar work in the 1970s established that monkeys could quickly learn to voluntarily control the firing rates of individual and multiple neurons in the primary motor cortex if they were rewarded for generating appropriate patterns of neural activity.

Studies that developed algorithms to reconstruct movements from motor cortex neurons, which control movement, date back to the 1970s. In the 1980s, Apostolos Georgopoulos at Johns Hopkins University found a mathematical relationship between the electrical responses of single motor cortex neurons in rhesus macaque monkeys and the direction in which they moved their arms (based on a cosine function). He also found that dispersed groups of neurons, in different areas of the monkey's brains, collectively controlled motor commands, but was able to record the firings of neurons in only one area at a time, because of the technical limitations imposed by his equipment.

There has been rapid development in BCIs since the mid-1990s. Several groups have been able to capture complex brain motor cortex signals by recording from neural ensembles (groups of neurons) and using these to control external devices.

Prominent Research Successes

Kennedy and Yang Dan

Phillip Kennedy (who later founded Neural Signals in 1987) and colleagues built the first intracortical brain–computer interface by implanting neurotrophic-cone electrodes into monkeys.

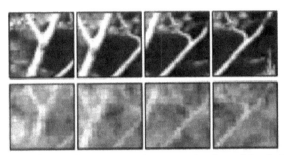

Yang Dan and colleagues' recordings of cat vision using a BCI implanted in the lateral geniculate nucleus (top row: original image; bottom row: recording)

In 1999, researchers led by Yang Dan at the University of California, Berkeley decoded neuronal firings to reproduce images seen by cats. The team used an array of electrodes embedded in the thalamus (which integrates all of the brain's sensory input) of sharp-eyed cats. Researchers targeted 177 brain cells in the thalamus lateral geniculate nucleus area, which decodes signals from the retina. The cats were shown eight short movies, and their neuron firings were recorded. Using mathematical filters, the researchers decoded the signals to generate movies of what the cats saw and were able to reconstruct recognizable scenes and moving objects. Similar results in humans have since been achieved by researchers in Japan.

Nicolelis

Miguel Nicolelis, a professor at Duke University, in Durham, North Carolina, has been a prominent proponent of using multiple electrodes spread over a greater area of the brain to obtain neuronal signals to drive a BCI.

After conducting initial studies in rats during the 1990s, Nicolelis and his colleagues developed BCIs that decoded brain activity in owl monkeys and used the devices to reproduce monkey movements in robotic arms. Monkeys have advanced reaching and grasping abilities and good hand manipulation skills, making them ideal test subjects for this kind of work.

By 2000 the group succeeded in building a BCI that reproduced owl monkey movements while the monkey operated a joystick or reached for food. The BCI operated in real time and could also control a separate robot remotely over Internet protocol. But the monkeys could not see the arm moving and did not receive any feedback, a so-called open-loop BCI.

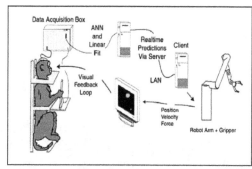

Diagram of the BCI developed by Miguel Nicolelis and colleagues for use on rhesus monkeys

Later experiments by Nicolelis using rhesus monkeys succeeded in closing the feedback loop and reproduced monkey reaching and grasping movements in a robot arm. With their deeply cleft and furrowed brains, rhesus monkeys are considered to be better models for human neurophysiology than owl monkeys. The monkeys were trained to reach and grasp objects on a computer screen by manipulating a joystick while corresponding movements by a robot arm were hidden. The monkeys were later shown the robot directly and learned to control it by viewing its movements. The BCI used velocity predictions to control reaching movements and simultaneously predicted handgripping force. In 2011 O'Doherty and colleagues showed a BCI with sensory feedback with rhesus monkeys. The monkey was brain controlling the position of an avatar arm while receiving sensory feedback through direct intracortical stimulation (ICMS) in the arm representation area of the sensory cortex.

Donoghue, Schwartz and Andersen

Other laboratories which have developed BCIs and algorithms that decode neuron signals include those run by John Donoghue at Brown University, Andrew Schwartz at the University of Pittsburgh and Richard Andersen at Caltech. These researchers have been able to produce working BCIs, even using recorded signals from far fewer neurons than did Nicolelis (15–30 neurons versus 50–200 neurons).

Donoghue's group reported training rhesus monkeys to use a BCI to track visual targets on a computer screen (closed-loop BCI) with or without assistance of a joystick. Schwartz's group created a BCI for three-dimensional tracking in virtual reality and also reproduced BCI control in a robotic arm. The same group also created headlines when they demonstrated that a monkey could feed itself pieces of fruit and marshmallows using a robotic arm controlled by the animal's own brain signals.

Andersen's group used recordings of premovement activity from the posterior parietal cortex in their BCI, including signals created when experimental animals anticipated receiving a reward.

Other Research

In addition to predicting kinematic and kinetic parameters of limb movements, BCIs that predict electromyographic or electrical activity of the muscles of primates are being developed. Such BCIs could be used to restore mobility in paralyzed limbs by electrically stimulating muscles.

Miguel Nicolelis and colleagues demonstrated that the activity of large neural ensembles can predict arm position. This work made possible creation of BCIs that read arm movement intentions and translate them into movements of artificial actuators. Carmena and colleagues programmed the neural coding in a BCI that allowed a monkey to control reaching and grasping movements by a robotic arm. Lebedev and colleagues argued that brain networks reorganize to create a new representation of the robotic appendage in addition to the representation of the animal's own limbs.

The biggest impediment to BCI technology at present is the lack of a sensor modality that provides safe, accurate and robust access to brain signals. It is conceivable or even likely, however, that such a sensor will be developed within the next twenty years. The use of such a sensor should greatly expand the range of communication functions that can be provided using a BCI.

Development and implementation of a BCI system is complex and time consuming. In response to this problem, Gerwin Schalk has been developing a general-purpose system for BCI research, called BCI2000. BCI2000 has been in development since 2000 in a project led by the Brain–Computer Interface R&D Program at the Wadsworth Center of the New York State Department of Health in Albany, New York, United States.

A new 'wireless' approach uses light-gated ion channels such as Channelrhodopsin to control the activity of genetically defined subsets of neurons in vivo. In the context of a simple learning task, illumination of transfected cells in the somatosensory cortex influenced the decision making process of freely moving mice.

The use of BMIs has also led to a deeper understanding of neural networks and the central nervous system. Research has shown that despite the inclination of neuroscientists to believe that neurons have the most effect when working together, single neurons can be conditioned through the use of BMIs to fire at a pattern that allows primates to control motor outputs. The use of BMIs has led to development of the single neuron insufficiency principle which states that even with a well tuned firing rate single neurons can only carry a narrow amount of information and therefore the highest level of accuracy is achieved by recording firings of the collective ensemble.

Other principles discovered with the use of BMIs include the neuronal multitasking principle, the neuronal mass principle, the neural degeneracy principle, and the plasticity principle.

BCIs are also proposed to be applied by users without disabilities. A user-centered categorization of BCI approaches by Thorsten O. Zander and Christian Kothe introduces the term passive BCI. Next to active an reactive BCI that are used for directed control, passive BCIs allow for assessing and interpreting changes in the user state during Human-Computer Interaction (HCI). In a secondary, implicit control loop the computer system adapts to its user improving its usability in general.

The BCI Award

The Annual BCI Research Award, endowed with 3,000 USD, is awarded in recognition of outstanding and innovative research in the field of Brain-Computer Interfaces. Each year, a renowned research laboratory is asked to judge the submitted projects and to award the prize. The jury consists of world-leading BCI experts recruited by the awarding laboratory. Following list consists the winners of the BCI Award:

- 2010: Cuntai Guan, Kai Keng Ang, Karen Sui Geok Chua and Beng Ti Ang, (A*STAR, Singapore)

Motor imagery-based Brain-Computer Interface robotic rehabilitation for stroke.

- 2011: Moritz Grosse-Wentrup and Bernhard Schölkopf, (Max Planck Institute for Intelligent Systems, Germany)

What are the neuro-physiological causes of performance variations in brain-computer interfacing?

- 2012: Surjo R. Soekadar and Niels Birbaumer, (Applied Neurotechnology Lab, University Hospital Tübingen and Institute of Medical Psychology and Behavioral Neurobiology, Eberhard Karls University, Tübingen, Germany)

Improving Efficacy of Ipsilesional Brain-Computer Interface Training in Neurorehabilitation of Chronic Stroke.

- 2013: M. C. Dadarlat[a,b], J. E. O'Doherty[a], P. N. Sabes[a,b] ([a]Department of Physiology, Center for Integrative Neuroscience, San Francisco, CA, US, [b]UC Berkeley-UCSF Bioengineering Graduate Program, University of California, San Francisco, CA, US),

A learning-based approach to artificial sensory feedback: intracortical microstimulation replaces and augments vision.

- 2014: Katsuhiko Hamada, Hiromu Mori, Hiroyuki Shinoda, Tomasz M. Rutkowski, (The University of Tokyo, JP, Life Science Center of TARA, University of Tsukuba, JP, RIKEN Brain Science Institute, JP),

Airborne Ultrasonic Tactile Display BCI

Human BCI Research

Invasive BCIs

Vision

Jens Naumann, a man with acquired blindness, being interviewed about his vision BCI on CBS's The Early Show

Invasive BCI research has targeted repairing damaged sight and providing new functionality for people with paralysis. Invasive BCIs are implanted directly into the grey matter of the brain during neurosurgery. Because they lie in the grey matter, invasive devices produce the highest quality signals of BCI devices but are prone to scar-tissue build-up, causing the signal to become weaker, or even non-existent, as the body reacts to a foreign object in the brain.

In *vision science*, direct brain implants have been used to treat non-congenital (acquired) blindness. One of the first scientists to produce a working brain interface to restore sight was private researcher William Dobelle.

Dobelle's first prototype was implanted into "Jerry", a man blinded in adulthood, in 1978. A single-array BCI containing 68 electrodes was implanted onto Jerry's visual cortex and succeeded in producing phosphenes, the sensation of seeing light. The system included cameras mounted on glasses to send signals to the implant. Initially, the implant allowed Jerry to see shades of grey in a limited field of vision at a low framerate. This also required him to be hooked up to a mainframe computer, but shrinking electronics and faster computers made his artificial eye more portable and now enable him to perform simple tasks unassisted.

In 2002, Jens Naumann, also blinded in adulthood, became the first in a series of 16 paying patients to receive Dobelle's second generation implant, marking one of the earliest commercial uses of BCIs. The second generation device used a more sophisticated implant enabling better mapping of phosphenes into coherent vision. Phosphenes are spread out across the visual field in what researchers call "the starry-night effect". Immediately after his implant, Jens was able to use his imperfectly restored vision to drive an automobile slowly around the parking area of the research institute. Unfortunately, Dobelle died in 2004 before his processes and developments were documented. Subsequently, when Mr. Naumann and the other patients in the program began having problems with their vision, there was no relief and they eventually lost their "sight" again. Naumann wrote about his experience with Dobelle's work in *Search for Paradise: A Patient's Account of the Artificial Vision Experiment* and has returned to his farm in Southeast Ontario, Canada, to resume his normal activities.

Dummy unit illustrating the design of a BrainGate interface

Movement

BCIs focusing on *motor neuroprosthetics* aim to either restore movement in individuals with paralysis or provide devices to assist them, such as interfaces with computers or robot arms.

Researchers at Emory University in Atlanta, led by Philip Kennedy and Roy Bakay, were first to install a brain implant in a human that produced signals of high enough quality to simulate movement. Their patient, Johnny Ray (1944–2002), suffered from 'locked-in syndrome' after suffering a brain-stem stroke in 1997. Ray's implant was installed in 1998 and he lived long enough to start working with the implant, eventually learning to control a computer cursor; he died in 2002 of a brain aneurysm.

Tetraplegic Matt Nagle became the first person to control an artificial hand using a BCI in 2005 as part of the first nine-month human trial of Cyberkinetics's BrainGate chip-implant. Implanted in Nagle's right precentral gyrus (area of the motor cortex for arm movement), the 96-electrode BrainGate implant allowed Nagle to control a robotic arm by thinking about moving his hand as well as a computer cursor, lights and TV. One year later, professor Jonathan Wolpaw received the prize of the Altran Foundation for Innovation to develop a Brain Computer Interface with electrodes located on the surface of the skull, instead of directly in the brain.

More recently, research teams led by the Braingate group at Brown University and a group led by University of Pittsburgh Medical Center, both in collaborations with the United States Department of Veterans Affairs, have demonstrated further success in direct control of robotic prosthetic limbs with many degrees of freedom using direct connections to arrays of neurons in the motor cortex of patients with tetraplegia.

Partially Invasive BCIs

Partially invasive BCI devices are implanted inside the skull but rest outside the brain rather than within the grey matter. They produce better resolution signals than non-invasive BCIs where the bone tissue of the cranium deflects and deforms signals and have a lower risk of forming scar-tissue in the brain than fully invasive BCIs. There has been preclinical demonstration of intracortical BCIs from the stroke perilesional cortex.

Electrocorticography (ECoG) measures the electrical activity of the brain taken from beneath the skull in a similar way to non-invasive electroencephalography, but the electrodes are embedded in a thin plastic pad that is placed above the cortex, beneath the dura mater. ECoG technologies were first trialled in humans in 2004 by Eric Leuthardt and Daniel Moran from Washington University in St Louis. In a later trial, the researchers enabled a teenage boy to play Space Invaders using his ECoG implant. This research indicates that control is rapid, requires minimal training, and may be an ideal tradeoff with regards to signal fidelity and level of invasiveness.

(Note: these electrodes had not been implanted in the patient with the intention of developing a BCI. The patient had been suffering from severe epilepsy and the electrodes were temporarily implanted to help his physicians localize seizure foci; the BCI researchers simply took advantage of this.)

Signals can be either subdural or epidural, but are not taken from within the brain parenchyma itself. It has not been studied extensively until recently due to the limited access of subjects. Currently, the only manner to acquire the signal for study is through the use of patients requiring invasive monitoring for localization and resection of an epileptogenic focus.

ECoG is a very promising intermediate BCI modality because it has higher spatial resolution, better signal-to-noise ratio, wider frequency range, and less training requirements than scalp-recorded EEG, and at the same time has lower technical difficulty, lower clinical risk, and probably superior long-term stability than intracortical single-neuron recording. This feature profile and recent evidence of the high level of control with minimal training requirements shows potential for real world application for people with motor disabilities.

Light reactive imaging BCI devices are still in the realm of theory. These would involve implanting a laser inside the skull. The laser would be trained on a single neuron and the neuron's reflectance measured by a separate sensor. When the neuron fires, the laser light pattern and wavelengths it reflects would change slightly. This would allow researchers to monitor single neurons but require less contact with tissue and reduce the risk of scar-tissue build-up.

In 2014, a BCI study using near-infrared spectroscopy for "locked-in" patients with amyotrophic lateral sclerosis (ALS) was able to restore some basic ability of the patients to communicate with other people.

Non-invasive BCIs

There have also been experiments in humans using non-invasive neuroimaging technologies as interfaces. The substantial majority of published BCI work involves non-invasive EEG-based BCIs. Noninvasive EEG-based technologies and interfaces have been used for a much broader variety of applications. Although EEG-based interfaces are easy to wear and do not require surgery, they have relatively poor spatial resolution and cannot effectively use higher-frequency signals because the skull dampens signals, dispersing and blurring the electromagnetic waves created by the neurons. EEG-based interfaces also require some time and effort prior to each usage session, whereas non-EEG-based ones, as well as invasive ones require no prior-usage training. Overall, the best BCI for each user depends on numerous factors.

Non EEG-based

Pupil-size Oscillation

In a recent 2016 article, an entirely new communication device and non EEG-based BCI was developed, requiring no visual fixation or ability to move eyes at all, that is based on covert interest in (i.e. without fixing eyes on) chosen letter on a virtual keyboard with letters each having its own (background) circle that is micro-oscillating in brightness in different time transitions, where the letter selection is based on best fit between, on one hand, unintentional pupil-size oscillation pattern, and, on the other hand, the circle-in-background's brightness oscillation pattern. Accuracy is additionally improved by user's mental rehearsing the words 'bright' and 'dark' in synchrony with the brightness transitions of the circle/letter.

EEG-based

Overview

Electroencephalography (EEG) is the most studied non-invasive interface, mainly due to its fine temporal resolution, ease of use, portability and low set-up cost. The technology is somewhat susceptible to noise however. In the early days of BCI research, another substantial barrier to using EEG as a brain–computer interface was the extensive training required before users can work the technology. For example, in experiments beginning in the mid-1990s, Niels Birbaumer at the University of Tübingen in Germany trained severely paralysed people to self-regulate the *slow cortical potentials* in their EEG to such an extent that these signals could be used as a binary signal to control a computer cursor. (Birbaumer had earlier trained epileptics to prevent impending fits by controlling this low voltage wave.) The experiment saw ten patients trained to move a computer cursor by controlling their brainwaves. The process was slow, requiring more than an hour for patients to write 100 characters with the cursor, while training often took many months. However, the slow cortical potential approach to BCIs has not been used in several years, since other approaches require little or no training, are faster and more accurate, and work for a greater proportion of users.

Recordings of brainwaves produced by an electroencephalogram

Another research parameter is the type of oscillatory activity that is measured. Birbaumer's later research with Jonathan Wolpaw at New York State University has focused on developing technology that would allow users to choose the brain signals they found easiest to operate a BCI, including *mu* and *beta* rhythms.

A further parameter is the method of feedback used and this is shown in studies of P300 signals. Patterns of P300 waves are generated involuntarily (stimulus-feedback) when people see something they recognize and may allow BCIs to decode categories of thoughts without training patients first. By contrast, the biofeedback methods described above require learning to control brainwaves so the resulting brain activity can be detected.

Lawrence Farwell and Emanuel Donchin developed an EEG-based brain–computer interface in the 1980s. Their "mental prosthesis" used the P300 brainwave response to allow subjects, including one paralyzed Locked-In syndrome patient, to communicate words, letters and simple commands to a computer and thereby to speak through a speech synthesizer driven by the computer. A number of similar devices have been developed since then. In 2000, for example, research by Jessica Bayliss at the University of Rochester showed that volunteers wearing virtual reality helmets could control elements in a virtual world using their P300 EEG readings, including turning lights on and off and bringing a mock-up car to a stop.

While an EEG based brain-computer interface has been pursued extensively by a number of research labs, recent advancements made by Bin He and his team at the University of Minnesota suggest the potential of an EEG based brain-computer interface to accomplish tasks close to invasive brain-computer interface. Using advanced functional neuroimaging including BOLD functional MRI and EEG source imaging, Bin He and co-workers identified the co-variation and co-localization of electrophysiological and hemodynamic signals induced by motor imagination. Refined by a neuroimaging approach and by a training protocol, Bin He and co-workers demonstrated the ability of a non-invasive EEG based brain-computer interface to control the flight of a virtual helicopter in 3-dimensional space, based upon motor imagination. In June 2013 it was announced that Bin He had developed the technique to enable a remote-control helicopter to be guided through an obstacle course.

In addition to a brain-computer interface based on brain waves, as recorded from scalp EEG electrodes, Bin He and co-workers explored a virtual EEG signal-based brain-computer interface by first solving the EEG inverse problem and then used the resulting virtual EEG for brain-computer interface tasks. Well-controlled studies suggested the merits of such a source analysis based brain-computer interface.

A 2014 study found that severely motor-impaired patients could communicate faster and more reliably with non-invasive EEG BCI, than with any muscle-based communication channel.

Dry Active Electrode Arrays

In the early 1990s Babak Taheri, at University of California, Davis demonstrated the first single and also multichannel dry active electrode arrays using micro-machining. The single channel dry EEG electrode construction and results were published in 1994. The arrayed electrode was also demonstrated to perform well compared to silver/silver chloride electrodes. The device consisted of four sites of sensors with integrated electronics to reduce noise by impedance matching. The advantages of such electrodes are: (1) no electrolyte used, (2) no skin preparation, (3) significantly reduced sensor size, and (4) compatibility with EEG monitoring systems. The active electrode array is an integrated system made of an array of capacitive sensors with local integrated circuitry housed in a package with batteries to power the circuitry. This level of integration was required to achieve the functional performance obtained by the electrode.

The electrode was tested on an electrical test bench and on human subjects in four modalities of EEG activity, namely: (1) spontaneous EEG, (2) sensory event-related potentials, (3) brain stem potentials, and (4) cognitive event-related potentials. The performance of the dry electrode compared favorably with that of the standard wet electrodes in terms of skin preparation, no gel requirements (dry), and higher signal-to-noise ratio.

In 1999 researchers at Case Western Reserve University, in Cleveland, Ohio, led by Hunter Peckham, used 64-electrode EEG skullcap to return limited hand movements to quadriplegic Jim Jatich. As Jatich concentrated on simple but opposite concepts like up and down, his beta-rhythm EEG output was analysed using software to identify patterns in the noise. A basic pattern was identified and used to control a switch: Above average activity was set to on, below average off. As well as enabling Jatich to control a computer cursor the signals were also used to drive the nerve controllers embedded in his hands, restoring some movement.

Prosthesis and Environment Control

Non-invasive BCIs have also been applied to enable brain-control of prosthetic upper and lower extremity devices in people with paralysis. For example, Gert Pfurtscheller of Graz University of Technology and colleagues demonstrated a BCI-controlled functional electrical stimulation system to restore upper extremity movements in a person with tetraplegia due to spinal cord injury. Between 2012 and 2013, researchers at the University of California, Irvine demonstrated for the first time that it is possible to use BCI technology to restore brain-controlled walking after spinal cord injury. In their spinal cord injury research study, a person with paraplegia was able to operate a BCI-robotic gait orthosis to regain basic brain-controlled ambulation. In 2009 Alex Blainey, an independent researcher based in the UK, successfully used the Emotiv EPOC to control a 5 axis robot arm. He then went on to make several demonstration mind controlled wheelchairs and home automation that could be operated by people with limited or no motor control such as those with paraplegia and cerebral palsy.

Other Research

Electronic neural networks have been deployed which shift the learning phase from the user to the computer. Experiments by scientists at the Fraunhofer Society in 2004 using neural networks led to noticeable improvements within 30 minutes of training.

Experiments by Eduardo Miranda, at the University of Plymouth in the UK, has aimed to use EEG recordings of mental activity associated with music to allow the disabled to express themselves musically through an encephalophone. Ramaswamy Palaniappan has pioneered the development of BCI for use in biometrics to identify/authenticate a person. The method has also been suggested for use as PIN generation device (for example in ATM and internet banking transactions. The group which is now at University of Wolverhampton has previously developed analogue cursor control using thoughts.

Researchers at the University of Twente in the Netherlands have been conducting research on using BCIs for non-disabled individuals, proposing that BCIs could improve error handling, task performance, and user experience and that they could broaden the user spectrum. They particularly focused on BCI games, suggesting that BCI games could provide challenge, fantasy and sociality to game players and could, thus, improve player experience.

The first BCI session with 100% accuracy (based on 80 right-hand and 80 left-hand movement imaginations) was recorded in 1998 by Christoph Guger. The BCI system used 27 electrodes overlaying the sensorimotor cortex, weighted the electrodes with Common Spatial Patterns, calculated the running variance and used a linear discriminant analysis.

Research is ongoing into military use of BCIs and since the 1970s DARPA has been funding research on this topic. The current focus of research is user-to-user communication through analysis of neural signals. The project "Silent Talk" aims to detect and analyze the word-specific neural signals, using EEG, which occur before speech is vocalized, and to see if the patterns are generalizable.

DIY and Open Source BCI

In 2001, The OpenEEG Project was initiated by a group of DIY neuroscientists and engineers. The ModularEEG was the primary device created the OpenEEG community; it was a 6-channel signal capture board that cost between $200 and $400 to make at home. The OpenEEG Project marked a significant moment in the emergence of DIY brain-computer interfacing.

In 2010, the Frontier Nerds of NYU's ITP program published a thorough tutorial titled How To Hack Toy EEGs. The tutorial, which stirred the minds of many budding DIY BCI enthusiasts, demonstrated how to create a single channel at-home EEG with an Arduino and a Mattel Mindflex at a very reasonable price. This tutorial amplified the DIY BCI movement.

In 2013, OpenBCI emerged from a DARPA solicitation and subsequent Kickstarter campaign. They created a high-quality, open-source 8-channel EEG acquisition board, known as the 32bit Board, that retailed for under $500. Two years later they created the first 3D-printed EEG Headset, known as the Ultracortex, as well as, a 4-channel EEG acquisition board, known as the Ganglion Board, that retailed for under $100.

In 2015, NeuroTechX was created with the mission of building an international network for neurotechnology. They bring hackers, researchers and enthusiasts all together in many different cities around the world. According to their rapid growth, the DIY neurotech / BCI community was already waiting for such initiative to see light.

MEG and MRI

Magnetoencephalography (MEG) and functional magnetic resonance imaging (fMRI) have both been used successfully as non-invasive BCIs. In a widely reported experiment, fMRI allowed two users being scanned to play Pong in real-time by altering their haemodynamic response or brain blood flow through biofeedback techniques.

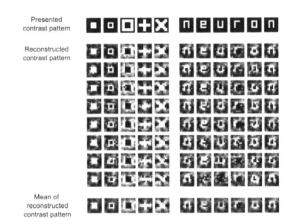

Presented contrast pattern

Reconstructed contrast pattern

Mean of reconstructed contrast pattern

ATR Labs' reconstruction of human vision using fMRI (top row: original image; bottom row: reconstruction from mean of combined readings)

fMRI measurements of haemodynamic responses in real time have also been used to control robot arms with a seven-second delay between thought and movement.

In 2008 research developed in the Advanced Telecommunications Research (ATR) Computational Neuroscience Laboratories in Kyoto, Japan, allowed the scientists to reconstruct images directly from the brain and display them on a computer in black and white at a resolution of 10x10 pixels. The article announcing these achievements was the cover story of the journal Neuron of 10 December 2008.

In 2011 researchers from UC Berkeley published a study reporting second-by-second reconstruction of videos watched by the study's subjects, from fMRI data. This was achieved by creating a statistical model relating visual patterns in videos shown to the subjects, to the brain activity caused by watching the videos. This model was then used to look up the 100 one-second video segments, in a database of 18 million seconds of random YouTube videos, whose visual patterns most closely matched the brain activity recorded when subjects watched a new video. These 100 one-second video extracts were then combined into a mashed-up image that resembled the video being watched.

Neurogaming

Currently, there is a new field of gaming called Neurogaming, which uses non-invasive BCI in order to improve gameplay so that users can interact with a console without the use of a traditional controller. Some Neurogaming software use a player's brain waves, heart rate, expressions, pupil dilation, and even emotions to complete tasks or affect the mood of the game. For example, game developers at Emotiv have created non-invasive BCI that will determine the mood of a player and adjust music or scenery accordingly. This new form of interaction between player and software will enable a player to have a more realistic gaming experience. Because there will be less disconnect between a player and console, Neurogaming will allow individuals to utilize their "psychological state" and have their reactions transfer to games in real-time.

However, since Neurogaming is still in its first stages, not much is written about the new industry. The first NeuroGaming Conference was held in San Francisco on May 1–2, 2013.

BCI Control Strategies in Neurogaming

Motor Imagery

Motor imagery involves the imagination of the movement of various body parts resulting in sensorimotor cortex activation,which modulates sensorimotor oscillations in the EEG. This can be detected by the BCI to infer a user's intent. Motor imagery typically requires a number of sessions of training before acceptable control of the BCI is acquired. These training sessions may take a number of hours over several days before users can consistently employ the technique with acceptable levels of precision. Regardless of the duration of the training session, users are unable to master the control scheme. This results in very slow pace of the gameplay. Advance machine learning methods were recently developed to compute a subject-specific model for detecting the performance of motor imagery. The top performing algorithm from BCI Competition IV (http://www.bbci.de/competition/iv/) dataset 2 for motor imagery is the Filter Bank Common Spatial Pattern, developed by Ang et al. from A*STAR, Singapore).

Bio/neurofeedback for Passive BCI Designs

Biofeedback is used to monitor a subject's mental relaxation. In some cases, biofeedback does not monitor electroencephalography (EEG), but instead bodily parameters such as electromyography(EMG), galvanic skin resistance (GSR), and heart rate variability (HRV).Many biofeedback systems are used to treat certain disorders such as attention deficit hyperactivity disorder (ADHD), sleep problems in children, teeth grinding, and chronic pain. EEG biofeedback systems typically monitor four different bands (theta: 4–7 Hz, alpha:8–12 Hz, SMR: 12–15 Hz, beta: 15–18 Hz) and challenge the subject to control them. Passive BCI involves using BCI to enrich human–machine interaction with implicit information on the actual user's state, for example, simulations to detect when users intend to push brakes during an emergency car stopping procedure. Game developers using passive BCIs need to acknowledge that through repetition of game levels the user's cognitive state will change or adapt. Within the first play of a level, the user will react to things differently from during the second play: for example, the user will be less surprised at an event in the game if he/she is expecting it.

Visual Evoked Potential (VEP)

A VEP is an electrical potential recorded after a subject is presented with a type of visual stimuli. There are several types of VEPs.

Steady-state visually evoked potentials (SSVEPs) use potentials generated by exciting the retina, using visual stimuli modulated at certain frequencies. SSVEP's stimuli are often formed from alternating checkerboard patterns and at times simply use flashing images . The frequency of the phase reversal of the stimulus used can be clearly distinguished in the spectrum of an EEG; this makes detection of SSVEP stimuli relatively easy . SSVEP has proved to be successful within many BCI systems . This is due to several factors, the signal elicited is measurable in as large a population as the transient VEP and blink movement and electro cardiographic artefacts do not affect the frequencies monitored. In addition, the SSVEP signal is exceptionally robust; the topographic organization of the primary visual cortex is such that a broader area obtains afferents from the central or fovial region of the visual field .SSVEP does have several problems however. As SSVEPs use flashing stimuli to infer a user's intent, the user must gaze at one of the flashing or iterating symbols in order to interact with the system. It is, therefore, likely that the symbols could become irritating and uncomfortable to use during longer play sessions, which can often last more than an hour which may not be an ideal gameplay.

Another type of VEP used with applications is the P300 potential. The P300 event-related potential is a positive peak in the EEG that occurs at roughly 300 ms after the appearance of a target stimulus (a stimulus for which the user is waiting or seeking) or oddball stimuli . The P300 amplitude decreases as the target stimuli and the ignored stimuli grow more similar.The P300 is thought to be related to a higher level attention process or an orienting response Using P300 as a control scheme has the advantage of the participant only having to attend limited training sessions. The first application to use the P300 model was the P300 matrix . Within this system, a subject would choose a letter from a grid of 6 by 6 letters and numbers. The rows and columns of the grid flashed sequentially and every time the selected "choice letter" was illuminated the user's P300 was (potentially) elicited. However, the communication process, at approximately 17 characters per minute, was quite slow. The P300 is a BCI that offers a discrete selection rather than a continuous control mechanism. The advantage of P300 use within games is that the player does not have to teach himself/herself how to use a completely new control system and so only has to undertake short training instances, to learn the gameplay mechanics and basic use of the BCI paradigm.

Synthetic Telepathy/Silent Communication

In a $6.3 million Army initiative to invent devices for telepathic communication, Gerwin Schalk, underwritten in a $2.2 million grant, found that it is possible to use ECoG signals to discriminate the vowels and consonants embedded in spoken and in imagined words. The results shed light on the distinct mechanisms associated with production of vowels and consonants, and could provide the basis for brain-based communication using imagined speech.

Research into synthetic telepathy using subvocalization is taking place at the University of California, Irvine under lead scientist Mike D'Zmura. The first such communication took place in the 1960s using EEG to create Morse code using brain alpha waves. Using

EEG to communicate imagined speech is less accurate than the invasive method of placing an electrode between the skull and the brain. On February 27, 2013 the group of Miguel Nicolelis at Duke University and IINN-ELS successfully connected the brains of two rats with electronic interfaces that allowed them to directly share information, in the first-ever direct brain-to-brain interface.

On 3 September 2014, scientists reported that direct communication between human brains was possible over extended distances through Internet transmission of EEG signals.

In March and in May 2014 a study conducted by Dipartimento di Psicologia Generale - Università di Padova, EVANLAB - Firenze, LiquidWeb s.r.l. company and Dipartimento di Ingegneria e Architettura - Università di Trieste, reports confirmatory results analyzing the EEG activity of two human partners spatially separated approximately 190 km apart when one member of the pair receives the stimulation and the second one is connected only mentally with the first.

Cell-culture BCIs

Researchers have built devices to interface with neural cells and entire neural networks in cultures outside animals. As well as furthering research on animal implantable devices, experiments on cultured neural tissue have focused on building problem-solving networks, constructing basic computers and manipulating robotic devices. Research into techniques for stimulating and recording from individual neurons grown on semiconductor chips is sometimes referred to as neuroelectronics or neurochips.

The world's first Neurochip, developed by Caltech researchers Jerome Pine and Michael Maher

Development of the first working neurochip was claimed by a Caltech team led by Jerome Pine and Michael Maher in 1997. The Caltech chip had room for 16 neurons.

In 2003 a team led by Theodore Berger, at the University of Southern California, started work on a neurochip designed to function as an artificial or prosthetic hippocampus. The neurochip was designed to function in rat brains and was intended as a prototype for the eventual development of higher-brain prosthesis. The hippocampus was chosen because it is thought to be the most ordered and structured part of the brain and is the most studied area. Its function is to encode experiences for storage as long-term memories elsewhere in the brain.

In 2004 Thomas DeMarse at the University of Florida used a culture of 25,000 neurons taken from a rat's brain to fly a F-22 fighter jet aircraft simulator. After collection, the cortical neurons were cultured in a petri dish and rapidly began to reconnect themselves to form a living neural network. The cells were arranged over a grid of 60 electrodes and used to control the pitch and yaw functions of the simulator. The study's focus was on understanding how the human brain performs and learns computational tasks at a cellular level.

Ethical Considerations

Important ethical, legal and societal issues related to brain-computer interfacing are:

- conceptual issues (researchers disagree over what is and what is not a brain-computer interface),
- obtaining informed consent from people who have difficulty communicating,
- risk/benefit analysis,
- shared responsibility of BCI teams (e.g. how to ensure that responsible group decisions can be made),
- the consequences of BCI technology for the quality of life of patients and their families,
- side-effects (e.g. neurofeedback of sensorimotor rhythm training is reported to affect sleep quality),
- personal responsibility and its possible constraints (e.g. who is responsible for erroneous actions with a neuroprosthesis),
- issues concerning personality and personhood and its possible alteration,
- therapeutic applications and their possible exceedance,
- questions of research ethics that arise when progressing from animal experimentation to application in human subjects,
- mind-reading and privacy,
- mind-control,
- use of the technology in advanced interrogation techniques by governmental authorities,

- selective enhancement and social stratification.

- communication to the media.

Clausen stated in 2009 that "BCIs pose ethical challenges, but these are conceptually similar to those that bioethicists have addressed for other realms of therapy". Moreover, he suggests that bioethics is well-prepared to deal with the issues that arise with BCI technologies. Haselager and colleagues pointed out that expectations of BCI efficacy and value play a great role in ethical analysis and the way BCI scientists should approach media. Furthermore, standard protocols can be implemented to ensure ethically sound informed-consent procedures with locked-in patients.

Researchers are well aware that sound ethical guidelines, appropriately moderated enthusiasm in media coverage and education about BCI systems will be of utmost importance for the societal acceptance of this technology. Thus, recently more effort is made inside the BCI community to create consensus on ethical guidelines for BCI research, development and dissemination.

Clinical and Research-grade BCI-based Interfaces

Some companies have been producing high-end systems that have been widely used in established BCI labs for several years. These systems typically entail more channels than the low-cost systems below, with much higher signal quality and robustness in real-world settings. Some systems from new companies have been gaining attention for new BCI applications for new user groups, such as persons with stroke or coma.

- In 2011, Nuamps EEG from www.neuroscan.com was used to study the extent of detectable brain signals from stroke patients who performed motor imagery using BCI in a large clinical trial, and the results showed that majority of the patients (87%) could use the BCI.

- In March 2012 g.tec introduced the intendiX-SPELLER, the first commercially available BCI system for home use which can be used to control computer games and apps. It can detect different brain signals with an accuracy of 99%. has hosted several workshop tours to demonstrate the intendiX system and other hardware and software to the public, such as a workshop tour of the US West Coast during September 2012.

- A German-based company called BrainProducts makes systems that are widely used within established BCI labs.

- In 2012 an Italian startup company, Liquidweb s.r.l., released "Braincontrol", a first prototype of an AAC BCI-based, designed for patients in locked-in state. It was validated from 2012 and 2014 with the involvement of LIS and CLIS patients. In 2014 the company introduced the commercial version of the product, with the CE mark class I as medical device.

Low-cost BCI-based Interfaces

Recently a number of companies have scaled back medical grade EEG technology (and in one case, NeuroSky, rebuilt the technology from the ground up) to create inexpensive BCIs. This technology has been built into toys and gaming devices; some of these toys have been extremely commercially successful like the NeuroSky and Mattel MindFlex.

- In 2006 Sony patented a neural interface system allowing radio waves to affect signals in the neural cortex.

- In 2007 NeuroSky released the first affordable consumer based EEG along with the game NeuroBoy. This was also the first large scale EEG device to use dry sensor technology.

- In 2008 OCZ Technology developed a device for use in video games relying primarily on electromyography.

- In 2008 the Final Fantasy developer Square Enix announced that it was partnering with NeuroSky to create a game, Judecca.

- In 2009 Mattel partnered with NeuroSky to release the Mindflex, a game that used an EEG to steer a ball through an obstacle course. By far the best selling consumer based EEG to date.

- In 2009 Uncle Milton Industries partnered with NeuroSky to release the Star Wars Force Trainer, a game designed to create the illusion of possessing The Force.

- In 2009 Emotiv released the EPOC, a 14 channel EEG device that can read 4 mental states, 13 conscious states, facial expressions, and head movements. The EPOC is the first commercial BCI to use dry sensor technology, which can be dampened with a saline solution for a better connection.

- In November 2011 Time Magazine selected "necomimi" produced by Neurowear as one of the best inventions of the year. The company announced that it expected to launch a consumer version of the garment, consisting of cat-like ears controlled by a brain-wave reader produced by NeuroSky, in spring 2012.

- In February 2014 They Shall Walk (a nonprofit organization fixed on constructing exoskeletons, dubbed LIFESUITs, for paraplegics and quadriplegics) began a partnership with James W. Shakarji on the development of a wireless BCI.

Future Directions for BCIs

A consortium consisting of 12 European partners has completed a roadmap to support the European Commission in their funding decisions for the new framework program Horizon 2020. The project, which was funded by the European Commission, started in November 2013 and ended in April 2015. The roadmap is now complete, and can be downloaded on the project's webpage. A 2015 publication describes some of the analyses and achievements of this project, as well as the emerging Brain-Computer Interface Society. For example, this article reviewed work within this project that further defined BCIs and applications, explored recent trends, discussed ethical issues, and evaluated different directions for new BCIs. As the article notes, their new roadmap generally extends and supports the recommendations from the Future BNCI project, which conveys some enthusiasm for emerging BCI directions.

In addition to, other recent publications have explored the most promising future BCI directions for new groups of disabled users (e.g.,). Some prominent examples are summarized below.

Disorders of Consciousness (DOC)

Some persons have a disorder of consciousness (DOC). This state is defined to include persons with coma, as well as persons in a vegetative state (VS) or minimally conscious state (MCS). New BCI research seeks to help persons with DOC in different ways. A key initial goal is to identify patients who are able to perform basic cognitive tasks, which would of course lead to a change in their diagnosis. That is, some persons who are diagnosed with DOC may in fact be able to process information and make important life decisions (such as whether to seek therapy, where to live, and their views on end-of-life decisions regarding them). Very sadly, some persons who are diagnosed with DOC die as a result of end-of-life decisions, which may be made by family members who sincerely feel this is in the patient's best interests. Given the new prospect of allowing these patients to provide their views on this decision, there would seem to be a strong ethical pressure to develop this research direction to guarantee that DOC patients are given an opportunity to decide whether they want to live.

These and other articles describe new challenges and solutions to use BCI technology to help persons with DOC. One major challenge is that these patients cannot use BCIs based on vision. Hence, new tools rely on auditory and/or vibrotactile stimuli. Patients may wear headphones and/or vibrotactile stimulators placed on the wrists, neck, leg, and/or other locations. Another challenge is that patients may fade in and out of consciousness, and can only communicate at certain times. This may indeed be a cause of mistaken diagnosis. Some patients may only be able to respond to physicians' requests during a few hours per day (which might not be predictable ahead of time) and thus may have been unresponsive during diagnosis. Therefore, new methods rely on tools that are easy to use in field settings, even without expert help, so family members and other persons without any medical or technical background can still use them. This reduces the cost, time, need for expertise, and other burdens with DOC assessment. Automated tools can ask simple questions that patients can easily answer, such as "Is your father named George?" or "Were you born in the USA?" Automated instructions inform patients that they may convey yes or no by (for example) focusing their attention on stimuli on the right vs. left wrist. This focused attention produces reliable changes in

EEG patterns that can help determine that the patient is able to communicate. The results could be presented to physicians and therapists, which could lead to a revised diagnosis and therapy. In addition, these patients could then be provided with BCI-based communication tools that could help them convey basic needs, adjust bed position and HVAC (heating, ventilation, and air conditioning), and otherwise empower them to make major life decisions and communicate.

This research effort was supported in part by different EU-funded projects, such as the DECODER project led by Prof. Andrea Kuebler at the University of Wuerzburg. This project contributed to the first BCI system developed for DOC assessment and communication, called mindBEAGLE. This system is designed to help non-expert users work with DOC patients, but is not intended to replace medical staff. An EU-funded project scheduled to begin in 2015 called ComAlert will conduct further research and development to improve DOC prediction, assessment, rehabilitation, and communication, called "PARC" in that project. Another project funded by the National Science Foundation is led by Profs. Dean Krusienski and Chang Nam. This project provides for improved vibrotactile systems, advanced signal analysis, and other improvements for DOC assessment and communication.

Functional Brain Mapping

Each year, about 400,000 people undergo brain mapping during neurosurgery. This procedure is often required for people with tumors or epilepsy that do not respond to medication. During this procedure, electrodes are placed on the brain to precisely identify the locations of structures and functional areas. Patients may be awake during neurosurgery and asked to perform certain tasks, such as moving fingers or repeating words. This is necessary so that surgeons can remove only the desired tissue while sparing other regions, such as critical movement or language regions. Removing too much brain tissue can cause permanent damage, while removing too little tissue can leave the underlying condition untreated and require additional neurosurgery. Thus, there is a strong need to improve both methods and systems to map the brain as effectively as possible.

In several recent publications, BCI research experts and medical doctors have collaborated to explore new ways to use BCI technology to improve neurosurgical mapping. This work focuses largely on high gamma activity, which is difficult to detect with non-invasive means. Results have led to improved methods for identifying key areas for movement, language, and other functions. A recent article addressed advances in functional brain mapping and summarizes a workshop.

BCI Society

Many people within the BCI community have been working toward an official Brain-Computer Interface Society over the last few years. At the Fifth International BCI Meeting in Asilomar, CA in 2013, a plenary session of the attendees unanimously voted in favor of forming this Society. Since then, several people have been active developing bylaws, articles of incorporation, official statements, a membership infrastructure, official website, and other details. The Board consists of many of the most established people in BCI research, including three officers: Prof. Jonathan Wolpaw (President), Prof. Nick Ramsey (Vice-President), and Dr. Christoph Guger (Treasurer).

Command-line Interface

Screenshot of a sample bash session in GNOME Terminal 3, Fedora 15

Screenshot of Windows PowerShell 1.0, running on Windows Vista

A command-line interface or command language interpreter (CLI), also known as command-line user interface, console user interface, and character user interface (CUI), is a means of interacting with a computer program where the user (or client) issues commands to the program in the form of successive lines of text (command lines).

The CLI was the primary means of interaction with most computer systems until the introduction of the video display terminal in the mid-1960s, and continued to be used throughout the 1970s and 1980s on OpenVMS, Unix systems and personal computer systems including MS-DOS, CP/M and Apple DOS. The interface is usually implemented with a command line shell, which is a program that accepts commands as text input and converts commands to appropriate operating system functions.

Command-line interfaces to computer operating systems are less widely used by casual computer users, who favor graphical user interfaces.

Alternatives to the command line include, but are not limited to text user interface menus, keyboard shortcuts, and various other desktop metaphors centered on the pointer (usually controlled with a mouse). Examples of this include the Windows versions 1, 2, 3, 3.1, and 3.11 (an OS shell that runs in DOS), DosShell, and Mouse Systems PowerPanel.

Command-line interfaces are often preferred by more advanced computer users, as they often provide a more concise and powerful means to control a program or operating system.

Programs with command-line interfaces are generally easier to automate via scripting.

Command line interfaces for software other than operating systems include a number of programming languages such as Tcl/Tk, PHP and others, as well as utilities such as the compression utilities WinZip and UltimateZip, and some FTP and ssh/telnet clients.

Advantages

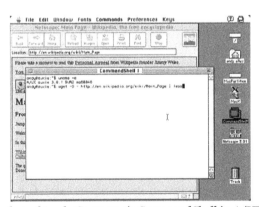

Screenshot of Apple Computer's CommandShell in A/UX 3.0.1

- Requires fewer resources.

- Concise and powerful.

- *Expert*-friendly.

- Easier to automate via scripting.

Criticisms

- Unintuitive

- Commands not obvious.

- Not visually rich.

- *Beginner*-unfriendly.

Operating System Command-line Interfaces

Operating system (OS) command line interfaces are usually distinct programs supplied with the operating system.

A program that implements such a text interface is often called a command-line interpreter, command processor or shell.

Examples of command-line interpreters include DEC's DIGITAL Command Language (DCL) in OpenVMS and RSX-11, the various Unix shells (sh, ksh, csh, tcsh, bash, etc.), the historical CP/M CCP, and MS-DOS/IBM-DOS/DR-DOS's COMMAND.COM, as well as the OS/2 and the Windows CMD.EXE programs, the latter groups being based heavily on DEC's RSX-11 and RSTS CLIs. Under most operating systems, it is possible to replace the default shell program with alternatives; examples include 4DOS for DOS, 4OS2 for OS/2, and 4NT or Take Command for Windows.

Although the term 'shell' is often used to describe a command-line interpreter, strictly speaking a 'shell' can be any program that constitutes the user-interface, including fully graphically oriented ones. For example, the default Windows GUI is a shell program named EXPLORER.EXE, as defined in the SHELL=EXPLORER.EXE line in the WIN. INI configuration file. These programs are shells, but not CLIs.

Application command-line Interfaces

Application programs (as opposed to operating systems) may also have command line interfaces.

An application program may support none, any, or all of these three major types of command line interface mechanisms:

1. Parameters: Most operating systems support a means to pass additional information to a program when it is launched. When a program is launched from an OS command line shell, additional text provided along with the program name is passed to the launched program.

2. Interactive command line sessions: After launch, a program may provide an operator with an independent means to enter commands in the form of text.

3. OS inter-process communication: Most operating systems support means of inter-process communication (for example; standard streams or named pipes). Command lines from client processes may be redirected to a CLI program by one of these methods.

CLI Software

Some applications support only a CLI, presenting a CLI prompt to the user and acting upon command lines as they are entered. Some examples of CLI-only applications are:

- DEBUG
- Diskpart
- Ed
- Edlin
- Fdisk
- Ping

Hybrid Software

Some computer programs support both a CLI and a GUI. In some cases, a GUI is simply a wrapper around a separate CLI executable file. In other cases, a program may provide a CLI as an optional alternative to its GUI. CLIs and GUIs often support different functionality. For example, all features of MATLAB, a numerical analysis computer program, are available via the CLI, whereas the MATLAB GUI exposes only a subset of features.

The early Sierra games, like the first three King's Quest games (1984–1986), used commands from an internal command line to move the character around in the graphic window.

History

The command-line interface evolved from a form of dialog once conducted by humans over teleprinter (TTY) machines, in which human operators remotely exchanged information, usually one line of text at a time. Early computer systems often used teleprinter machines as the means of interaction with a human operator. The computer became one end of the human-to-human teleprinter model. So instead of a human communicating with another human over a teleprinter, a human communicated with a computer.

In time, the actual mechanical teleprinter was replaced by a "glass tty" (keyboard and screen, but emulating the teleprinter), and then by a "smart" terminal (where a microprocessor in the terminal could address all of the screen, rather than only print successive lines). As the microcomputer revolution replaced the traditional – minicomputer + terminals – time sharing architecture, hardware terminals were replaced by terminal emulators — PC software that interpreted terminal signals sent through the PC's serial ports. These were typically used to interface an organization's new PC's with their existing mini- or mainframe computers, or to connect PC to PC. Some of these PCs were running Bulletin Board System software.

Early operating system CLIs were implemented as part of resident monitor programs, and could not easily be replaced. The concept of implementing the shell as a replaceable component is usually attributed to Multics.

Early microcomputers themselves were based on a command-line interface such as CP/M, MS-DOS or AppleSoft BASIC. Throughout the 1980s and 1990s—especially after the introduction of the Apple Macintosh and Microsoft Windows—command line interfaces were replaced in popular usage by the Graphical User Interface. The command line remains in use, however, by system administrators and other advanced users for system administration, computer programming, and batch processing.

In November 2006, Microsoft released version 1.0 of Windows PowerShell (formerly codenamed *Monad*), which combined features of traditional Unix shells with their proprietary object-oriented .NET Framework. MinGW and Cygwin are open-source packages for Windows that offer a Unix-like CLI. Microsoft provides MKS Inc.'s ksh implementation *MKS Korn shell* for Windows through their Services for UNIX add-on.

Since 2001, the Macintosh operating system is based on a variation of Unix called Darwin. On these computers, users can access a Unix-like command-line interface called Terminal found in the Applications Utilities folder. This terminal uses bash by default.

Screenshot of the MATLAB 7.4 command-line interface and GUI

Usage

A CLI is used whenever a large vocabulary of commands or queries, coupled with a wide (or arbitrary) range of options, can be entered more rapidly as text than with a pure GUI. This is typically the case with operating system command shells. CLIs are also used by systems with insufficient resources to support a graphical user interface. Some computer language systems (such as Python, Forth, LISP, Rexx, and many dialects of BASIC) provide an interactive command-line mode to allow for rapid evaluation of code.

CLIs are often used by programmers and system administrators, in engineering and scientific environments, and by technically advanced personal computer users. CLIs are also popular among people with visual disability, since the commands and responses can be displayed using Refreshable Braille displays.

Anatomy of a Shell CLI

The general pattern of an OS command line interface is:

Prompt command param1 param2 param3 ... paramN

- Prompt - generated by the program to provide context for the client.

- Command — provided by the client. Commands are usually one of three classes:

    1. Internal — recognized and processed by the command line interpreter itself and not dependent upon any external executable file.

    2. Included — A separate executable file generally considered part of the operating environment and always included with the OS.

    3. External — External executable files not part of the basic OS, but added by other parties for specific purposes and applications.

- param1 ...paramN — Optional parameters provided by the client. The format and meaning of the parameters depends upon the command issued. In the case of Included or External commands, the values of the parameters are delivered to the program (specified by the Command) as it is launched by the OS. Parameters may be either Arguments or Options.

In this example, the delimiters between command line elements are whitespace characters and the end-of-line delimiter is the newline delimiter. This is a widely used (but not universal) convention for command-line interfaces.

A CLI can generally be considered as consisting of syntax and semantics. The *syntax* is the grammar that all commands must follow. In the case of operating systems (OS), MS-DOS and Unix each define their own set of rules that all commands must follow. In the case of embedded systems, each vendor, such as Nortel, Juniper Networks or Cisco Systems, defines their own proprietary set of rules that all commands within their CLI conform to. These rules also dictate how a user navigates through the system of commands. The *semantics* define what sort of operations are possible, on what sort of data these operations can be performed, and how the grammar represents these operations and data—the symbolic meaning in the syntax.

Two different CLIs may agree on either syntax or semantics, but it is only when they agree on both that they can be considered sufficiently similar to allow users to use both CLIs without needing to learn anything, as well as to enable re-use of scripts.

A simple CLI will display a prompt, accept a "command line" typed by the user terminated by the Enter key, then execute the specified command and provide textual display of results or error messages. Advanced CLIs will validate, interpret and parameter-expand the command line before executing the specified command, and optionally capture or redirect its output.

Unlike a button or menu item in a GUI, a command line is typically self-documenting, stating exactly what the user wants done. In addition, command lines usually include many defaults that can be changed to customize the results. Useful command lines can be saved by assigning a character string or alias to represent the full command, or several commands can be grouped to perform a more complex sequence – for instance, compile the program, install it, and run it — creating a single entity, called a command procedure or script which itself can be treated as a command. These advantages mean that a user must figure out a complex command or series of commands only once, because they can be saved, to be used again.

The commands given to a CLI shell are often in one of the following forms:

- *doSomething how toFiles*

- *doSomething how sourceFile destinationFile*

- *doSomething how < inputFile > outputFile*

- *doSomething how | doSomething how | doSomething how > outputFile*

where *doSomething* is, in effect, a verb, *how* an adverb (for example, should the command be executed "verbosely" or "quietly") and *toFiles* an object or objects (typically one or more files) on which the command should act. The > in the third example is a redirection operator, telling the command-line interpreter to send the output of the command not to its own standard output (the screen) but to the named file. This will overwrite the file. Using >> will redirect the output and append it to the file. Another redirection operator is the vertical bar (|), which creates a pipeline where the output of one command becomes the input to the next command.

CLI and Resource Protection

One can modify the set of available commands by modifying which paths appear in the PATH environment variable. Under Unix, commands also need be marked as executable files. The directories in the path variable are searched in the order they are given. By re-ordering the path, one can run e.g. \OS2\MDOS\E.EXE instead of \OS2\E.EXE, when the default is the opposite. Renaming of the executables also works: people often rename their favourite editor to EDIT, for example.

The command line allows one to restrict available commands, such as access to advanced internal commands. The Windows CMD.EXE does this. Often, shareware programs will limit the range of commands, including printing a command 'your administrator has disabled running batch files' from the prompt.

Some CLIs, such as those in network routers, have a hierarchy of modes, with a different set of commands supported in each mode. The set of commands are grouped by association with security, system, interface, etc. In these systems the user might traverse through a series of sub-modes. For example, if the CLI had two modes called *interface* and *system*, the user might use the command *interface* to enter the interface mode. At this point, commands from the system mode may not be accessible and the user exits the interface mode and enters the system mode.

Command Prompt

A command prompt (or just *prompt*) is a sequence of (one or more) characters used in a command-line interface to indicate readiness to accept commands. Its intent is to literally prompt the user to take action. A prompt usually ends with one of the characters $, %, #, :, > and often includes other information, such as the path of the current working directory and hostname.

On many Unix and derivative systems, it is common for the prompt to end in $ or % if the user is a normal user, but in # if the user is a superuser ("root" in Unix terminology).

It is common for prompts to be modifiable by the user. Depending on the environment, they may include colors, special characters, and other elements like variables and functions for the current time, user, shell number or working directory, in order, for instance, to make the prompt more informative or visually pleasing, to distinguish sessions on various machines, or to indicate the current level of nesting of commands. On some systems, special tokens in the definition of the prompt can be used to cause external programs to be called by the command-line interpreter while displaying the prompt.

In DOS's COMMAND.COM and in Windows NT's cmd.exe the prompt is modifiable by issuing a prompt command or by directly changing the value of the corresponding %PROMPT% environment variable. The default of most modern systems, the C:\> style is obtained, for instance, with prompt PG. The default of older DOS systems, C> is obtained by just prompt, although on some systems this produces the newer C:\> style, unless used on floppy drives A: or B:; on those systems prompt NG can be used to override the automatic default and explicitly switch to the older style.

On many Unix systems, the $PS1 variable can be used, although other variables also may affect the prompt (depending on what shell is being used). In the bash shell, a prompt of the form:

[time] user@host: work_dir $

could be set by issuing the command

export PS1='[\t] \u@\H: \W $'

In zsh the $RPROMPT variable controls an optional "prompt" on the right hand side of the display. It is not a real prompt in that the location of text entry does not change. It is used to display information on the same line as the prompt, but right justified.

In RISC OS, the command prompt is a * symbol, and thus (OS)CLI commands are often referred to as "star commands". It is also possible to access the same commands from other command lines (such as the BBC BASIC command line), by preceding the command with a *.

Arguments

An MS DOS command line, illustrating parsing into command and arguments

A command-line argument or parameter is an item of information provided to a program when it is started. A program can have many command-line arguments that identify sources or destinations of information, or that alter the operation of the program.

When a command processor is active a program is typically invoked by typing its name followed by command-line arguments (if any). For example, in Unix and Unix-like environments, an example of a command-line argument is:

rm file.s

"file.s" is a command-line argument which tells the program rm to remove the file "file.s".

Some programming languages, such as C, C++ and Java, allow a program to interpret the command-line arguments by handling them as string parameters in the main function. Other languages, such as Python, expose these arguments as global variables.

In Unix-like operating systems, a single hyphen-minus by itself is usually a special value specifying that a program should handle data coming from the standard input or send data to the standard output.

Command-line Option

A command-line option or simply option (also known as a flag or switch) modifies the operation of a command; the effect is determined by the command's program. Options follow the command name on the command line, separated by spaces. A space before the first option is not always required, for example Dir/? and DIR /? have the same effect in DOS (list the DIR command's options) whereas dir --help (in many versions of Unix) *does* require the option to be preceded by at least one space (and is case-sensitive).

The format of options varies widely between operating systems. In most cases the syntax is by convention rather than an operating system requirement; the entire command line is simply a string passed to a program, which can process it in any way the programmer wants, so long as the interpreter can tell where the command name ends and its arguments and options begin.

A few representative samples of command-line options, all relating to listing files in a directory, to illustrate some conventions:

Operating system	Command	Valid alternative	Notes
OpenVMS	directory/owner	Dir /Owner	instruct the *directory* command to also display the ownership of the files. *Note the Directory command name is not case sensitive, and can be abbreviated to as few letters as required to remain unique.*
DOS	dir/Q/O:S d*	diR /q d* /o:s	display ownership of files whose names begin with "D", sorted by size, smallest first. *Note spaces around argument d* are required.*
Unix-like systems	ls -lS D*	ls -S -l D*	display in long format files and directories beginning with "D" (but not "d"), sorted by size (largest first). *Note spaces are required around all arguments and options, but some can be run together, e.g. -lS is the same as -l -S.*
Data General RDOS CLI	list/e/s 04-26-80/b	List /S/E 4-26-80/B	list every attribute for files created before 26 April 1980. *Note the /B at the end of the date argument is a local switch, that modifies the meaning of that argument, while /S and /E are global switches, i.e. apply to the whole command.*

Abbreviating Commands

In Multics, command-line options and subsystem keywords may be abbreviated. This idea appears to derive from the PL/I programming language, with its shortened keywords (e.g., STRG for STRINGRANGE and DCL for DECLARE). For example, in the Multics "forum" subsystem, the *-long_subject* parameter can be abbreviated *-lgsj*. It is also common for Multics commands to be abbreviated, typically corresponding to the initial letters of the words that are strung together with underscores to form command names, such as the use of *did* for *delete_iacl_dir*.

In some other systems abbreviations are automatic, such as permitting enough of the first characters of a command name to uniquely identify it (such as SU as an abbreviation for SUPERUSER) while others may have some specific abbreviations pre-programmed (e.g. MD for MKDIR in COMMAND.COM) or user-defined via batch scripts and aliases (e.g. alias md mkdir in tcsh).

Option conventions in DOS, Windows, OS/2

On DOS, OS/2 and Windows, different programs called from their COMMAND.COM or CMD.EXE (or internal their commands) may use different syntax within the same operating system. For example:

- Options may be indicated by either of the "switch characters": -, /, or either may be allowed.

- They may or may not be case-sensitive.

- Sometimes options and their arguments are run together, sometimes separated by whitespace, and sometimes by a character, typically : or =; thus Prog -fFilename, Prog -f Filename, Prog -f:Filename, Prog -f=Filename.

- Some programs allow single-character options to be combined; others do not. The switch -fA may mean the same as -f -A, or it may be incorrect, or it may even be a valid but different parameter.

In DOS, OS/2 and Windows, the forward slash (/) is most prevalent, although the hyphen-minus is also sometimes used. In many versions of DOS (MS-DOS/PC DOS 2.xx and higher, all versions of DR-DOS since 5.0, as well as PTS-DOS, Embedded DOS, FreeDOS and RxDOS) the switch character (sometimes abbreviated switchar or switchchar) to be used is defined by a value returned from a system call (INT 21h/AH=37h). The default character returned by this API is /, but can be changed to a hyphen-minus on the above-mentioned systems, except for Datalight ROM-DOS and MS-DOS/PC DOS 5.0 and higher, which always return / from this call (unless one of many available TSRs to reenable the SwitChar feature is loaded). In some of these systems (MS-DOS/PC DOS 2.xx, DOS Plus 2.1, DR-DOS 7.02 and higher, PTS-DOS, Embedded DOS, FreeDOS and RxDOS), the setting can also be pre-configured by a SWITCHAR directive in CONFIG.SYS. Embedded DOS provides a SWITCH command for the same purpose, whereas 4DOS allows the setting to be changed via SETDOS /W:n. Under DR-DOS, if the setting has been changed from /, the first directory separator \ in the display of the PROMPT parameter $G will change to a forward slash / (which is also a valid directory separator in DOS, FlexOS, 4680 OS, 4690 OS, OS/2 and Windows) thereby serving as a visual clue to indicate the change. Some versions of DR-DOS COMMAND.COM also support a PROMPT token $/ to display the current setting. COMMAND.COM since DR-DOS 7.02 and 4DOS also provide a pseudo-environment variable named %/% to allow portable batchjobs to be written. Several external DR-DOS commands additionally support an environment variable %SWITCHAR% to override the system setting.

However, many programs are hardwired to use / only, rather than retrieving the switch setting before parsing command line arguments. A very small number, mainly ports from Unix-like systems, are programmed to accept "-" even if the switch character is not set to it (for example netstat and ping, supplied with Windows, will accept the /? option to list available options, and yet the list will specify the "-" convention).

Option Conventions in Unix-like Systems

In Unix-like systems, the ASCII hyphen-minus begins options; the new (and GNU) convention is to use *two* hyphens then a word (e.g. --create) to identify the option's use while the old convention (and still available as an option for frequently-used options) is to use one hyphen then one letter (e.g. -c); if one hyphen is followed by two or more letters it may mean two options are being specified, or it may mean the second and subsequent letters are a parameter (such as filename or date) for the first option.

Two hyphen-minus characters without following letters (--) may indicate that the remaining arguments should not be treated as options, which is useful for example if a file name itself begins with a hyphen, or if further arguments are meant for an inner command (e.g. sudo). Double hyphen-minuses are also sometimes used to prefix "long options" where more descriptive option names are used. This is a common feature of GNU software. The *getopt* function and program, and the *getopts* command are usually used for parsing command-line options.

Unix command names, arguments and options are case-sensitive (except in a few examples, mainly where popular commands from other operating systems have been ported to Unix).

Options Conventions in Other Systems

FlexOS, 4680 OS and 4690 OS use -.

CP/M typically used.

Conversational Monitor System (CMS) uses a single left parenthesis to separate options at the end of the command from the other arguments. For example, in the following command the options indicate that the target file should be replaced if it exists, and the date and time of the source file should be retained on the copy: COPY source file a target file b (REPLACE OLDDATE

Data General's CLI under their RDOS, AOS, etc. operating systems, as well as the version of CLI that came with their Business Basic, uses only / as the switch character, is case-insensitive, and allows "local switches" on some arguments to control the way they are interpreted, such as MAC/U LIB/S A B C $LPT/L has the global option "U" to the macro assembler command to appemd user symbols, but two local switches, one to specify LIB should be skipped on pass 2 and the other to direct listing to the printer, $LPT.

Built-in Usage Help

One of the criticisms of a CLI is the lack of cues to the user as to the available actions. In contrast, GUIs usually inform the user of available actions with menus, icons, or other visual cues. To overcome this limitation, many CLI programs display a brief summary of its valid parameters, typically when invoked with no arguments or one of ?, -?, -h, -H, /?, /h, /H, -help, or --help.

However, entering a program name without parameters in the hope that it will display usage help can be hazardous, as some programs and scripts execute without further notice.

Although desirable at least for the help parameter, programs may not support all option lead-in characters exemplified above. Under DOS, where the default command line option character can be changed from / to -, programs may query the SwitChar API in order to determine the current setting. So, if a program is not hard-wired to support them all, a user may need to know the current setting even to be able to reliably request help. If the SwitChar has been changed to - and therefore the / character is accepted as alternative path delimiter also at the DOS command line, programs may misinterpret options like /h or /H as paths rather than help parameters. However, if given as first or only parameter, most DOS programs will, by convention, accept it as request for help regardless of the current SwitChar setting.

In some cases, different levels of help can be selected for a program. Some programs supporting this allow to give a verbosity level as an optional argument to the help parameter (as in /H:1, /H:2, etc.) or they give just a short help on help parameters with question mark and a longer help screen for the other help options.

Depending on the program, additional or more specific help on accepted parameters is sometimes available by either providing the parameter in question as an argument to the help parameter or vice versa (as in /H:W or in /W:? (assuming /W would be another parameter supported by the program)).

In a similar fashion to the help parameter, but much less common, some programs provide additional information about themselves (like mode, status, version, author, license or contact information) when invoked with an "about" parameter like -!, /!, -about, or --about.

Since the ? and ! characters typically also serve other purposes at the command line, they may not be available in all scenarios, therefore, they should not be the only options to access the corresponding help information.

If more detailed help is necessary than provided by a program's built-in internal help, many systems support a dedicated external "HELP *command*" command (or similar), which accepts a command name as calling parameter and will invoke an external help system.

In the DR-DOS family, typing /? or /H at the COMMAND.COM prompt instead of a command itself will display a dynamically generated list of available internal commands; 4DOS and NDOS support the same feature by typing ? at the prompt (which is also accepted by newer versions of DR-DOS COMMAND.COM); internal commands can be individually disabled or reenabled via SETDOS /I. In addition to this, some newer versions of DR-DOS COMMAND.COM also accept a ?% command to display a list of available built-in pseudo-environment variables. Besides their purpose as quick help reference this can be used in batchjobs to query the facilities of the underlying command line processor.

Command Description Syntax

Built-in usage help and man pages commonly employ a small syntax to describe the valid command form:

- angle brackets for *required* parameters: ping <hostname>

- square brackets for *optional* parameters: mkdir [-p] <dirname>

- ellipses for *repeated* items: cp <dest>

- vertical bars for *choice* of items: netstat {-t|-u}

Notice that these characters have different meanings than when used directly in the shell. Angle brackets may be omitted when confusing the parameter name with a literal string is not likely.

The Space Character

In many areas of computing, but particularly in the command line, the space character can cause problems as it has two distinct and incompatible functions: as part of a command or parameter, or as a parameter or name separator. Ambiguity can be prevented either by prohibiting embedded spaces in file and directory names in the first place (for example, by substituting them with underscores _), or by enclosing a name with embedded spaces between quote characters or using an escape character before the space, usually a backslash (\). For example

Long path/Long program name Parameter one Parameter two ...

is ambiguous (is "program name" part of the program name, or two parameters?); however

Long_path/Long_program_name Parameter_one Parameter_two ...,

LongPath/LongProgramName ParameterOne ParameterTwo ...,

"Long path/Long program name" "Parameter one" "Parameter two" ...

and

Long\ path/Long\ program\ name Parameter\ one Parameter\ two ...

are not ambiguous. Unix-based operating systems minimize the use of embedded spaces to minimize the need for quotes. In Microsoft Windows, one often has to use quotes because embedded spaces (such as in directory names) are common.

Command-line Interpreter

Although most users think of the shell as an interactive command interpreter, it is really a programming language in which each statement runs a command. Because it must satisfy both the interactive and programming aspects of command execution, it is a strange language, shaped as much by history as by design.

— Brian Kernighan & Rob Pike

The terms command-line interpreter, command line shell, command language interpreter, or identical abbreviation CLI, are applied to computer programs designed to interpret a sequence of lines of text which may be entered by a user, read from a file or another kind of data stream. The context of interpretation is usually one of a given operating system or programming language.

Command-line interpreters allow users to issue various commands in a very efficient (and often terse) way. This requires the user to know the names of the commands and their parameters, and the syntax of the language that is interpreted.

The Unix #! mechanism and OS/2 EXTPROC command facilitate the passing of batch files to external processors. One can use these mechanisms to write specific command processors for dedicated uses, and process external data files which reside in batch files.

Many graphical interfaces, such as the OS/2 Presentation Manager and early versions of Microsoft Windows use command-lines to call helper programs to open documents and programs. The commands are stored in the graphical shell or in files like the registry or the OS/2 os2user.ini file.

Early History

The earliest computers did not support interactive input/output devices, often relying on sense switches and lights to communicate with the computer operator. This was adequate for batch systems that ran one program at a time, often with the programmer acting as operator. This also had the advantage of low overhead, since lights and switches could be tested and set with one machine instruction. Later a single system console was added to allow the operator to communicate with the system.

From the 1960s onwards, user interaction with computers was primarily by means of command-line interfaces, initially on machines like the Teletype Model 33 ASR, but then on early CRT-based computer terminals such as the VT52.

All of these devices were purely text based, with no ability to display graphic or pictures. For business application programs, text-based menus were used, but for more general interaction the command line was the interface.

Around 1964 Louis Pouzin introduced the concept and the name *shell* in Multics, building on earlier, simpler facilities in the Compatible Time-Sharing System (CTSS).

From the early 1970s the Unix operating system adapted the concept of a powerful command-line environment, and introduced the ability to *pipe* the output of one command in as input to another. Unix also had the capability to save and re-run strings of commands as "shell scripts" which acted like custom commands.

The command-line was also the main interface for the early home computers such as the Commodore PET, Apple II and BBC Micro – almost always in the form of a BASIC interpreter. When more powerful business oriented microcomputers arrived with CP/M and later MS-DOS computers such as the IBM PC, the command-line began to borrow some of the syntax and features of the Unix shells such as globbing and piping of output.

The command-line was first seriously challenged by the PARC GUI approach used in the 1983 Apple Lisa and the 1984 Apple Macintosh. The majority of IBM PC users did not replace their command.com shell with a GUI until Windows 95 was released in 1995.

Modern Usage As an Operating System Shell

While most computer users now use a GUI almost exclusively, more advanced users have access to powerful command-line environments:

- The default VAX/VMS command shell, using the DCL language, has been ported to Windows systems at least three times, including PC-DCL and Acceler8 DCL Lite. MS-DOS 6.22 has been ported to Linux type systems, Unix command shells have been ported to VMS and MS-DOS/Windows 95 and Windows NT types of operating systems. Command.com and Windows NT cmd.exe have been ported to Windows CE and presumably works on Microsoft Windows NT Embedded 4.0

- Windows Resource Kit and Windows Services for Unix include Korn and the Bourne shells along with a Perl interpreter (Services of Unix contains Active State ActivePerl in later versions and Interix for versions 1 and 2 and a shell compiled by Microsoft)

- IBM OS/2 has the cmd.exe processor. This copies the command.com commands, with extensions to REXX.

- A different interpreter Cmd.exe is, along with Command.com are part of the Windows NT stream operating systems.

- Yet another Cmd.exe is a stripped-down shell for Windows CE 3.0

- An MS-DOS type interpreter called PocketDOS has been ported to Windows CE machines; the most recent release is almost identical to MS-DOS 6.22 and can also run Windows 1, 2, and 3.0, QBasic and other development tools, 4NT and 4DOS. The latest release includes several shells, namely MS-DOS 6.22, PC-DOS 7, DR DOS 3, and others

- PocketConsole is a Windows NT 4.0 shell for Windows CE that is much like 4NT

- Windows users have a CLI environment named Windows Command Prompt, which might use the CScript interface to alternate programs. PowerShell provides a command-line interface, but its applets are not written in shell-script. Implementations of the Unix shell are also available as part of the POSIX sub-system, Cygwin, MKS Toolkit, UWIN, Hamilton C shell and other software packages. Available shells for these interoperability tools include csh, ksh, sh, bash, rsh, tclsh and less commonly zsh, ysh, psh

- Command.com (4DOS), Windows NT cmd.exe (4NT, TCC), and OS/2 cmd.exe (4OS2) and others based on them are enhanced shells which can be a replacement for the native shell or a means of enhancement of the default shell

- Implementations of PHP have a shell for interactive use called php-cli

- Standard Tcl/Tk has two interactive shells, Tclsh and Wish, that latter being the GUI version.

- Python, Ruby, Lua, XLNT, and other interpreters also have command shells for interactive use

- FreeBSD uses tcsh as its default interactive shell for the superuser.

- Apple Mac OS X and many Linux distributions have the Bash implementation of the Unix shell. Early versions of OS X used tcsh as the default shell.

- Embedded Linux (and other embedded Unix-like) devices often use the Ash implementation of the Unix shell, as part of Busybox.

- Android uses the mksh shell, (a shell derived from ash in older versions) with commands from the separate *toolbox*.

- Routers with Cisco IOS, Junos and many others are commonly configured from the command line.

Scripting

Most command-line interpreters support scripting, to various extents. (They are, after all, interpreters of an interpreted programming language, albeit in many cases the language is unique to the particular command-line interpreter.) They will interpret scripts (variously termed shell scripts or batch files) written in the language that they interpret. Some command-line interpreters also incorporate the interpreter engines of other languages, such as REXX, in addition to their own, allowing the executing of scripts, in those languages, directly within the command-line interpreter itself.

Conversely, scripting programming languages, in particular those with an eval function (such as REXX, Perl, Python, Ruby or Jython), can be used to implement command-line interpreters and filters. For a few operating systems, most notably DOS, such a command interpreter provides a more flexible command line interface than the one supplied. In other cases, such a command interpreter can present a highly customised user interface employing the user interface and input/output facilities of the language.

Other Command-line Interfaces

The command line provides an interface between programs as well as the user. In this sense, a command line is an alternative to a dialog box. Editors and data-bases present a command line, in which alternate command processors might run. On the other hand, one might have options on the command line which opens a dialog box. The latest version of 'Take Command' has this feature. DBase used a dialog box to construct command lines, which could be further edited before use.

Programs like Basic, Diskpart, Edlin, and QBasic all provide command-line interfaces, some of which use the system shell. Basic is modeled on the default interface for 8-bit Intel computers. Calculators can be run as command-line or dialog interfaces.

Emacs provides a command line interface in the form of its minibuffer. Commands and arguments can be entered using Emacs standard text editing support, and output is displayed in another buffer.

There are a number of pre-mouse games, like *Adventure* or *King's Quest 1-3*, which relied on the user typing commands at the bottom of the screen. One controls the character by typing commands like 'get ring' or 'look'. The program returns a text which describes how the character sees it, or makes the action happen. The text adventure *The Hitchhiker's Guide to the Galaxy*, a piece of interactive fiction based on Douglas Adam's book of the same name, is a teletype-style command-line game.

The most notable of these interfaces is the standard streams interface, which allows the output of one command to be passed to the input of another. Text files can serve either purpose as well. This provides the interfaces of piping, filters and redirection. Under

Unix, devices are files too, so the normal type of file for the shell used for stdin,stdout and stderr is a tty device file.

Another command-line interface allows a shell program to launch helper programs, either to launch documents or start a program. The command is processed internally by the shell, and then passed on to another program to launch the document. The graphical interface of Windows and OS/2 rely heavily on command-lines passed through to other programs – console or graphical, which then usually process the command line without presenting a user-console.

Programs like the OS/2 E editor and some other IBM editors, can process command-lines normally meant for the shell, the output being placed directly in the document window.

A web browser's URL input field can be used as a command line. It can be used to "launch" web apps, access browser configuration, as well as perform a search. Google, which has been called "the command line of the internet" will perform a domain-specific search when it detects search parameters in a known format. This functionality is present whether the search is triggered from a browser field or one on Google's web site.

Command (Computing)

In computing, a command is a directive to a computer program acting as an interpreter of some kind, in order to perform a specific task. Most commonly a command is either a directive to some kind of command-line interface, such as a shell, or an event in a graphical user interface triggered by the user selecting an option in a menu.

Specifically, the term *command* is used in imperative computer languages. These languages are called this, because statements in these languages are usually written in a manner similar to the imperative mood used in many natural languages. If one views a statement in an imperative language as being like a sentence in a natural language, then a command is generally like a verb in such a language.

Many programs allow specially formatted arguments, known as flags or options, which modify the default behaviour of the command, while further arguments describe what the command acts on. Comparing to a natural language: the flags are adverbs, whilst the other arguments are objects.

Examples

Here are some commands given to a command-line interpreter (Unix shell).

The following command changes the user's place in the directory tree from their current position to the directory /home/pete. The command is cd and the argument is /home/pete:

cd /home/pete

The following command prints the text Hello World out to the standard output stream, which, in this case, will just print the text out on the screen. The command is echo and the argument is "Hello World". The quotes are used to prevent Hello and World being treated as separate arguments:

echo "Hello World"

The following commands are equivalent. They list files in the directory /bin. The command is ls, the argument is /bin and there are three flags: -l, -t and -r.

ls -l -t -r /bin

ls -ltr /bin

The following command displays the contents of the files ch1.txt and ch2.txt. The command is cat, and ch1.txt and ch2.txt are both arguments.

cat ch1.txt ch2.txt

Here are some commands given to a different command-line interpreter (the DOS, OS/2 and Microsoft Windows command prompt). Notice that the flags are identified differently but that the concepts are the same:

The following command lists all the contents of the current directory. The command is dir, and "A" is a flag. There is no argument.

dir /A

The following command displays the contents of the file readme.txt. The command is type. The argument is "readme.txt". "P" is a parameter.

type /P readme.txt

References

- "Introduction Section". Recent advances in business administration. [S.l.]: Wseas. 2010. p. 190. ISBN 978-960-474-161-8.

- Raskin, Jef (2000). The human interface : new directions for designing interactive systems (1. printing. ed.). Reading, Mass. [u.a.]: Addison Wesley. ISBN 0-201-37937-6.

- Naumann, J. Search for Paradise: A Patient's Account of the Artificial Vision Experiment (2012), Xlibris Corporation, ISBN 1-479-7092-04

- Errett, Joshua. "As app fatigue sets in, Toronto engineers move on to chatbots". CBC. CBC/Radio-Canada. Retrieved July 4, 2016.

Understanding Graphical User Interface

Electronic devices interact with users with the help of a graphical user interface. Multiple document interface is a user interface which allows windows to reside under a single window. The chapter also focuses on object-action interfaces, pointers and widgets.

Graphical User interface

In computer science, a graphical user interface (GUI), is a type of user interface that allows users to interact with electronic devices through graphical icons and visual indicators such as secondary notation, instead of text-based user interfaces, typed command labels or text navigation. GUIs were introduced in reaction to the perceived steep learning curve of command-line interfaces (CLIs), which require commands to be typed on a computer keyboard.

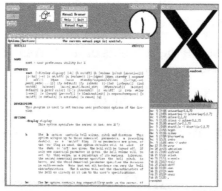

A Unix-based X Window System desktop

The actions in a GUI are usually performed through direct manipulation of the graphical elements. Beyond computers, GUIs are used in many handheld mobile devices such as MP3 players, portable media players, gaming devices, smartphones and smaller household, office and industrial equipment. The term *GUI* tends not to be applied to other lower-display resolution types of interfaces, such as video games (where *head-up display* (HUD) is preferred), or not restricted to flat screens, like volumetric displays because the term is restricted to the scope of two-dimensional display screens able to describe generic information, in the tradition of the computer science research at the Xerox Palo Alto Research Center (PARC).

User Interface and Interaction Design

The graphical user interface is presented (displayed) on the computer screen. It is the result of processed user input and usually the main interface for human-machine interaction. The touch user interfaces popular on small mobile devices are an overlay of the visual output to the visual input.

Designing the visual composition and temporal behavior of a GUI is an important part of software application programming in the area of human–computer interaction. Its goal is to enhance the efficiency and ease of use for the underlying logical design of a stored program, a design discipline named *usability*. Methods of user-centered design are used to ensure that the visual language introduced in the design is well-tailored to the tasks.

The visible graphical interface features of an application are sometimes referred to as *chrome* or *GUI* (pronounced *gooey*). Typically, users interact with information by manipulating visual widgets that allow for interactions appropriate to the kind of data they hold. The widgets of a well-designed interface are selected to support the actions necessary to achieve the goals of users. A model–view–controller allows a flexible structure in which the interface is independent from and indirectly linked to application functions, so the GUI can be customized easily. This allows users to select or design a different *skin* at will, and eases the designer's work to change the interface as user needs evolve. Good user interface design relates to users more, and to system architecture less.

Large widgets, such as windows, usually provide a frame or container for the main presentation content such as a web page, email message or drawing. Smaller ones usually act as a user-input tool.

A GUI may be designed for the requirements of a vertical market as application-specific graphical user interfaces. Examples include automated teller machines (ATM), point of sale (POS) touchscreens at restaurants, self-service checkouts used in a retail store, airline self-ticketing and check-in, information kiosks in a public space, like a train station or a museum, and monitors or control screens in an embedded industrial application which employ a real-time operating system (RTOS).

By the 1990s, cell phones and handheld game systems also employed application specific touchscreen GUIs. Newer automobiles use GUIs in their navigation systems and multimedia centers, and/or navigation multimedia center combinations.

Components

A GUI uses a combination of technologies and devices to provide a platform that users can interact with, for the tasks of gathering and producing information.

A series of elements conforming a visual language have evolved to represent information stored in computers. This makes it easier for people with few computer skills to work with and use computer software. The most common combination of such elements in GUIs is the *windows, icons, menus, pointer* (WIMP) paradigm, especially in personal computers.

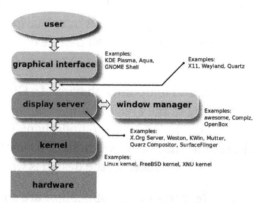

Layers of a GUI based on a windowing system

The WIMP style of interaction uses a virtual input device to control the position of a pointing device, most often a mouse, and presents information organized in windows and represented with icons. Available commands are compiled together in menus, and actions are performed making gestures with the pointing device. A window manager facilitates the interactions between windows, applications, and the windowing system. The windowing system handles hardware devices such as pointing devices, graphics hardware, and positioning of the pointer.

In personal computers, all these elements are modeled through a desktop metaphor to produce a simulation called a desktop environment in which the display represents a desktop, on which documents and folders of documents can be placed. Window managers and other software combine to simulate the desktop environment with varying degrees of realism.

Post-WIMP Interfaces

Smaller mobile devices such as personal digital assistants (PDAs) and smartphones typically use the WIMP elements with different unifying metaphors, due to constraints in space and available input devices. Applications for which WIMP is not well suited may use newer interaction techniques, collectively termed *post-WIMP* user interfaces.

As of 2011, some touchscreen-based operating systems such as Apple's iOS (iPhone) and Android use the class of GUIs named post-WIMP. These support styles of interaction using more than one finger in contact with a display, which allows actions such as pinching and rotating, which are unsupported by one pointer and mouse.

Interaction

Human interface devices, for the efficient interaction with a GUI include a computer keyboard, especially used together with keyboard shortcuts, pointing devices for the cursor (or rather pointer) control: mouse, pointing stick, touchpad, trackball, joystick, virtual keyboards, and head-up displays (translucent information devices at the eye level).

There are also actions performed by programs that affect the GUI. For example, there are components like inotify or D-Bus to facilitate communication between computer programs.

History

The Xerox Alto was the first device to use a graphical user interface.

Precursors

A precursor to GUIs was invented by researchers at the Stanford Research Institute, led by Douglas Engelbart. They developed the use of text-based hyperlinks manipulated with a mouse for the On-Line System (NLS). The concept of hyperlinks was further refined and extended to graphics by researchers at Xerox PARC and specifically Alan Kay, who went beyond text-based hyperlinks and used a GUI as the main interface for the Xerox Alto computer, released in 1973. Most modern general-purpose GUIs are derived from this system.

Ivan Sutherland developed a pointer-based system called the Sketchpad in 1963. It used a light pen to guide creating and manipulating objects in engineering drawings.

PARC User Interface

The PARC user interface consisted of graphical elements such as windows, menus, radio buttons, and check boxes. The concept of icons was later introduced by David Canfield Smith, who had written a thesis on the subject under the guidance of Kay. The PARC user interface employs a pointing device along with a keyboard. These aspects can be emphasized by using the alternative term and acronym for *windows, icons, menus, pointing device* (WIMP).

The Xerox Star 8010 workstation introduced the first commercial GUI.

Evolution

Following PARC the first GUI-centric computer operating model was the *Xerox 8010 Information System* (Xerox Star) in 1981, followed by the Apple Lisa (which presented the concept of menu bar and window controls) in 1983, the Apple Macintosh 128K in 1984, and the Atari ST and Commodore Amiga in 1985.

Visi On was released in 1983 for the IBM PC compatible computers, but was never popular due to its high hardware demands. Nevertheless, it was a crucial influence on the contemporary development of Microsoft Windows.

Apple, IBM and Microsoft used many of Xerox's ideas to develop products, and IBM's Common User Access specifications formed the basis of the user interfaces used in Microsoft Windows, IBM OS/2 Presentation Manager, and the Unix Motif toolkit and window manager. These ideas evolved to create the interface found in current versions of Microsoft Windows, and in various desktop environments for Unix-like operating systems, such as macOS and Linux. Thus most current GUIs have largely common idioms.

Macintosh 128K, the first Macintosh (1984)

Popularization

GUIs were a hot topic in the early 1980s. The Apple Lisa was released in 1983, and various windowing systems existed for DOS operating systems. Individual applications for many platforms presented their own GUI variants. Despite the GUIs advantages, many reviewers questioned the value of the entire concept, citing hardware limits, and problems in finding compatible software.

In 1984, Apple released a television commercial which introduced the Apple Macintosh during the telecast of Super Bowl XVIII by CBS, with allusions to George Orwell's noted novel, *Nineteen Eighty-Four*. The commercial was aimed at making people think about computers, identifying the user-friendly interface as a personal computer which departed from prior business-oriented systems, and becoming a signature representation of Apple products.

Accompanied by an extensive marketing campaign, Windows 95 was a major success in the marketplace at launch and shortly became the most popular desktop operating system.

In 2007, with the iPhone and later in 2010 with the introduction of the iPad, Apple popularized the post-WIMP style of interaction for multi-touch screens, and those devices were considered to be milestones in the development of mobile devices.

The GUIs familiar to most people as of the mid-2010s are Microsoft Windows, OS X, and the X Window System interfaces for desktop and laptop computers, and Android, Apple's iOS, Symbian, BlackBerry OS, Windows Phone, Palm OS-WebOS, and Firefox OS for handheld (smartphone) devices.

Comparison to Other Interfaces

Command-line Interfaces

A modern CLI

Since the commands available in command line interfaces can be many, complex operations can be performed using a short sequence of words and symbols. This allows greater efficiency and productivity once many commands are learned, but reaching this level takes some time because the command words may not be easily discoverable or mnemonic. Also, using the command line can become slow and error-prone when users must enter long commands comprising many parameters and/or several different filenames at once. However, *windows, icons, menus, pointer* (WIMP) interfaces present users with many widgets that represent and can trigger some of the system's available commands.

GUIs can be made quite hard when dialogs are buried deep in a system, or moved about to different places during redesigns. Also, icons and dialog boxes are usually harder for users to script.

WIMPs extensively use modes, as the meaning of all keys and clicks on specific positions on the screen are redefined all the time. Command line interfaces use modes only in limited forms, such as for current directory and environment variables.

Most modern operating systems provide both a GUI and some level of a CLI, although the GUIs usually receive more attention. The GUI is usually WIMP-based, although occasionally other metaphors surface, such as those used in Microsoft Bob, 3dwm, or File System Visualizer (FSV).

GUI Wrappers

Graphical user interface (GUI) wrappers circumvent the command-line interface versions (CLI) of (typically) Linux and Unix-like software applications and their text-based user interfaces or typed command labels. While command-line or text-based application allow users to run a program non-interactively, GUI wrappers atop them avoid the steep learning curve of the command-line, which requires commands to be typed on the keyboard. By starting a GUI wrapper, users can intuitively interact with polipo, start, stop, and change its working parameters, through graphical icons and visual indicators of a desktop environment, for example. Applications may also provide both interfaces, and when they do the GUI is usually a WIMP wrapper around the command-line version. This is especially common with applications designed for Unix-like operating systems. The latter used to be implemented first because it allowed the developers to focus exclusively on their product's functionality without bothering about interface details such as designing icons and placing buttons. Designing programs this way also allows users to run the program in a shell script. An example of this basic design could be the specialized polipo command-line web proxy server, which has some connected GUI wrapper projects, e.g., for Windows OS (*solipo*), OS X (*dolipo*), and Android (*polipoid*).

Three-dimensional User Interfaces

For typical computer displays, *three-dimensional* is a misnomer—their displays are two-dimensional. Semantically, however, most graphical user interfaces use three dimensions. With height and width, they offer a third dimension of layering or stacking screen elements over one another. This may be represented visually on screen through an illusionary transparent effect, which offers the advantage that information in background windows may still be read, if not interacted with. Or the environment may simply hide the background information, possibly making the distinction apparent by drawing a drop shadow effect over it.

Some environments use the methods of 3D graphics to project virtual three dimensional user interface objects onto the screen. These are often shown in use in science fiction films. As the processing power of computer graphics hardware increases, this becomes less of an obstacle to a smooth user experience.

Three-dimensional graphics are currently mostly used in computer games, art, and computer-aided design (CAD). A three-dimensional computing environment can also be useful in other uses, like molecular graphics and aircraft design.

Several attempts have been made to create a multi-user three-dimensional environment, including the Croquet Project and Sun's Project Looking Glass.

Technologies

The use of three-dimensional graphics has become increasingly common in mainstream operating systems, from creating attractive interfaces, termed eye candy, to functional purposes only possible using three dimensions. For example, user switching is represented by rotating a cube which faces are each user's workspace, and window management is represented via a Rolodex-style flipping mechanism in Windows Vista. In both cases, the operating system transforms windows on-the-fly while continuing to update the content of those windows.

Interfaces for the X Window System have also implemented advanced three-dimensional user interfaces through compositing window managers such as Beryl, Compiz and KWin using the AIGLX or XGL architectures, allowing use of OpenGL to animate user interactions with the desktop.

Another branch in the three-dimensional desktop environment is the three-dimensional GUIs that take the desktop metaphor a step further, like the BumpTop, where users can manipulate documents and windows as if they were physical documents, with realistic movement and physics.

The zooming user interface (ZUI) is a related technology that promises to deliver the representation benefits of 3D environments without their usability drawbacks of orientation problems and hidden objects. It is a logical advance on the GUI, blending some three-dimensional movement with two-dimensional or *2.5D* vector objects. In 2006, Hillcrest Labs introduced the first zooming user interface for television.

In Science Fiction

Three-dimensional GUIs appeared in science fiction literature and films before they were technically feasible or in common use. For example; the 1993 American film *Jurassic Park* features Silicon Graphics' three-dimensional file manager File System Navigator, a real-life file manager for Unix operating systems. The film Minority Report has scenes of police officers using specialized 3d data systems. In prose fiction, three-dimensional user interfaces have been portrayed as immersible environments like William Gibson's Cyberspace or Neal Stephenson's Metaverse. Many futuristic imaginings of user interfaces rely heavily on object-oriented user interface (OOUI) style and especially object-oriented graphical user interface (OOGUI) style.

Multiple Document Interface

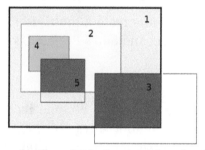

An example of a multiple document interface layout

A multiple document interface (MDI) is a graphical user interface in which multiple windows reside under a single parent window. Such systems often allow child windows to embed other windows inside them as well, creating complex nested hierarchies. This contrasts with single document interfaces (SDI) where all windows are independent of each other.

Comparison with Single Document Interface

In the usability community, there has been much debate about whether the multiple document or single document interface is preferable. Software companies have used both interfaces with mixed responses. For example, Microsoft changed its Office applications from SDI to MDI mode and then back to SDI, although the degree of implementation varies from one component to another. SDI can be more useful in cases where users switch more often between separate applications than among the windows of one application.

The disadvantage of MDI usually cited is its lack of information about the currently opened windows: In MDI applications, the application developer must provide a way to switch between documents or view a list of open windows, and the user might have to use an application-specific menu ("window list" or something similar) to switch between open documents. This is in contrast to SDI applications, where the window manager's task bar or task manager displays the currently opened windows. However, in recent years it has become increasingly common for MDI applications to use "tabs" to display the currently opened windows, which has made this criticism somewhat obsolete. An interface in which tabs are used to manage open documents is referred to as a "tabbed document interface" (TDI).

Another option is "tiled" panes or windows, which make it easier to prevent content from overlapping.

Some applications allow the user to switch between these modes at their choosing, depending on personal preference or the task at hand.

Nearly all graphical user interface toolkits to date provide at least one solution for designing MDIs, with an exception being Apple's Cocoa API. The Java GUI toolkit, Swing, for instance, provides the class javax.swing.JDesktopPane which serves as a container for individual frames (class javax.swing.JInternalFrame). GTK+ lacks any standardized support for MDI.

Advantages

- With multiple document interfaces (and also tabbed document interfaces), a single menu bar and/or toolbar is shared between all child windows, reducing clutter and increasing efficient use of screen space. This argument is less relevant on an operating system which uses a common menu bar.

- An application's child windows can be hidden/shown/minimized/maximized as a whole.

- Features such as "Tile" and "Cascade" can be implemented for the child windows.

- Authors of cross-platform applications can provide their users with consistent application behaviour between platforms.

- If the windowing environment and OS lack good window management, the application author can implement it themselves.

- Modularity: An advanced window manager can be upgraded independently of the applications

Disadvantages

- Can be tricky to implement on desktops using multiple monitors as the parent window may need to span two or more monitors, hiding sections.

- Virtual desktops cannot be spanned by children of the MDI. However, in some cases, this is solveable by initiating another parent window; this is the case in Opera and Chrome, for example, which allows tabs/child windows to be dragged outside of the parent window to start their own parent window. In other cases, each child window is also a parent window, forming a new, "virtual" MDI .

- MDI can make it more difficult to work with several applications at once, by restricting the ways in which windows from multiple applications can be arranged together without obscuring each other.

- The shared menu might change, which may cause confusion to some users.

- MDI child windows behave differently from those in single document interface applications, requiring users to learn two subtly different windowing concepts. Similarly, the MDI parent window behaves like the desktop in many respects, but has enough differences to confuse some users.

- Deeply nested, branching hierarchies of child windows can be confusing.

- Many window managers have built-in support for manipulating groups of separate windows, which is typically more flexible than MDI in that windows can be grouped and ungrouped arbitrarily. A typical policy is to group automatically windows that belong to the same application. This arguably makes MDI redundant by providing a solution to the same problem.

- Controls and hotkeys learned for the MDI application may not apply to others, whereas with an advanced Window Manager, more behavior and user preference settings are shared across client applications on the same system

- Without an MDI frame window, floating toolbars from one application can clutter the workspace of other applications, potentially confusing users with the jumble of interfaces.

Application Examples

- Internet Explorer 6: a typical SDI application

- Visual Studio 6 development environment: a typical modern MDI

- Visual Studio .NET: MDI or TDI with "Window" menu, but not both

- Opera: Combination of MDI and TDI (a true MDI interface with a tab bar for quick access).

- Chrome: Combination of MDI and TDI.

- Paint.NET: Thumbnail-based, TDI

- Firefox: TDI by default, can be SDI

- Kate: Text editor designed for the KDE Software Compilation, with advanced features and a sophisticated MDI

- KWrite: Another text editor designed for the KDE Software Compilation, with a simplified SDI but sharing many of Kate's features via a mutual back end

- GIMP: SDI with floating windows (MDI is available as an option called "Single-Window Mode" since version 2.8).

- GIMPshop: A fork of GIMP aiming to be more like Adobe Photoshop. The Windows version has limited MDI.

- AmiBroker: is a multiple document interface (MDI) application (for technical analysis and financial market trading). In short it means that it allows you to open and work with multiple windows at the same time.

- Adobe Photoshop: MDI under MS Windows. In newer versions, toolbars can move outside the frame window. Child windows can be outside the frame unless they are minimized or maximized.

- Adobe Acrobat: MDI until version 7.0 (Windows-only); SDI default in 8.0 (configurable to MDI); SDI only in 9.0; MDI (with a tabbed interface) in version 2015.

- Microsoft Excel 2003: SDI if you start new instances of the application, but MDI if you click the "File → New" menu (but child windows optionally appear on the OS taskbar). SDI only as of 2013.

- Microsoft Word 2003: MDI until Microsoft Office 97. After 2000, Word has a Multiple Top-Level Windows Interface, thus exposing to shell individual SDI instances, while the operating system recognizes it as a single instance of an MDI application. In Word 2000, this was the only interface available, but 2002 and later offer MDI as an option. Microsoft Foundation Classes (which Office is loosely based on) supports this metaphor since version 7.0, as a new feature in Visual Studio 2002. SDI only as of 2013.

- UltraEdit: Combination of MDI and TDI (a true MDI interface with a tab bar for quick access).

- VEDIT: Combination of MDI and TDI (a true MDI interface with a tab bar for quick access). Special "Full size" windows act like maximized windows, but allow smaller overlapping windows to be used at the same time. Multiple instances of Vedit can be started, which allows it to be used like an SDI application.

- Notepad++, PSPad, TextMate and many other text editors: TDI

- EmEditor: Options for either SDI or MDI.

- Macromedia Studio for Windows: a hybrid interface; TDI unless document windows are un-maximized. (They are maximized by default.)

- Corel Wordperfect: MDI. A user can open multiple instances of WP with a single document in each, if they have multiple versions of WordPerfect installed on their computer. Recent versions maintain a list of open documents for a given window on the status bar at the bottom of the window, providing a variant of the TDI.

- Zeus for Windows: Combination of MDI and TDI (a true MDI interface with a tab bar for quick access).

- mIRC: MDI by default, can also work on SDI mode

IDE-style Interface

Graphical computer applications with an IDE-style interface (IDE) are those whose child windows reside under a single parent window (usually with the exception of modal windows). An IDE-style interface is distinguishable from the Multiple Document Interface (MDI), because all child windows in an IDE-style interface are enhanced with added functionality not ordinarily available in MDI applications. Because of this, IDE-style applications can be considered a functional superset and descendant of MDI applications.

Examples of enhanced child-window functionality include:

- Dockable child windows

- Collapsible child windows

- Tabbed document interface for sub-panes

- Independent sub-panes of the parent window

- GUI splitters to resize sub-panes of the parent window

- Persistence for window arrangements

Collapsible Child Windows

A common convention for child windows in IDE-style applications is the ability to collapse child windows, either when inactive, or when specified by the user. Child windows that are collapsed will conform to one of the four outer boundaries of the parent window, with some kind of label or indicator that allows them to be expanded again.

Tabbed Document Interface for Sub-panes

In contrast to (MDI) applications, which ordinarily allow a single tabbed interface for the parent window, applications with an IDE-style interface allow tabs for organizing one or more subpanes of the parent window.

IDE-style Application Examples

- NetBeans

- dBASE

- Eclipse

- Visual Studio 6

- Visual Studio .NET

- RSS Bandit

- JEdit

- MATLAB

- Microsoft Excel when in MDI mode

Macintosh

Mac OS and its GUI are document-centric instead of window-centric or application-centric. Every document window is an object with which the user can work. The menu bar changes to reflect whatever application the front window belongs to. Application windows can be hidden and manipulated as a group, and the user may switch between applications (i.e., groups of windows) or between individual windows, automatically hiding palettes, and most programs will stay running even with no open windows. Indeed, prior to Mac OS X, it was purposely impossible to interleave windows from multiple applications.

In spite of this, some unusual applications breaking the human interface guidelines (most notably Photoshop) do exhibit different behavior.

Object–action Interface

Object–action interface, also abbreviated as OAI, is an extension to the graphical user interface, especially related to direct manipulation user interface and it can help to create better human-computer interfaces and increase the usability of a product.

There are basically two similar models regarding OAI.

This model focuses on the priority of the object over the actions (i.e. it emphasizes the object being selected first, and then any action performed on it. OAI adheres to this model.

Action–object Interface

This model suggests that the user of the interface specify the action before stating what object the action be performed upon. An example of this model can be command-line interface (e.g. copy <Source_File> <Destination_File>, here the action "copy" is specified prior to the object "file").

In the present context, the interface design is overwhelmed by GUIs. And hence more concern is given to the visual representation of the user's task objects and actions.It helps to reduces the adverse effect in case the users switch their mind mode from task domain to tool domain.

OAI Model

The OAI model graphically represents the users' workplace using metaphors and let the users perform action(s) on the object. The sequence of work is to first select the object graphically (using mouse or other pointing device), and then performing an action on the selected object. The result/effect of the action is then shown graphically to the user. This way, the user is relieved from memory limitation, and syntactical complexity of the actions. Moreover, it emulates WYSIWYG. This feature of OAI lets the user control their sequence of action and visualize the effects at the runtime. If an action results in an undesired effect, the user simply reverses his sequence of actions.

In the action–object model, the computer is seen as a tool to perform different action. Whereas in the object–action model, the user gains a great sense of control from the feeling of a direct involvement. The computer in this case is seen as a medium through which different tools are represented, which is isomorphic to interacting with objects in the real world.

Designing an OAI model starts with examining and understanding the tasks to be performed by the system. The domain of tasks include the universe of objects within which the user works to accomplish a certain goal as well as the domain of all possible actions performed by the user. Once these tasks objects and actions are agreed upon, the designer starts by creating an isomorphic representation of the corresponding interface objects and actions.

The figure above shows how the designer maps the objects of the user's world to metaphors and actions to plans. The interface actions are usually performed by pointing device or keyboard and hence have to be visual to the user so that the latter can decompose his plan into steps of actions such as pointing, clicking, dragging, etc.

This way DMUIs provide a snapshot of the real world situations and map the natural way of user's work sequence through the interface. This means that the users do not have to memorize the course of actions and it reduces the time required to familiarize themselves with the new model of work. Moreover, it reduces the memory load of the users significantly and therefore enhances the usability.

Task Hierarchies of Objects and Actions

Tasks are composed of objects and actions at different levels. The positional hierarchy of any object and its related action may not be suitable for every user, but by being comprehensible they provide a great deal of usefulness.

For the User

The most natural way of solving a complex problem is to divide it into sub-problems and then tackle them independently. Then by merging the solutions, a solution for the main problem is reached. This is basically a Divide-and-Conquer approach to problem-solving. This approach is followed in the real world by users when they perform tasks. Each complex task is divided into simple tasks. It is easy to see then, that by managing different levels within a hierarchy, the process is simplified. Through this method, users learn to execute tasks without considering the issues of implementation.

For the Designer

Ben Shneiderman suggests the following steps for designers to build a correct task hierarchy:

1. Know about the users and their tasks (Interviewing users, reading workbooks and taking training sessions)

2. Generate hierarchies of tasks and objects to model the users' tasks

3. Design interface objects and actions that metaphorically map to the real world universe

Interface Hierarchy of Objects and Actions

This hierarchy is similar to that of the task hierarchy and contains:

Interface Objects

Users interacting with system build up a basic concept/model of computer related objects like files, buttons, dialog box etc. They also acquire a brief experience of the properties of the objects and how to manipulate the object through its properties. Moreover, they learn how to perform actions on those objects to achieve their computing goals. Hence, a hierarchy of such objects is maintained (which represent the resource of the interface).

Interface Actions

This hierarchy consists of decomposed low level units of complex actions that could be performed on objects relevant to the domain of computers as assigned in the interface objects hierarchy. Each level in the hierarchy represent different level of decompositions. A high level plan to create a text file might involve mid-level actions such as creating a file, inserting text and saving that file. The mid-level action of saving a file the file can be decomposed into lower level actions such as storing the file with a backup copy and applying the access control rights. Further lower level actions might involve choosing the name of the file, the folder to save in, dealing with errors such as space shortage and so on.

For the User

There are several ways users learn interface objects and actions such as demonstrations, sessions, or trial and error sessions. When these objects and actions have logical structure that can be related to other familiar task objects and actions, this knowledge becomes stable in the user's memory.

For the Designer

The OAI model helps a designer to understand the complex processes that a user has to perform in order to successfully use an interface to perform a certain task. Designers model the interface actions and objects based on familiar example and then fine tune these models to fit the task and the user.

Pointer (User Interface)

Common pointer types (enlarged)

In computing, a pointer or mouse cursor (as part of a personal computer WIMP style of interaction) is a symbol or graphical image on the computer monitor or other display device that echoes movements of the pointing device, commonly a mouse, touchpad, or stylus pen. It signals the point where actions of the user take place. It can be used in text-based or graphical user interfaces to select and move other elements. It is distinct from the cursor, which responds to keyboard input. The cursor may also be repositioned using the pointer.

The pointer commonly appears as an angled arrow, (angled because historically that improved appearance on low resolution screens) but it can vary within different programs or operating systems. The use of a pointer is employed when the input method, or pointing device, is a device that can move fluidly across a screen and select or highlight objects on the screen. In GUIs where the input method relies on hard keys, such as the five-way key on many mobile phones, there is no pointer employed, and instead the GUI relies on a clear focus state.

Appearance

The pointer "hotspot" is the active pixel of the pointer, used to target a click or drag. The hotspot is normally along the pointer edges or in its center, though it may reside at any location in the pointer.

In many GUIs, moving the pointer around the screen may reveal other screen hotspots as the pointer changes shape depending on the circumstances. For example:

- In text that the user can select or edit, the pointer changes to a vertical bar with little cross-bars (or curved serif-like extensions) at the top and bottom — sometimes called an "I-beam" since it resembles the cross-section of the construction detail of the same name.

- When displaying a document, the pointer can appear as a hand with all fingers extended allowing scrolling by "pushing" the displayed page around.

- Graphics-editing pointers such as brushes, pencils or paint buckets may display when the user edits an image.

- On an edge or corner of a window the pointer usually changes into a double arrow (horizontal, vertical, or diagonal) indicating that the user can drag the edge/corner in an indicated direction in order to adjust the size and shape of the window.

- The corners and edges of the whole screen may also act as hotspots. According to Fitts's law, which predicts the time it takes to reach a target area, moving mouse and stylus pointers to those spots is easy and fast. As the pointer usually stops when reaching a screen edge, the size of those spots can be considered of virtual infinite size, so the hot corners and edges can be reached quickly by throwing the pointer toward the edges.

The default wait cursor for Windows XP replaces the pointer with an hourglass.

- While a computer process is performing tasks and cannot accept user input, a wait pointer (an hourglass in Windows before Vista and many other systems, spinning ring in Windows Vista, watch in classic Mac OS, or spinning ball in Mac OS X) is displayed when the mouse pointer is in the corresponding window.

- When the pointer hovers over a hyperlink, a mouseover event changes the pointer into a hand with an outstretched index finger. Often some informative text about the link may pop up in a tooltip, which disappears when the user moves the pointer away. The tooltips revealed in the box depend on the implementation of the web browser; many web browsers will display the "title" of the element, the "alt" attribute, or the non-standard "tooltips" attribute. This pointer shape was first used for hyperlinks in Apple Computer's HyperCard.

- The mouseover or hover gesture can also present information about what the pointer is hovering over; the information is a description of what selecting an active element is for or what it will do, it appears only when stationary over content. A common use of viewing the information is when browsing the internet to know the destination of a link before selecting it, if the URL of the text is not recognisable.

Pointer Trails and Animation

ɲnhance the visibility of the r

at follow the actual pointer. \

An example of mouse pointer trails.

Pointer trails can be used to enhance its visibility during movement. Pointer trails are a feature of GUI operating systems to enhance the visibility of the pointer. Although disabled by default, pointer trails have been an option in every version of Microsoft Windows since Windows 3.1x.

When pointer trails are active and the mouse or stylus is moved, the system waits a moment before removing the pointer image from the old location on the screen. A copy of the pointer persists at every point that the pointer has visited in that moment, resulting in a snake-like trail of pointer icons that follow the actual pointer. When the user stops moving the mouse or removes the stylus from the screen, the trails disappear and the pointer returns to normal.

Pointer trails have been provided as a feature mainly for users with poor vision and for screens where low visibility may become an issue, such as LCD screens in bright sunlight.

In Windows, pointer trails may be enabled in the Control Panel, usually under the Mouse applet.

Introduced with Windows NT, an *animated pointer* was a small looping animation that was played at the location of the pointer. This is used, for example, to provide a visual cue that the computer is busy with a task. After their introduction, many animated pointers became available for download from third party suppliers. Unfortunately, animated pointers are not without their problems. In addition to imposing a small additional load on the CPU, the animated pointer routines did introduce a security vulnerability. A client-side exploit known as the *Windows Animated Cursor Remote Code Execution Vulnerability* used a buffer overflow vulnerability to load malicious code via the animated cursor load routine of Windows.

Widget (GUI)

gtk3-demo, a program to demonstrate the widgets in GTK+ version 3.

Qt widgets rendered according to three different skins (artistic design): Plastik, Keramik, and Windows

Various widgets shown in Ubuntu.

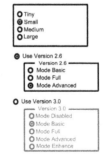

Example of enabled and disabled widgets; the frame at the bottom is disabled, they are grayed out.

A widget (also graphical control element or control) is an element of interaction in a graphical user interface (GUI), such as a button or a scroll bar. Controls are software components that a computer user interacts with through direct manipulation to read or edit information about an application. User interface libraries, such as e.g. GTK+ or Cocoa, contain a collection of widgets and the logic to render these.

Each widget facilitates a specific type of user-computer interaction, and appears as a visible part of the application's GUI as defined by the theme and rendered by the rendering engine. The theme makes all widgets adhere to a unified aesthetic design and creates a sense of overall cohesion. Some widgets support interaction with the user, for example labels, buttons, and check boxes. Others act as containers that group the widgets added to them, for example windows, panels, and tabs.

Structuring a user interface with widget toolkits allow developers to reuse code for similar tasks, and provides users with a common language for interaction, maintaining consistency throughout the whole information system.

Graphical user interface builders, such as e.g. Glade Interface Designer, facilitate the authoring of GUIs in a WYSIWYG manner employing a user interface markup language such as in this case GtkBuilder. It automatically generates all the source code for a widget from general descriptions provided by the developer, usually through direct manipulation.

History and Use

Any widget displays an information arrangement changeable by the user, such as a window or a text box. The defining characteristic of a widget is to provide a single interaction point for the direct manipulation of a given kind of data. In other words, widgets are basic visual building blocks which, combined in an application, hold all the data processed by the application and the available interactions on this data.

GUI widgets are graphical elements used to build the human-machine-interface of a program. GUI widgets are implemented like software components. Widget toolkits and software frameworks, like e.g. GTK+ or Qt, contain them in software libraries so that programmers can use them to build GUIs for their programs.

A family of common reusable widgets has evolved for holding general information based on the Palo Alto Research Center Inc. research for the Xerox Alto User Interface. Various implementations of these generic widgets are often packaged together in widget toolkits, which programmers use to build graphical user interfaces (GUIs). Most operating systems include a set of ready-to-tailor widgets that a programmer can incorporate in an application, specifying how it is to behave. Each type of widget generally is defined as a class by object-oriented programming (OOP). Therefore, many widgets are derived from class inheritance.

In the context of an application, a widget may be *enabled* or *disabled* at a given point in time. An enabled widget has the capacity to respond to events, such as keystrokes or mouse actions. A widget that cannot respond to such events is considered disabled. The appearance of disabled widget is typically different from an enabled widget; the disabled widget may be drawn in a lighter color, or may be visually obscured in some way.

Widgets are sometimes qualified as *virtual* to distinguish them from their physical counterparts, e.g. *virtual* buttons that can be clicked with a pointer, vs. physical buttons that can be pressed with a finger.

A related (but different) concept is the desktop widget, a small specialized GUI application that provides some visual information and/or easy access to frequently used functions such as clocks, calendars, news aggregators, calculators and desktop notes. These kinds of widgets are hosted by a widget engine.

Etymology

"Widget" entered American English around 1920, as a generic term for any useful device, particularly a product manufactured for sale. In computer use it has been borrowed as a shortened form of "window gadget," and was first applied to user interface elements during Project Athena in 1988. The word was chosen because "all other common terms were overloaded with inappropriate connotations" – since the project's Intrinsics toolkit associated each widget with a window of the underlying X Window System – and because of the common prefix with the word *window*.

List of Common Generic Widgets

- Selection and display of collections

  o Button – control which can be clicked upon to perform an action. An equivalent to a push-button as found on mechanical or electronic instruments.

    □ Radio button – control which can be clicked upon to select one option from a selection of options, similar to selecting a radio station from a group of buttons dedicated to radio tuning. Radio buttons always appear in pairs or larger groups, and only one option in the group can be selected at a time; selecting a new item from the group's buttons also de-selects the previously selected button.

    □ Check box – control which can be clicked upon to enable or disable an option. Also called a tick box. The box indicates an "on" or "off" state via a check mark/tick ☑ or a cross ☒. Can be shown in an intermediate state (shaded or with a dash) to indicate that various objects in a multiple selection have different values for the property represented by the check box. Multiple check boxes in a group may be selected, in contrast with radio buttons.

- ☐ Split button – control combining a button (typically invoking some default action) and a drop-down list with related, secondary actions

- ☐ Cycle button - a button that cycles its content through two or more values, thus enabling selection of one from a group of items.

o   Slider – control with a handle that can be moved up and down (vertical slider) or right and left (horizontal slider) on a bar to select a value (or a range if two handles are present). The bar allows users to make adjustments to a value or process throughout a range of allowed values.

o   List box - a graphical control element that allows the user to select one or more items from a list contained within a static, multiple line text box.

o   Spinner – value input control which has small up and down buttons to step through a range of values

o   Drop-down list. A list of items from which to select. The list normally only displays items when a special button or indicator is clicked.

o   Menu – control with multiple actions which can be clicked upon to choose a selection to activate

- ☐ Context menu – a type of menu whose contents depend on the *context* or state in effect when the menu is invoked

- ☐ Pie menu - a circular context menu where selection depends on direction

o   Menu bar -a graphical control element which contains drop down menus

o   Toolbar - a graphical control element on which on-screen buttons, icons, menus, or other input or output elements are placed

- ☐ Ribbon - a hybrid of menu and toolbar, displaying a large collection of commands in a visual layout through a tabbed interface.

o   Combo box (text box with attached menu or List box). A combination of a single-line text box and a drop-down list or list box, allowing the user to either type a value directly into the control or choose from the list of existing options.

o   Icon - a quickly comprehensible symbol of a software tool, function, or a data file,

- Tree view - a graphical control element that presents a hierarchical view of information

- Grid view or datagrid - a spreadsheet-like tabular view of data that allows numbers or text to be entered in rows and columns.

- Navigation

  - Link. Text with some kind of indicator (usually underlining and/or color) that indicates that clicking it will take one to another screen or page.

  - Tab - a graphical control element that allows multiple documents or panels to be contained within a single window

  - Scrollbar - a graphical control element by which continuous text, pictures, or any other content can be scrolled in a predetermined direction (up, down, left, or right)

- Text/value input

  - Text box (edit field) - a graphical control element intended to enable the user to input text

  - Combo box -a graphical control element combining a drop-down list or list box and a single-line editable textbox

- Output

  - Label – text used to describe another widget

  - Tooltip – informational window which appears when the mouse hovers over another control

  - Balloon help

  - Status bar - a graphical control element which poses an information area typically found at the window's bottom

  - Progress bar - a graphical control element used to visualize the progression of an extended computer operation, such as a download, file transfer, or installation

  - Infobar - a graphical control element used by many programs to display non-critical information to a user

- Container

  - Window - a graphical control element consisting of a visual area containing some of the graphical user interface elements of the program it belongs to

- ☐ Collapsible panel - a panel that can compactly store content which is hidden or revealed by clicking the tab of the widget

- ☐ Accordion - a vertically stacked list of items, such as labels or thumbnails where each item can be "expanded" to reveal the associated content

- ☐ Modal window - a graphical control element subordinate to an application's main window which creates a mode where the main window can't be used.

- ☐ Dialog box - a small window that communicates information to the user and prompts for a response

- ☐ Palette window, also known as "Utility window" - a graphical control element which floats on top of all regular windows and offers ready access tools, commands or information for the current application

  - ☐ Inspector window - a type of dialog window that shows a list of the current attributes of a selected object and allows these parameters to be changed on the fly

- ☐ Frame - a type of box within which a collection of graphical control elements can be grouped as a way to show relationships visually

- ☐ Canvas - generic drawing element for representing graphical information

References

- Friedman, Ted (2005). "Chapter 5: 1984". Electric Dreams: Computers in American Culture. New York University Press. ISBN 0-8147-2740-9. Retrieved October 6, 2011.

- Lock & Philander (2009). Michael Sangster, ed. FCS Systems Analysis & Design L4. Pearson Education South Africa. p. 149. ISBN 1-77025-428-5.

- McClure, Stuart; Scambray, Joel; Kurtz, George (2009). Hacking exposed: network security secrets & solutions (6th ed.). McGraw Hill Professional. p. 177. ISBN 0-07-161374-9.

- Grote, Patrick (October 29, 2006). "Review of Pirates of Silicon Valley Movie". DotJournal.com. Archived from the original on November 7, 2006. Retrieved January 24, 2014.

- Washington Post (August 24, 1995). "With Windows 95's Debut, Microsoft Scales Heights of Hype". Washington Post. Retrieved November 8, 2013.

Designs of User Interface

User interface has a number of designs. Some of these are user interface design, user-centered design, usage-centered design, contextual design, user experience design etc. The interface of machines, such as computers, mobiles and electronic devices is known as the user interface design. The topics discussed in the text are of great importance to broaden the existing knowledge on user interface.

UserInterface Design

The graphical user interface is presented (displayed) on the computer screen. It is the result of processed user input and usually the primary interface for human-machine interaction. The touch user interfaces popular on small mobile devices are an overlay of the visual output to the visual input.

User interface design (UI) or user interface engineering is the design of user interfaces for machines and software, such as computers, home appliances, mobile devices, and other electronic devices, with the focus on maximizing usability and the user experience. The goal of user interface design is to make the user's interaction as simple and efficient as possible, in terms of accomplishing user goals (user-centered design).

Good user interface design facilitates finishing the task at hand without drawing unnecessary attention to itself. Graphic design and typography are utilized to support its usability, influencing how the user performs certain interactions and improving the aesthetic appeal of the design; design aesthetics may enhance or detract from the ability of users to use the functions of the interface. The design process must balance technical functionality and visual elements (e.g., mental model) to create a system that is not only operational but also usable and adaptable to changing user needs.

Interface design is involved in a wide range of projects from computer systems, to cars, to commercial planes; all of these projects involve much of the same basic human interactions yet also require some unique skills and knowledge. As a result, designers tend to specialize in certain types of projects and have skills centered on their expertise, whether that be software design, user research, web design, or industrial design.

Processes

User interface design requires a good understanding of user needs. There are several phases and processes in the user interface design, some of which are more demanded upon than others, depending on the project. (Note: for the remainder of this section, the word *system* is used to denote any project whether it is a website, application, or device.)

- Functionality requirements gathering – assembling a list of the functionality required by the system to accomplish the goals of the project and the potential needs of the users.

- User and task analysis – a form of field research, it's the analysis of the potential users of the system by studying how they perform the tasks that the design must support, and conducting interviews to elucidate their goals. Typical questions involve:

  o   What would the user want the system to do?

  o   How would the system fit in with the user's normal workflow or daily activities?

  o   How technically savvy is the user and what similar systems does the user already use?

  o   What interface look & feel styles appeal to the user?

- Information architecture – development of the process and/or information flow of the system (i.e. for phone tree systems, this would be an option tree flowchart and for web sites this would be a site flow that shows the hierarchy of the pages).

- Prototyping – development of wire-frames, either in the form of paper proto-types or simple interactive screens. These prototypes are stripped of all look & feel elements and most content in order to concentrate on the interface.

- Usability inspection – letting an evaluator inspect a user interface. This is generally considered to be cheaper to implement than usability testing, and can be used early on in the development process since it can be used to evaluate prototypes or specifications for the system, which usually can't be tested on users. Some common usability inspection methods include cognitive walkthrough, which focuses the simplicity to accomplish tasks with the system for new users, heuristic evaluation, in which a set of heuristics are used to identify usability problems in the UI design, and pluralistic walkthrough, in which a selected group of people step through a task scenario and discuss usability issues.

- Usability testing – testing of the prototypes on an actual user—often using a technique called think aloud protocol where you ask the user to talk about their thoughts during the experience. User interface design testing allows the designer to understand the reception of the design from the viewer's standpoint, and thus facilitates creating successful applications.

- Graphical user interface design – actual look and feel design of the final graphical user interface (GUI). It may be based on the findings developed during the user research, and refined to fix any usability problems found through the results of testing.

Requirements

The dynamic characteristics of a system are described in terms of the dialogue requirements contained in seven principles of part 10 of the ergonomics standard, the ISO 9241. This standard establishes a framework of ergonomic "principles" for the dialogue techniques with high-level definitions and illustrative applications and examples of the principles. The principles of the dialogue represent the dynamic aspects of the interface and can be mostly regarded as the "feel" of the interface. The seven dialogue principles are:

- Suitability for the task: the dialogue is suitable for a task when it supports the user in the effective and efficient completion of the task.

- Self-descriptiveness: the dialogue is self-descriptive when each dialogue step is immediately comprehensible through feedback from the system or is explained to the user on request.

- Controllability: the dialogue is controllable when the user is able to initiate and control the direction and pace of the interaction until the point at which the goal has been met.

- Conformity with user expectations: the dialogue conforms with user expectations when it is consistent and corresponds to the user characteristics, such as task knowledge, education, experience, and to commonly accepted conventions.

- Error tolerance: the dialogue is error tolerant if despite evident errors in input, the intended result may be achieved with either no or minimal action by the user.

- Suitability for individualization: the dialogue is capable of individualization when the interface software can be modified to suit the task needs, individual preferences, and skills of the user.

- Suitability for learning: the dialogue is suitable for learning when it supports and guides the user in learning to use the system.

The concept of usability is defined of the ISO 9241 standard by effectiveness, efficiency, and satisfaction of the user. Part 11 gives the following definition of usability:

- Usability is measured by the extent to which the intended goals of use of the overall system are achieved (effectiveness).

- The resources that have to be expended to achieve the intended goals (efficiency).

- The extent to which the user finds the overall system acceptable (satisfaction).

Effectiveness, efficiency, and satisfaction can be seen as quality factors of usability. To evaluate these factors, they need to be decomposed into sub-factors, and finally, into usability measures.

The information presentation is described in Part 12 of the ISO 9241 standard for the organization of information (arrangement, alignment, grouping, labels, location), for the display of graphical objects, and for the coding of information (abbreviation, color, size, shape, visual cues) by seven attributes. The "attributes of presented information" represent the static aspects of the interface and can be generally regarded as the "look" of the interface. The attributes are detailed in the recommendations given in the standard. Each of the recommendations supports one or more of the seven attributes. The seven presentation attributes are:

- Clarity: the information content is conveyed quickly and accurately.

- Discriminability: the displayed information can be distinguished accurately.

- Conciseness: users are not overloaded with extraneous information.

- Consistency: a unique design, conformity with user's expectation.

- Detectability: the user's attention is directed towards information required.

- Legibility: information is easy to read.

- Comprehensibility: the meaning is clearly understandable, unambiguous, interpretable, and recognizable.

The user guidance in Part 13 of the ISO 9241 standard describes that the user guidance information should be readily distinguishable from other displayed information and should be specific for the current context of use. User guidance can be given by the following five means:

- Prompts indicating explicitly (specific prompts) or implicitly (generic prompts) that the system is available for input.

- Feedback informing about the user's input timely, perceptible, and non-intrusive.

- Status information indicating the continuing state of the application, the system's hardware and software components, and the user's activities.

- Error management including error prevention, error correction, user support for error management, and error messages.

- On-line help for system-initiated and user initiated requests with specific information for the current context of use.

Research

User interface design has been a topic of considerable research, including on its aesthetics. Standards have been developed as far back as the 1980s for defining the usability of software products. One of the structural bases has become the IFIP user interface reference model. The model proposes four dimensions to structure the user interface:

- The input/output dimension (the look)

- The dialogue dimension (the feel)

- The technical or functional dimension (the access to tools and services)

- The organizational dimension (the communication and co-operation support)

This model has greatly influenced the development of the international standard ISO 9241 describing the interface design requirements for usability. The desire to understand application-specific UI issues early in software development, even as an application was being developed, led to research on GUI rapid prototyping tools that might offer convincing simulations of how an actual application might behave in production use. Some of this research has shown that a wide variety of programming tasks for GUI-based software can, in fact, be specified through means other than writing program code.

Research in recent years is strongly motivated by the increasing variety of devices that can, by virtue of Moore's law, host very complex interfaces.

Research has also been conducted on generating user interfaces automatically, to match a user's level of ability for different levels of interaction.

At the moment, in addition to traditional prototypes the literature proposes new solutions, such as an experimental mixed prototype based on a configurable physical prototype that allow to achieve a complete sense of touch, thanks to the physical mock-up, and a realistic visual experience, thanks to the superimposition of the virtual interface on the physical prototype with Augmented Reality techniques.

User-centered Design

User-centered design (UCD) or user-driven development (UDD) is a framework of processes (not restricted to interfaces or technologies) in which the needs, wants, and limitations of end users of a product, service or process are given extensive attention at each stage of the design process. User-centered design can be characterized as a multi-stage problem solving process that not only requires designers to analyse and foresee how users are likely to use a product, but also to test the validity of their assumptions with regard to user behavior in real world tests with actual users at each stage of the process from requirements, concepts, pre-production models, mid production and post production creating a circle of proof back to and confirming or modifying the original requirements. Such testing is necessary as it is often very difficult for the designers of a product to understand intuitively what a first-time user of their design experiences, and what each user's learning curve may look like.

The chief difference from other product design philosophies is that user-centered design tries to optimize the product around how users can, want, or need to use the product, rather than forcing the users to change their behavior to accommodate the product.

UCD Models and Approaches

For example, the user-centered design process can help software designers to fulfill the goal of a product engineered for their users. User requirements are considered right from the beginning and included into the whole product cycle. These requirements are noted and refined through investigative methods including: ethnographic study, contextual inquiry, prototype testing, usability testing and other methods. Generative methods may also be used including: card sorting, affinity diagramming and participatory design sessions. In addition, user requirements can be inferred by careful analysis of usable products similar to the product being designed.

- Cooperative design: involving designers and users on an equal footing. This is the Scandinavian tradition of design of IT artifacts and it has been evolving since 1970.

- Participatory design (PD), a North American term for the same concept, inspired by Cooperative Design, focusing on the participation of users. Since 1990, there has been a bi-annual Participatory Design Conference.

- Contextual design, "customer-centered design" in the actual context, including some ideas from Participatory design

Here are principles that will ensure a design is user centered:

1. The design is based upon an explicit understanding of users, tasks and environments.

2. Users are involved throughout design and development.

3. The design is driven and refined by user-centered evaluation.

4. The process is iterative.

5. The design addresses the whole user experience.

6. The design team includes multidisciplinary skills and perspectives.

Purpose

UCD answers questions about users and their tasks and goals, then uses the findings to make decisions about development and design. UCD of a web site, for instance, seeks to answer the following questions:

- Who are the users of the document?

- What are the users' tasks and goals?

- What are the users' experience levels with the document, and documents like it?

- What functions do the users need from the document?

- What information might the users need, and in what form do they need it?

- How do users think the document should work?

- What are the extreme environments?

- Is the user multitasking?

- Does the interface utilize different inputs modes such as touching, spoken, gestures, or orientation?

Elements

As examples of UCD viewpoints, the essential elements of UCD of a web site are considerations of visibility, accessibility, legibility and language.

Visibility

Visibility helps the user construct a mental model of the document. Models help the user predict the effect(s) of their actions while using the document. Important elements (such as those that aid navigation) should be emphatic. Users should be able to tell from a glance what they can and cannot do with the document.

Accessibility

Users should be able to find information quickly and easily throughout the document, regardless of its length. Users should be offered various ways to find information (such as navigational elements, search functions, table of contents, clearly labeled sections, page numbers, color-coding, etc.). Navigational elements should be consistent with the genre of the document. 'Chunking' is a useful strategy that involves breaking information into small pieces that can be organized into some type meaningful order or hierarchy. The ability to skim the document allows users to find their piece of information by scanning rather than reading. Bold and italic words are often used.

Legibility

Text should be easy to read: Through analysis of the rhetorical situation, the designer should be able to determine a useful font style. Ornamental fonts and text in all capital letters are hard to read, but italics and bolding can be helpful when used correctly. Large or small body text is also hard to read. (Screen size of 10-12 pixel sans serif and 12-16 pixel serif is recommended.) High figure-ground contrast between text and background increases legibility. Dark text against a light background is most legible.

Language

Depending on the rhetorical situation, certain types of language are needed. Short sentences are helpful, as are well-written texts used in explanations and similar bulk-text situations. Unless the situation calls for it, jargon or technical terms should not be used. Many writers will choose to use active voice, verbs (instead of noun strings or nominals), and simple sentence structure.

Rhetorical Situation

A user-centered design is focused around the rhetorical situation. The rhetorical situation shapes the design of an information medium. There are three elements to consider in a rhetorical situation: Audience, Purpose, and Context.

Audience

The audience is the people who will be using the document. The designer must consider their age, geographical location, ethnicity, gender, education, etc.

Purpose

The purpose is what the document targets or what problem the document is trying to address.

Context

The context is the circumstances surrounding the situation. The context often answers the question: What situation has prompted the need for this document? Context also includes any social or cultural issues that may surround the situation.

Analysis Tools

There are a number of tools that are used in the analysis of user-centered design, mainly: personas, scenarios, and essential use cases.

Persona

During the UCD process, a Persona representing the user may be created. A persona is a user archetype used to help guide decisions about product features, navigation, interactions, and even visual design. In most cases, personas are synthesized from a series of ethnographic interviews with real people, then captured in 1-2 page descriptions that include behavior patterns, goals, skills, attitudes, and environment, with a few fictional personal details to bring the persona to life.

For each product, or sometimes for each set of tools within a product, there is a small set of personas, one of whom is the primary focus for the design. There are also what's called a secondary persona, where the character is not the main target of the design, but their needs should be met and problems solved if possible. They exist to help account for further possible problems and difficulties that may occur even though the primary persona is satisfied with their solution. There is also an anti-persona, which is the character that the design is specifically not made for.

Personas are useful in the sense that they create a common shared understanding of the user group for which the design process is built around. Also, they help to prioritize the design considerations by providing a context of what the user needs and what functions are simply nice to add and have. They can also provide a human face and existence to a diversified and scattered user group, and can also create some empathy and add emotions when referring to the users. However, since personas are a generalized perception of the primary stakeholder group from collected data, the characteristics may be too broad and typical, or too much of an "average Joe". Sometimes, personas can have stereotypical properties also, which may hurt the entire design process. Overall, personas can be a useful tool to be used by designers to make informed design decisions around, opposed to referring to a set of data or a wide range of individuals.

Scenario

A scenario created in the UCD process is a fictional story about the "daily life of" or a sequence of events with the primary stakeholder group as the main character. Typically, a persona that was created earlier is used as the main character of this story. The story should be specific of the events happening that relate to the problems of the primary stakeholder group, and normally the main research questions the design process is built upon. These may turn out to be a simple story about the daily life of an individual, but small details from the events should imply details about the users, and may include emotional or physical characteristics. There can be the "best-case scenario", where everything works out best for the main character, the "worst-case scenario", where the main character experiences everything going wrong around him or her, and an "average-case scenario", which is the typical life of the individual, where nothing really special or really depressing occurs, and the day just moves on.

Scenarios create a social context in which the personas exist, and also create an actual physical world, instead of imagining a character with internal characteristics from gathered data and nothing else; there is more action involved in the persona's existence. A scenario is also more easily understood by people, since it is in the form of a story, and is easier to follow. Yet, like the personas, these scenarios are assumptions made by the researcher and designer, and is also created from a set of organized data. Some even say such scenarios are unrealistic to real life occurrences. Also, it is difficult to explain and inform low level tasks that occur, like the thought process of the persona before acting.

Use Case

In short, a use case describes the interaction between an individual and the rest of the world. Each use case describes an event that may occur for a short period of time in real life, but may consist of intricate details and interactions between the actor and the world. It is represented as a series of simple steps for the character to achieve his or her goal, in the form of a cause-and effect scheme. Use cases are normally written in the form of a chart with two columns: first column labelled actor, second column labelled world, and the actions performed by each side written in order in the respective columns. The following is an example of a use case for performing a song on a guitar in front of an audience.

The interaction between actor and the world is an act that can be seen in everyday life, and we take them as granted and don't think too much about the small detail that needs to happen in order for an act like performing a piece of music to exist. It is similar to the fact that when speaking our mother tongue, we don't think too much about grammar and how to phrase words; they just come out since we are so used to saying them. The actions between an actor and the world, notably, the primary stakeholder (user) and the world in this case, should be thought about in detail, and hence use cases are created to understand how these tiny interactions occur.

An essential use case is a special kind of use case, also called an "abstract use case." Essential use cases describe the essence of the problem, and deals with the nature of the problem itself. While writing use cases, no assumptions about unrelated details should be made. In additions, the goals of the subject should be separated from the process and implementation to reach that particular goal. Below is an example of an essential use case with the same goal as the former example.

Use cases are useful because they help identify useful levels of design work. They allow the designers to see the actual low level processes that are involved for a certain problem, which makes the problem easier to handle, since certain minor steps and details the user makes are exposed. The designers' job should take into consideration of these small problems in order to arrive at a final solution that works. Another way to say this is that use cases breaks a complicated task into smaller bits, where these bits are useful units. Each bit completes a small task, which then builds up to the final bigger task.

Like writing code on a computer, it is easier to write the basic smaller parts and make them work first, and then put them together to finish the larger more complicated code, instead to tackling the entire code from the very beginning.

The first solution is less risky because if something goes wrong with the code, it is easier to look for the problem in the smaller bits, since the segment with the problem will be the one that does not work, while in the latter solution, the programmer may have to look through the entire code to search for a single error, which proves time consuming. The same reasoning goes for writing use cases in UCD. Lastly, use cases convey useful and important tasks where the designer can see which one are of higher importance than others. Some drawbacks of writing use cases include the fact that each action, by the actor or the world, consist of little detail, and is simply a small action. This may possibly lead to further imagination and different interpretation of action from different designers.

Also, during the process, it is really easy to oversimplify a task, since a small task from a larger task may consist of even smaller tasks. Picking up a guitar may involve thinking of which guitar to pick up, which pick to use, and think about where the guitar is located first. These tasks may then be divided into smaller tasks, such as first thinking of what colour of guitar fits the place to perform the piece, and other related details. Tasks may be split further down into even tinier tasks, and it is up to the designer to determine what is a suitable place to stop splitting up the tasks. Tasks may not only be oversimplified, they may also be omitted in whole, thus the designer should be aware of all the detail and all the key steps that are involved in an event or action when writing use cases.

Needs and Emotions

The book "The Design of Everyday Things" (originally called "The Psychology of Everyday Things") was first published in 1986. In this book, Donald A. Norman describes the psychology behind what he deems 'good' and 'bad' design through examples and offers principles of 'good' design. He exalts the importance of design in our everyday lives, and the consequences of errors caused by bad designs.

In his book, Norman uses the term user-centered design to describe design based on the needs of the user, leaving aside what he considers secondary issues like aesthetics. User-centered design involves simplifying the structure of tasks, making things visible, getting the mapping right, exploiting the powers of constraint, and designing for error. Norman's overly reductive approach in this text was readdressed by him later in his own publication "Emotional Design."

Other books in a similar vein include "Designing Pleasurable Products" by Patrick W. Jordan, in which the author suggests that different forms of pleasure should be included in a user-centered approach in addition to traditional definitions of usability.

In Product Lifecycle Management Systems

Software applications (or often suites of applications) used in product lifecycle management (typically including CAD, CAM and CAx processes) can be typically characterized by the need for these solutions to serve the needs of a broad range of users, with each user having a particular job role and skill level. For example, a CAD digital mockup might be utilized by a novice analyst, design engineer of moderate skills, or a manufacturing planner of advanced skills.

Usage-centered Design

Usage-centered design is an approach to user interface design based on a focus on user intentions and usage patterns. It analyzes users in terms of the roles they play in relation to systems and employs abstract (essential) use cases for task analysis. It derives visual and interaction design from abstract prototypes based on the understanding of user roles and task cases.

Usage-centered design was introduced by Larry Constantine and Lucy Lockwood. The primary reference is their book.

Usage-centered Design Methods

Usage-centered design is largely based on formal, abstract models such as models of interaction between user roles, UML workflow models and task case and role profiles. Usage-centered design proponents argue for abstract modelling while many designers use realistic personas, scenarios and high-fidelity prototypes. The techniques have been applied with particular success in complex software projects, some of which have been reported in case studies.

Usage-Centered Design And Activity-Centered Design Approach

Usage-centered design share some common ideas with activity-centered design. It is concerned more with the activities of users but not the users per se. In [Constantine, 2006] an integrated framework is presented where the models of Usage-centered design are enriched with concepts from the Activity theory.

Contextual Design

Contextual design (CD) is a user-centered design process developed by Hugh Beyer and Karen Holtzblatt. It incorporates ethnographic methods for gathering data relevant to the product via field studies, rationalizing workflows, and designing human-computer interfaces. In practice, this means that researchers aggregate data from customers in the field where people are living and applying these findings into a final product. Contextual design can be seen as an alternative to engineering and feature driven models of creating new systems.

Process Overview

The contextual design process consists of the following top-level steps: contextual inquiry, interpretation, data consolidation, visioning, storyboarding, user environment design, and prototyping.

Collecting Data – contextual Inquiry

Contextual inquiry is a field data collection technique used to capture detailed information about how users of a product interact with the product in their normal work environment. This information is captured by both observations of user behavior and conversations with the user while she or he works. A key aspect of the technique is to partner with the user, letting their work and the issues they encounter guide the interview. Key takeaways from the technique are to learn what users actually do, why they do it that way, latent needs, and core values.

Interpretation

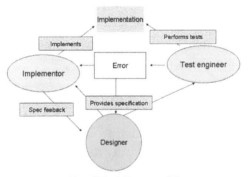

Simplified flow model

Data from each interview is analyzed and key issues and insights are captured. Detailed work models are also created in order to understand the different aspects of the work that matter for design. Contextual design consists of five work models which are used to model the work tasks and details of the working environment. These work models are:

- Flow model – represents the coordination, communication, interaction, roles, and responsibilities of the people in a certain work practice

- Sequence model – represents the steps users go through to accomplish a certain activity, including breakdowns

- Cultural model – represents the norms, influences, and pressures that are present in the work environment

- Artifact model – represents the documents or other physical things that are created while working or are used to support the work. Artifacts often have a structure or styling that could represent the user's way of structuring the work

- Physical model – represents the physical environment where the work tasks are accomplished; often, there are multiple physical models representing, e.g., office layout, network topology, or the layout of tools on a computer display.

Data Consolidation

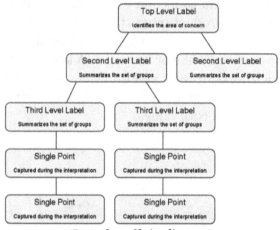

Part of an affinity diagram

Data from individual customer interviews are analyzed in order to reveal patterns and the structure across distinct interviews. Models of the same type can be consolidated together (but not generalized—detail must be maintained). Another method of processing the observations is making an affinity diagram ("wall"), as described by Beyer & Holtzblatt:

- A single observation is written on each piece of paper.

- Individual notes are grouped according to the similarity of their contents.

- These groups are labeled with colored Post-it notes, each color representing a distinct level in the hierarchy.

- Then the groups are combined with other groups to get the final construct of observations in a hierarchy of up to three levels.

Beyer & Holtzblatt propose the following color-coding convention for grouping the notes, from lowest to highest level in the hierarchy:

- White notes – individual notes captured during interpretation, also known as "affinity notes"

- Blue notes – summaries of groups of white notes that convey all the relevant details

- Pink notes – summaries of groups of blue notes that reveal key issues in the data

- Green notes – labels identifying an area of concern indicated by pink notes

Beyer & Holtzblatt emphasize the importance of building the entire affinity diagram in one or two sessions rather than building smaller affinity diagrams over many sessions. This immersion in the data for an extended period of time helps teams see the broad scope of a problem quickly and encourages a paradigm shift of thought rather than assimilation of ideas.

The design ideas and relevant issues that arise during the process should be included in the affinity diagram. Any holes in the data and areas that need more information should also be labeled. After completing the wall, participants "walk" the affinity diagram to stimulate new ideas and identify any remaining issues or holes in data. The affinity diagram is a bottom-up method. Consolidated data may also be used to create a cause-and-effect diagram or a set of personas describing typical users of the proposed system.

Visioning

In visioning, a cross-functional team comes together to create stories of how new product concepts, services, and technology can better support the user work practice. The visioning team starts by reviewing the data to identify key issues and opportunities. The data walking session is followed by a group visioning session during which the visioning team generates a variety of new product concepts by telling stories of different usage scenarios based on the data collected. A vision includes the system, its delivery, and support structures to make the new work practice successful, but is told from the user's point of view.

Storyboarding

After visioning, the team develops the vision in storyboards, capturing scenarios of how people will work with the new system. Understanding the current way of working, its structure and the complete workflow helps the design team address the problems and design the new workflow. Storyboards work out the details of the vision, guided by the consolidated data, using pictures and text in a series of hand-drawn cells.

User Environment Design

The User Environment Design captures the floor plan of the new system. It shows each part of the system, how it supports the user's work, exactly what function is available in that part, and how the user gets to and from other parts of the system. Contextual design uses the User Environment Design (UED) diagram, which displays the focus areas, i.e., areas which are visible to the user or which are relevant to the user. Focus areas can be defined further as functions in a system that support a certain type or part of the work. The UED also presents how the focus areas relate to each other and shows the links between focus areas.

Prototyping

Testing the design ideas with paper prototypes or even with more sophisticated interactive prototypes before the implementation phase helps the designers communicate with users about the new system and develop the design further. Prototypes test the structure of a User Environment Design and initial user interface ideas, as well as the understanding of the work, before the implementation phase. Depending on the results of the prototype test, more iterations or alternative designs may be needed.

-by Eko Nurwahyudi

Uses and Adaptations

Contextual design has primarily been used for the design of computer information systems, including hardware, software. Parts of contextual design have been adapted for use as a usability evaluation method and for contextual application design. Contextual design has also been applied to the design of digital libraries and other learning technologies.

Contextual design has also been used as a means of teaching user-centered design/ Human–computer interaction at the university level.

A more lightweight approach to contextual design has been developed by its originators to address an oft-heard criticism that the method is too labor-intensive or lengthy for some needs. Yet others find the designer/user engagement promoted by contextual design to be too brief.

User Experience Design

User experience design (UX, UXD, UED or XD) is the process of enhancing user satisfaction by improving the usability, accessibility, and pleasure provided in the interaction between the user and the product. User experience design encompasses traditional human–computer interaction (HCI) design, and extends it by addressing all aspects of a product or service as perceived by users.

History

The field of user experience design is a conceptual design discipline and has its roots in human factors and ergonomics, a field that, since the late 1940s, has focused on the interaction between human users, machines, and the contextual environments to design systems that address the user's experience. With the proliferation of workplace computers in the early 1990s, user experience became an important concern for designers. It was Donald Norman, a user experience architect, who coined the term "user experience," and brought it to a wider audience.

I invented the term because I thought human interface and usability were too narrow. I wanted to cover all aspects of the person's experience with the system including industrial design graphics, the interface, the physical interaction and the manual. Since then the term has spread widely, so much so that it is starting to lose its meaning.

— Donald Norman

The term also has a more recent connection to user-centered design, human–computer interaction, and also incorporates elements from similar user-centered design fields.

Elements

User experience design includes elements of interaction design, information architecture, user research, and other disciplines, and is concerned with all facets of the overall experience delivered to users. Following is a short analysis of its constituent parts.

Visual Design

Visual design, also commonly known as graphic design, user interface design, communication design, and visual communication, represents the aesthetics or look-and-feel of the front end of any user interface. Graphic treatment of interface elements is often perceived as the visual design. The purpose of visual design is to use visual elements like colors, images, and symbols to convey a message to its audience. Fundamentals of Gestalt psychology and visual perception give a cognitive perspective on how to create effective visual communication.

Information Architecture

Information architecture is the art and science of structuring and organizing the information in products and services to support usability and findability.

In the context of information architecture, information is separate from both knowledge and data, and lies nebulously between them. It is information about objects. The objects can range from websites, to software applications, to images et al. It is also concerned with metadata: terms used to describe and represent content objects such as documents, people, process, and organizations.

Structuring, Organization, and Labeling

Structuring is reducing information to its basic building units and then relating them to each other. Organization involves grouping these units in a distinctive and meaningful manner. Labeling means using appropriate wording to support easy navigation and findability.

Finding and Managing

Findability is the most critical success factor for information architecture. If users are not able to find required information without browsing, searching or asking, then the findability of the information architecture fails. Navigation needs to be clearly conveyed to ease finding of the contents.

Interaction Design

There are many key factors to understanding interaction design and how it can enable a pleasurable end user experience. It is well recognized that building great user experience requires interaction design to play a pivotal role in helping define what works best for the users. High demand for improved user experiences and strong focus on the end-users have made interaction designers critical in conceptualizing design that matches user expectations and standards of the latest UI patterns and components. While working, interaction designers take several things in consideration. A few of them are:

- Defining interaction patterns best suited in the context

- Incorporating user needs collected during user research into the designs

- Features and information that are important to the user

- Interface behavior like drag-drop, selections, and mouse-over actions

- Effectively communicating strengths of the system

- Making the interface intuitive by building affordances

- Maintaining consistency throughout the system.

In the last few years, the role of interaction designer has shifted from being just focused on specifying UI components and communicating them to the engineers to a situation now where designers have more freedom to design contextual interfaces which are based on helping meet the user needs. Therefore, User Experience Design evolved into a multidisciplinary design branch that involves multiple technical aspects from motion graphics design and animation to programming.

Usability

Usability is the extent to which a product can be used by specified users to achieve specified goals with effectiveness, efficiency and satisfaction in a specified context of use.

Usability is attached with all tools used by humans and is extended to both digital and non-digital devices. Thus, it is a subset of user experience but not wholly contained. The section of usability that intersects with user experience design is related to humans' ability to use a system or application. Good usability is essential to a positive user experience but does not alone guarantee it.

Accessibility

Accessibility of a system describes its ease of reach, use and understanding. In terms of user experience design it can also be related to the overall comprehensibility of the information and features. It contributes to shorten the learning curve attached with the system. Accessibility in many contexts can be related to the ease of use for people with disabilities and comes under usability.

Human–computer Interaction

Human–computer interaction is concerned with the design, evaluation and implementation of interactive computing systems for human use and with the study of major phenomena surrounding them.

Human–computer interaction is the main contributor to user experience design because of its emphasis on human performance rather than mere usability. It provides key research findings which inform the improvement of systems for the people. Human-computer interaction extends its study towards more integrated interactions, such as tangible interactions, which is generally not covered in the practice of user experience. User experience cannot be manufactured or designed; it has to be incorporated in the design. Understanding the user's emotional quotient plays a key role while designing a user experience. The first step while designing the user experience is determining the reason a visitor will be visiting the website or use the application in question. Then the user experience can be designed accordingly.

Design

User experience design incorporates most or all of the above disciplines to positively impact the overall experience a person has with a particular interactive system and its provider. User experience design most frequently defines a sequence of interactions between a user (individual person) and a system, virtual or physical, designed to meet or support user needs and goals, primarily, while also satisfying systems requirements and organizational objectives.

Typical outputs include:

- Persona (an archetypal user for whom the product or service is being designed)

- Wireframes (screen blueprints or storyboards)

- Prototypes (for interactive or in-the-mind simulation)

- Written specifications (describing the behavior or design)

- Site audit (usability study of existing assets)

- Flows and navigation maps

- User stories or scenarios

- Sitemaps and content inventory

- High-fidelity visual mockups (precise visual layout and design of the expected product or interface)

General Design Process

While designing a product or service for a client, it is of utmost importance that the designers are on the same page as the client. All the information collected, plans made, design executed will reflect on the final product. Rigorous analysis must be done before proceeding to the design stage and then numerous testings done to optimize the site as per best standards so that the competitive edge is maintained. Leading Digital marketing companies combine three elements to provide the best responsive product to the customer. These are:

1. Researching about the target audience

2. Understanding the company's business goals

3. And most importantly apply out of the box thinking.

Brainstorming and testing ultimately leads them to finalize the design for their customers. Let's have a detailed look at the step by step process of product design:

- Collecting information about the problem

The UX designer needs to find out as much as they can about people, processes, and products before the design phase. Designers can do this by meeting with the clients or business stakeholders frequently to know what their requirements are, or by conducting interviews with users in their home or work spaces. This kind of qualitative research helps designers create products and services that better serve user needs.

- Getting ready to design

After research, the designer must make sense of the data they've collected. Typically this is done through modeling of the users and their environments. User modeling or personas are composite archetypes based on behavior patterns uncovered during research. Personas provide designers a precise way of thinking and communicating about how groups of users behave, how they think, what they want to accomplish and why. Once created, personas help the designer to understand the users' goals in specific contexts, which is particularly useful during ideation and for validating design concepts. Other types of models include work flow models, artifact models, and physical models.

- Design

When the designer has a firm grasp on the user's needs and goals, they begin to sketch out the interaction framework (also known as wireframes). This stage defines the high-level structure of screen layouts, as well as the product's flow, behavior, and organization. There are many kinds of materials that can be involved in during this iterative phase, from whiteboards to paper prototypes. As the interaction framework establishes an overall structure for product behavior, a parallel process focused on the visual and industrial designs. The visual design framework defines the experience attributes, visual language, and the visual style.

Once a solid and stable framework is established, wireframes are translated from sketched storyboards to full-resolution screens that depict the user interface at the pixel level. At this point, it's critical for the programming team to collaborate closely with the designer. Their input is necessary to creating a finished design that can and will be built while remaining true to the concept.

- Test and iterate

Usability testing is carried out through prototypes. The target users are given various tasks to perform on the prototypes. Any issues or problems faced by the users are collected as field notes and these notes are used to make changes in the design and reiterate the testing phase. Usability testing is, at its core, a means to "evaluate, not create".

UX Deliverables

UX designers' main goal is to solve the end-users' problems, and thus the ability to communicate the design to stakeholders and developers is critical to the ultimate success of the design. Regarding UX specification documents, these requirements depend on the client or the organization involved in designing a product. The four major deliverables are: a title page, an introduction to the feature, wireframes and a version history. Depending on the type of project, the specification documents can also include flow models, cultural models, personas, user stories, scenarios and any prior user research.

Documenting design decisions, in the form of annotated wireframes, gives the developer the necessary information they may need to successfully code the project.

Depending on the company, a user experience designer may need to be a jack of all trades. It is not uncommon to see a user experience designer jump in at the beginning of the project lifecycle, where the problem set and project definition is vague, or after the project requirements document has been finalized and wireframes and functional annotations need to be created.

The following details the responsibilities a user experience designer may have at each phase of a project:

At the beginning, when the project is more conceptual:

- Ethnographic research
- Surveying
- Customer feedback and testing
- Focus group administration
- Non-directed interview
- Contextual Interview
- Mental modeling
- Mood boards
- Card sorting
- Competitive analysis
- Contextual Inquiry

While the project is underway:

- Wireframing
- Heuristic analysis
- Expert evaluation
- Pluralistic walkthrough
- Personas
- Scenario
- Prototypes

- System mapping

- Experience mapping

- User testing/usability testing

After the project has launched:

- User testing/usability testing

- A/B testing

- Additional wireframing as a result of test results and fine-tuning

Designers

As with the fields mentioned above, user experience design is a highly multi-disciplinary field, incorporating aspects of psychology, anthropology, architecture, sociology, computer science, graphic design, industrial design, cognitive science, and business. Depending on the purpose of the product, UX may also involve content design disciplines such as communication design, instructional design, and game design. The subject matter of the content may also warrant collaboration with a subject-matter expert on planning the UX from various backgrounds in business, government, or private groups. More recently, content strategy has come to represent a sub-field of UX.

Graphic Designers

Graphic designers focus on the aesthetic appeal of the design. Information is communicated to the users through text and images. Much importance is given to how the text and images look and attract the users. Graphic designers have to make stylistic choices about things like font color, font type, and image locations. Graphic designers focus on grabbing the user's attention with the way the design looks. Graphic designers create visual concepts, using computer software or by hand, to communicate ideas that inspire, inform, and captivate consumers. They develop the overall layout and production design for various applications such as advertisements, brochures, magazines, and corporate reports.

Visual Designers

The visual designer (VisD) ensures that the visual representation of the design effectively communicates the data and hints at the expected behavior of the product. At the same time, the visual designer is responsible for conveying the brand ideals in the product and for creating a positive first impression; this responsibility is shared with the industrial designer if the product involves hardware. In essence, a visual designer must aim for maximum usability combined with maximum desirability.

Interaction Designers

Interaction designers (IxD) are responsible for understanding and specifying how the product should behave. This work overlaps with the work of both visual and industrial designers in a couple of important ways. When designing physical products, interaction designers must work with industrial designers early on to specify the requirements for physical inputs and to understand the behavioral impacts of the mechanisms behind them. Interaction designers cross paths with visual designers throughout the project. Visual designers guide the discussions of the brand and emotive aspects of the experience, Interaction designers communicate the priority of information, flow, and functionality in the interface.

Testing the Design

Usability testing is the most common method used by designers to test their designs. The basic idea behind conducting a usability test is to check whether the design of a product or brand works well with the target users. While carrying out usability testing, two things are being tested for: Whether the design of the product is successful and if it is not successful, how can it be improved. While designers are testing, they are testing the design and not the user. Also, every design is evolving. The designers carry out usability testing at every stage of the design process.

Benefits

User experience design is integrated into software development and other forms of application development to inform feature requirements and interaction plans based upon the users' goals. Every new software introduced must keep pace with the rapid technological advancements. The benefits associated with integration of these design principles include:

- Avoiding unnecessary product features

- Simplifying design documentation and customer-centric technical publications

- Improving the usability of the system and therefore its acceptance by customers

- Expediting design and development through detailed and properly conceived guidelines

- Incorporating business and marketing goals while protecting the user's freedom of choice

Principles of User Interface Design

The principles of user interface design are intended to improve the quality of user interface design. According to Larry Constantine and Lucy Lockwood in their usage-centered design, these principles are:

- *The structure principle*: Design should organize the user interface purposefully, in meaningful and useful ways based on clear, consistent models that are apparent and recognizable to users, putting related things together and separating unrelated things, differentiating dissimilar things and making similar things resemble one another. The structure principle is concerned with overall user interface architecture.

- *The simplicity principle*: The design should make simple, common tasks easy, communicating clearly and simply in the user's own language, and providing good shortcuts that are meaningfully related to longer procedures.

- *The visibility principle*: The design should make all needed options and materials for a given task visible without distracting the user with extraneous or redundant information. Good designs don't overwhelm users with alternatives or confuse with unneeded information.

- *The feedback principle*: The design should keep users informed of actions or interpretations, changes of state or condition, and errors or exceptions that are relevant and of interest to the user through clear, concise, and unambiguous language familiar to users.

- *The tolerance principle*: The design should be flexible and tolerant, reducing the cost of mistakes and misuse by allowing undoing and redoing, while also preventing errors wherever possible by tolerating varied inputs and sequences and by interpreting all reasonable actions.

- *The reuse principle*: The design should reuse internal and external components and behaviors, maintaining consistency with purpose rather than merely arbitrary consistency, thus reducing the need for users to rethink and remember.

According to Jef Raskin in his book *The Humane Interface*, there are two laws of user interface design, based on the fictional laws of robotics created by Isaac Asimov:

- *First Law*: A computer shall not harm your work or, through inactivity, allow your work to come to harm.

- *Second Law*: A computer shall not waste your time or require you to do more work than is strictly necessary.

Jef Raskin also mentions that "users should set the pace of an interaction," meaning that a user should not be kept waiting unnecessarily.

References

- Beyer, H. & Holtzblatt, K. (1998). Contextual Design: Defining Customer-Centered Systems. San Francisco: Morgan Kaufmann. ISBN 1-55860-411-1

- Marcus, Aaron (2015). Design, User Experience, and Usability: Design Discourse. p. 340. ISBN 3319208861. Retrieved 26 July 2015.

- "Graphic Designers". Occupational Outlook Handbook. Bureau of Labor Statistics, U.S. Department of Labor. December 17, 2015. Retrieved July 1, 2016.

- "Curricula for Human-Computer Interaction, Chapter 2. Definition and Overview of Human-Computer Interaction". ACM SIGCHI. Retrieved 2015-06-18.

- Treder, Marcin (2012-08-29). "Beyond Wireframing: The Real-Life UX Design Process". Smashing Magazine. Retrieved 2015-06-18.

- "What's the Difference Between a User Experience (UX) Designer and a User Interface (UI) Designer? - Zanthro". Retrieved 2015-09-24.

- Norman, D. A. (2002). "Emotion & Design: Attractive things work better". Interactions Magazine, ix (4). pp. 36–42. Retrieved 20 April 2014.

- Ann Blandford. "Semi-structured qualitative studies". The Encyclopedia of Human-Computer Interaction, 2nd Ed. Interaction Design Foundation. Retrieved 20 April 2014.

- Karen Holtzblatt and Hugh R. Beyer. "Contextual design". The Encyclopedia of Human-Computer Interaction, 2nd Ed. Interaction Design Foundation. Retrieved 20 April 2014.

- Wolf, Lauren (23 May 2012). "6 Tips for Designing an Optimal User Interface for Your Digital Event". INXPO. Retrieved 22 May 2013.

- "SUPPLE: Automatically Generating Personalized User Interfaces". Intelligent Interactive Systems Group (website). Harvard University. 2007-05-07. Retrieved 2010-07-07.

Allied fields of Human-computer Interaction

The branch of human computer interaction that focuses on the response of computer interface to human touch is known as hands-on computing. This chapter is a compilation of the allied fields related to human-computer interaction. Some of the fields explained are hands-on computing, human-centered computing, interactive computing, mobile interaction and mobile computing.

Hands-on Computing

Hands-On Computing is a branch of Human-Computer Interaction research, which focuses on computer interfaces that respond to human touch or expression, allowing the machine and the user to interact physically. Hands-on computing can make complicated computer tasks more natural to users by attempting to respond to motions and interactions that are natural to human behavior. Thus hands-on computing is a component of user-centered design, focusing on how users physically respond to virtual environments.

Implementations

- Keyboards
- Stylus Pens and Tablets
- Touchscreens
- Human Signaling

Keyboards

Keyboards and typewriters are some of the earliest hands-on computing devices. These devices are effective because users receive kinesthetic feedback, tactile feedback, auditory feedback, and visual feedback. The QWERTY layout of the keyboard is one of the first designs, dating to 1878 New designs such as the split keyboard increase the comfortability of typing for users. Keyboards input directions to the computer via keys; however, keyboards do not allow the user direct interaction with the computer through touch or expression.

Stylus Pens and Tablets

Tablets are touch-sensitive surfaces that detect the pressure applied by a stylus pen. This works via changes in magnetic fields or by bringing together two resistive sheets, for magnetic tablets and resistive tablets respectively. Tablets allow users to interact with computers by touching through a stylus pen, yet they do not respond directly to a user's touch.

Touchscreens

Touchscreen allow users to directly interact with computers by touching the screen with his or her finger. It is natural for humans to point to objects in order to show a preference or a selection. Touchscreens allow users to take this natural action and use it to interact with computers. Problems arise due to inaccuracy: people attempt to make a selection, but due to incorrect calibration, the computer does not accurately process the touch.

Human Signaling

New developments in Hands-On Computing have led to the creation of interfaces that can respond to gestures and facial signaling. Often haptic devices like a glove have to be worn to translate the gesture into a recognizable command. The natural actions of pointing, grabbing, and tapping are common ways to interact with the computer interface. The latest studies include using the eye signals to indicate selection or control the cursor. Blinking and the gaze of the eye are used to communicate selections. Computers can also respond to speech inputs. Developments in this technology have made it possible for users to dictate phrases to the computer instead of type them to display text on an interface. Utilizing human signal inputs allows more people to interact with computers and do so in a way that is humanly natural.

Current Problems

There are still many problems with hands-on computing interfaces that are currently being eradicated through continuing research and development. The problem of creating a simple, user-friendly interface and developing it in an inexpensive and mass producible way is the main complication in hands-on computing technologies. Because some interactions between human and machine are ambiguous, the mechanical response is not always the desired result for the user. Different hand gestures and facial expressions can lead the computer to interpret one command, while the user wished to convey another one entirely. Solving this problem is currently one of the main focuses in research and development.

Researchers are also working to find the best way to design hands-on computing devices, so that the consumer can use the product easily. Focusing on user-centered design while creating hands-on computing products helps developers make the best and easiest to use product.

Research and Development

This new field has a lot of room for contributions in research and product development. Hands-on computing technologies require scientists and engineers to approach a different problem solving strategy which considers the devices for interaction rather than just input; the interaction devices in terms of tool use; how interaction will mediate user-performance; and the context in which the devices will be used.

In order for a machine to be successfully used, people need to be able to transfer some of their current skill set to operate the machine. This can be done directly by comparing the interface to a known and familiar topic to help people understand, or by aiding the user to draw new inferences through feedback. Users have to be able to understand how to use and manipulate the interface in order to use it to its full capability. By applying their current skills, users can operate the machine without learning new concepts and approaches

Human-centered Computing

Human-centered computing (HCC) studies the design, development, and deployment of mixed-initiative human-computer systems. It is emerged from the convergence of multiple disciplines that are concerned both with understanding human beings and with the design of computational artifacts. Human-centered computing is closely related to human-computer interaction and information science. Human-centered computing is usually concerned with systems and practices of technology use while human-computer interaction is more focused on ergonomics and the usability of computing artifacts and information science is focused on practices surrounding the collection, manipulation, and use of information.

Human-centered computing researchers and practitioners usually come from one or more of disciplines such as computer science, human factors, sociology, psychology, cognitive science, anthropology, communication studies, graphic design and industrial design. Some researchers focus on understanding humans, both as individuals and in social groups, by focusing on the ways that human beings adopt and organize their lives around computational technologies. Others focus on designing and developing new computational artifacts.

Overview

Scope

HCC aims at bridging the existing gaps between the various disciplines involved with the design and implementation of computing systems that support human's activities. Meanwhile, it is a set of methodologies that apply to any field that uses computers in applications in which people directly interact with devices or systems that use computer technologies.

HCC facilitates the design of effective computer systems that take into account personal, social, and cultural aspects and addresses issues such as information design, human information interaction, human-computer interaction, human-human interaction, and the relationships between computing technology and art, social, and cultural issues.

HCC Topics

The National Science Foundation (NSF) defines the trends of HCC research as "a three dimensional space comprising human, computer, and environment." According to the NSF, the human dimension ranges from research that supports individual needs, through teams as goal-oriented groups, to society as an unstructured collection of connected people. The computer dimension ranges from fixed computing devices, through mobile devices, to computational systems of visual/audio devices that are embedded in the surrounding physical environment. The environment dimension ranges from discrete physical computational devices, through mixed reality systems, to immersive virtual environments. Some examples of topics in the field are listed below.

List of Topics in HCC Field

- Problem-solving in distributed environments, ranging across Internet-based information systems, grids, sensor-based information networks, and mobile and wearable information appliances.

- Multimedia and multi-modal interfaces in which combinations of speech, text, graphics, gesture, movement, touch, sound, etc. are used by people and machines to communicate with one another.

- Intelligent interfaces and user modeling, information visualization, and adaptation of content to accommodate different display capabilities, modalities, bandwidth and latency.

- Multi-agent systems that control and coordinate actions and solve complex problems in distributed environments in a wide variety of domains, such as disaster response teams, e-commerce, education, and successful aging.

- Models for effective computer-mediated human-human interaction under a variety of constraints, (e.g., video conferencing, collaboration across high vs. low bandwidth networks, etc.).

- Definition of semantic structures for multimedia information to support cross-modal input and output.

- Specific solutions to address the special needs of particular communities.

- Collaborative systems that enable knowledge-intensive and dynamic interactions for innovation and knowledge generation across organizational boundaries, national borders, and professional fields.

- Novel methods to support and enhance social interaction, including innovative ideas like social orthotics, affective computing, and experience capture.

- Studies of how social organizations, such as government agencies or corporations, respond to and shape the introduction of new information technologies, especially with the goal of improving scientific understanding and technical design.

- Knowledge-driven human-computer interaction that uses ontologies to addresss the semantic ambiguities between human and computer's understandings towards mutual behaviors

- Human-centered semantic relatedness measure that employs human power to measure the semantic relatedness between two concepts

Human-centered Systems

Human-centered systems (HCS) are systems designed for human-centered computing. HCS focuses on the design of interactive systems as they relate to human activities. According to Kling et al., the Committee on Computing, Information, and Communication of the National Science and Technology Council, identified human-centered systems, or HCS, as one of five components for a High Performance Computing Program. Human-centered systems can be referred to in terms of human-centered automation. According to Kling et al., HCS refers to "systems that are:

1. based on the analysis of the human tasks the system is aiding

2. monitored for performance in terms of human benefits

3. built to take account of human skills and

4. adaptable easily to changing human needs."

In addition, Kling et al. defines four dimensions of human-centeredness that should be taken into account when classifying a system: systems that are human centered must analyze the complexity of the targeted social organization, and the varied social units that structure work and information; human centeredness is not an attribute of systems, but a process in which the stakeholder group of a particular system assists in evaluating the benefit of the system; the basic architecture of the system should reflect a realistic relationship between humans and machines; the purpose and audience the system is designed for should be an explicit part of the design, evaluation, and use of the system.

Human-centered Activities in Multimedia

The human-centered activities in multimedia, or HCM, can be considered as follows according to: media production, annotation, organization, archival, retrieval, sharing, analysis, and communication, which can be clustered into three areas: production, analysis, and interaction.

Wikimania human-centered design visualization, created by *Myriapoda*.

Multimedia Production

Multimedia production is the human task of creating media. For instance, photographing, recording audio, remixing, etc. It is important that all aspects of media production concerned should directly involve humans in HCM. There are two main characteristics of multimedia production. The first is culture and social factors. HCM production systems should consider cultural differences and be designed according to the culture in which they will be deployed. The second is to consider human abilities. Participants involved in HCM production should be able to complete the activities during the production process.

Multimedia Analysis

Multimedia analysis can be considered as a type of HCM applications which is the automatic analysis of human activities and social behavior in general. There is a broad area of potential relevant uses from facilitating and enhancing human communications, to allowing for improved information access and retrieval in the professional, entertainment, and personal domains.

Multimedia Interaction

Multimedia interaction can be considered as the interaction activity area of HCM. It is paramount to understand both how humans interact with each other and why, so that we can build systems to facilitate such communication and so that people can interact with computers in natural ways. To achieve natural interaction, cultural differences and social context are primary factors to consider, due to the potential different cultural backgrounds. For instance, a couple of examples include: face-to-face communications where the interaction is physically located and real-time; live-computer mediated communications where the interaction is physically remote but remains real-time; and non-real time computer-mediated communications such as instant SMS, email, etc.

Career

Academic Programs

As human-centered computing has become increasingly popular, many universities have create special programs for HCC research and study for both graduate and undergraduate students. Here is a list of major universities that provide HCC programs.

- University of Florida – https://www.cise.ufl.edu/academics/grad/phdhcc

- Georgia Institute of Technology – http://www.cc.gatech.edu/human-centered-computing-phd-program

- Clemson University – http://www.clemson.edu/ces/computing/divisions/hcc.html

- Drexel University – http://drexel.edu/cci/disciplines/human-centered-computing/

- Indiana University – Purdue University Indianapolis – http://soic.iupui.edu/hcc/about/

- University of Colorado – http://www.colorado.edu/cs/researchtopics/human-centered-computing

- University of Pittsburgh – http://www.ischool.pitt.edu/ist/degrees/specializations/hcc.php

- University of Maryland – http://informationsystems.umbc.edu/home/graduate-programs/doctor-of-philosophy-programs/doctor-of-philosophy-in-human-centered-computing-hcc/

- Hang Seng Management College – http://www.hsmc.edu.hk/index.php/academic-programmes/undergraduate/ahcc

- Reutlingen University – http://www.inf.reutlingen-university.de/studienangebot/studienangebot-master/huc-master/huc-aufbau.html

User Interface Designer

A user interface designer is an individual who usually with a relevant degree or high level of knowledge, not only on technology, cognitive science, human–computer interaction, learning sciences, but also on psychology and sociology. A user interface designer develops and applies user-centered design methodologies and agile development processes that includes consideration for overall usability of interactive software applications, emphasizing interaction design and front-end development.

Information Architect (IA)

Information architects mainly work to understand user and business needs in order to organize information to best satisfy these needs. Specifically, information architects often act as a key bridge between technical and creative development in a project team. Currently, almost all IAs work on web sites so most of them are hired by companies with a large enough web presence to support a full-time information architect as well as service firms and agencies that create web sites for clients.

Projects

NASA/Ames Computational Sciences Division

NASA Mars Project

The Human-Centered Computing (HCC) group at NASA/Ames Computational Sciences Division is conducting research at Haughton as members of the Haughton-Mars Project (HMP) to determine, via an analog study, how we will live and work on Mars.

1. HMP/Carnegie Mellon University (CMU) Field Robotics Experiments—HCC is collaborating with researchers on the HMP/CMU field robotics research program at Haughton to specify opportunities for robots assisting scientists. Researchers in this project has carried out a parallel investigation that documents work during traverses. A simulation module has been built, using a tool that represents people, their tools, and their work environment, that will serve as a partial controller for a robot that assist scientists in the field work in mars. When it comes to take human, computing and environment all into consideration, theory and techniques in HCC filed will be the guideline.

2. Ethnography of Human Exploration of Space—HCC lab is carrying out an ethnographic study of scientific field work, covering all aspects of a scientist's life in the field. This study involves observing as participants at Haughton and writing about HCC lab`s experiences. HCC lab then look for patterns in how people organize their time, space, and objects and how they relate to each other to accomplish their goals. In this study, HCC lab is focusing on learning and conceptual change.

Interactive Computing

In computer science, interactive computing refers to software which accepts input from humans as it runs. Interactive software includes most popular programs, such as word processors or spreadsheet applications. By comparison, noninteractive programs operate without human contact; examples of these include compilers and batch processing applications.

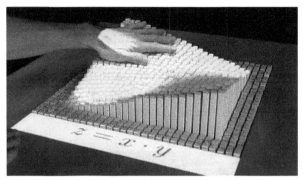

Physically interactive computing - MIT

Interactive computing focuses on real-time interaction ("dialog") between computers and people, and the technologies that enable this.

If the response of the computer system is complex enough, it is said that the system is conducting social interaction; some systems try to achieve this through the implementation of social interfaces.

History of Interactive Computing Systems

Ivan Sutherland is considered the Father of Interactive Computing for his work on *Sketchpad*, the interactive display graphics program he developed in 1963. He later worked at the ARPA Information Processing Techniques Office under the direction of J.C.R. Licklider. There he facilitated ARPA's research grant to Douglas Engelbart for developing the NLS system at SRI based on his visionary manifesto published in a 1962 Report, in which Engelbart envisioned interactive computing as a vehicle for human interaction with computers, with each other, and with their knowledge, all in a vast virtual information space. In a 1965 Report he published his early experiments with pointing devices, including the mouse, for composing and editing on interactive display workstations. Engelbart's work on interactive computing at SRI migrated directly to Xerox PARC, from there to Apple, and out into the mainstream. Thus, the tree of evolution for interactive computing generally traces back to Engelbart's lab at SRI.

In December 2008, on the 40th anniversary of his 1968 demo, SRI sponsored the public commemorative event Engelbart and the Dawn of Interactive Computing in his honor.

Some common computing systems previously were:

- Batch interfaces

- Conversational interfaces

- Graphical interfaces

Later Examples

inFORM is a Dynamic Shape Display that can render 3D content physically, so users can interact with digital information in a tangible way. inFORM can also interact with the physical world around it, for example moving objects on the table's surface. Remote participants in a video conference can be displayed physically, allowing for a strong sense of presence and the ability to interact physically at a distance. HP Sprout released at the end of the 2014 by HP Inc is a projector-camera (pro-cam) system that enables users to interact with physical and digital content while working.

Tools

IPython provides a rich architecture for interactive computing IPython with:

- A powerful interactive shell.

- A kernel for Jupyter.

- Support for interactive data visualization and use of GUI toolkits.

- Flexible, embeddable interpreters to load into your own projects.

- Easy to use, high performance tools for parallel computing.

Current Research on Interactive Computing

The need of constant user interaction in interactive computing systems makes it different in many ways from batch processing systems. Thus different aspects of computing systems are significantly different for interactive computing systems and they have been focused on different research. The design of a different programming model has been discussed. Another article describes the importance of security and reliability in interactive computing.

The nature of interactive computing as well as its impact on humans, are studied extensively in the field of Human-computer interaction.

Georgia Institute of Technology has a school named School of Interactive Computing which has formed in 2007. It is still active and offering masters and doctoral degree by collaborations of more than 40 faculties.

The Tangible Media Group of MIT, led by Professor Hiroshi Ishii, explores the Tangible Bits & Radical Atoms visions to seamlessly couple the dual world of bits and atoms by giving dynamic physical form to digital information and computation.

Mobile Interaction

Mobile Phone Device

Mobile interaction is the study of interaction between mobile users and computers. Mobile interaction is an aspect of human–computer interaction that emerged when computers became small enough to enable mobile usage around 1990's.

Mobile devices are a pervasive part of our everyday lives. People use mobile phones, PDAs, and portable media players almost everywhere. These devices are the first truly pervasive interaction devices that are currently used for a huge variety of services and applications. Mobile devices affect the way we interact, share, and communicate with others. They are growing in diversity and complexity, featuring new interaction paradigms, modalities, shapes, and purposes (e.g., e-readers, portable media players, handheld game consoles). The strong differentiating factors that characterize mobile devices from traditional personal computing (e.g., desktop computers), are their ubiquitous use, usual small size, and mixed interaction modalities.

The history of mobile interaction includes different design trends. The main six design trends are Portability, Miniaturization, Connectivity, Convergence, Divergence, and Apps. The main reason behind those trends is to understand the requirements and needs of mobile users which is the main goal for mobile interaction. Mobile interaction is a multidisciplinary area with various academic subjects making contributions to it. The main disciplines involved in mobile interaction are Psychology, Computer Science, Sociology, Design, and Information Systems. The processes in mobile interaction design includes three main activities: understanding users, developing prototype designs, and evaluation.

History

The history of mobile interaction can be divided into a number of eras, or waves, each characterized by a particular technological focus, interaction design trends, and by leading to fundamental changes in the design and use of mobile devices. Although not strictly sequential, they provide a good overview of the legacy on which current mobile computing research and design is built.

1.   Portability

One of the first work in the mobile interaction discipline was the concept of the Dynabook by Alan Kay in 1968. However, at that time the necessary hardware to build such system was not available. When the first laptops were built in the early 1980s they were seen as transportable desktop computers.

2.   Miniaturization

By the early 1990s, many types of handheld devices were introduced such as labelled palmtop computers, digital organizers, or personal digital assistants (PDAs).

3.   Connectivity

By 1973, Martin Cooper worked at Motorola developed a handheld mobile phone concept, which later on by 1983, led to the introduction of the first commercial mobile phone called the DynaTAC 8000X.

Apple iPhone

4.   Convergence

During this era, different types of specialized mobile devices started to converge into new types of hybrid devices with primarily different form factors and interaction designs. On 1992, the first device of such technique, the "smartphones" was introduced. The first smart phone was the IBM Simon and it was used for making phone calls, calendars, addresses, notes, e-mail, fax and games.

5.   Divergence

During the 2000s, a trend toward a single function many devices started to spread. the basic idea behind divergence is that specialized tools facilitate optimization of functionality over time and enhancement of use. The most famous device of this era was the Apple iPod on 2001.

6. Apps

During 2007, Apple Inc. introduced the first truly "smart" cellular phone; the iPhone. It was a converged mobile device with different features functionality. The most important thing is that it represents a significant rethinking of the design of mobile interactions and a series of notable interaction design choices. In less than a decade Apple Inc. would sell over one-billion iPhones

Goals

With the evolution of both software and hardware on the mobile devices, the users are becoming more demanding of the user interface that provide both functionality and pleasant user experience. The goal of mobile interaction researches is to understand the requirements and needs of mobile users. Compared with stationary devices mobile devices have specific, often restricted, input and output requirements. A goal that is often named is to overcome the limitations of mobile devices. However, exploiting the special opportunities of mobile usage can also be seen as a central goal.

Disciplines Involved in Mobile Interaction

Mobile interaction is a multidisciplinary area with various academic subjects making contributions. This is a reflection of the complicated nature of an individual's interaction with a computer system. This includes factors such as an understanding of the user and the task the user wants to perform with the system, understanding of the design tools, software packages that are needed to achieve this and an understanding of software engineering tools. The following are the main disciplines involved in mobile interaction:

1. Psychology

Many of the research methods and system evaluation techniques currently used in mobile Human Computer Interaction research are borrowed from Psychology. As well as attitude measures, performance measures that are used in mobile Human Computer Interaction research studies come from the area of experimental psychology. Understanding users and their needs is a key aspect in the design of mobile systems, devices, and applications so that they will be easy and enjoyable to use. Individual user characteristics such as age, or personality physical disabilities such as blindness, all have an affect on users' performance when they are using mobile applications and systems, and these individual differences can also affect people's attitude towards the mobile service or device that they interact with.

2. Computer Science

Computer Science (along with Software Engineering) is responsible for providing software tools to develop the interfaces that users need to interact with system. These include the software development tools.

3. Sociology

Sociologists working in this area are responsible for looking at socio-technical aspects of Human Computer Interaction. They bring methods and techniques from the social sciences (e.g., observational studies, ethnography) that can be used in the design and evaluation of mobile devices and applications.

4. Design

People working in this area are concerned with looking at the design layout of the interface (e.g., colors, positioning of text or graphics on a screen of a PDA). This is a crucial area of mobile Human Computer Interaction research due to the limited screen space available for most mobile devices. Therefore, it is crucial that services and applications reflect this limitation by reducing information complexity to fit the parameters of the mobile device, without losing any substantial content.

5. Information Systems

People who work in this area are interested in investigating how people interact with information and technologies in an organisational, managerial, and business context. In an organisational context, information system professionals and researchers are interested in looking at ways in which mobile technologies and mobile applications can be used to make an organisation more effective in conducting its business on a day-to-day business.

Mobile Interaction Design

Mobile interaction design is part of the interaction design which heavily focused on satisfying the needs and desires of the majority of people who will use the product. The processes in mobile interaction design are in the following main types of activity:

1. Understanding users - having a sense of people's capabilities and limitations; gaining a rich picture of what makes up the detail of their lives, the things they do and use.

2. Developing prototype designs - representing a proposed interaction design in such a way that it can be demonstrated, altered, and discussed.

3. Evaluation - each prototype is a stepping stone to the next, better, refined design. Evaluation techniques identify the strengths and weaknesses of a design

but can also lead the team to propose a completely different approach, discarding the current line of design thinking for a radical approach.

Mobile Computing

The Galaxy Nexus, capable of web browsing, e-mail access, video playback, document editing, file transfer, image editing, among many other tasks common on smartphones. A smartphone is a tool of mobile computing.

Telxon PTC-710 is a 16-bit mobile computer PTC-710 with MP 830-42 microprinter 42-column version.

Mobile computing is human–computer interaction by which a computer is expected to be transported during normal usage, which allows for transmission of data, voice and video. Mobile computing involves mobile communication, mobile hardware, and mobile software. Communication issues include ad hoc networks and infrastructure networks as well as communication properties, protocols, data formats and concrete technologies. Hardware includes mobile devices or device components. Mobile software deals with the characteristics and requirements of mobile applications.

Principles of Mobile Computing

Portability

Facilitates movement of device(s) within the mobile computing environments.

Connectivity

Ability to continuously stay connected with minimal amount of lag/downtime, without being affected by movements of the device.

Social Interactivity

Maintaining the connectivity to collaborate with other users, at least within the same environment.

Individuality

Adapting the technology to suit individual needs.

Devices

Some of the most common forms of mobile computing devices are as follows.

- portable computers, compacted lightweight units including a full character set keyboard and primarily intended as hosts for software that may be parameterized, as laptops, notebooks, notepads, etc.

- *mobile phones* including a restricted key set primarily intended but not restricted to for vocal communications, as smartphones, cell phones, feature phones, etc.

- Smart cards that can run multiple applications but typically payment, travel and secure area access

- *wearable computers*, mostly limited to functional keys and primarily intended as incorporation of software agents, as watches, wristbands, necklaces, keyless implants, etc.

The existence of these classes is expected to be long lasting, and complementary in personal usage, none replacing one the other in all features of convenience.

Other types of mobile computers have been introduced since the 1990s including the:

- Portable computer (discontinued)

- Personal digital assistant/Enterprise digital assistant (discontinued)

- Ultra-Mobile PC (discontinued)

- Laptop

- Smartphone

- Robots

- Tablet computer

- Wearable computer

- Carputer

- Application-specific computer

Limitations

- Range & Bandwidth: Mobile Internet access is generally slower than direct cable connections, using technologies such as GPRS and EDGE, and more recently HSDPA, HSUPA, 3G and 4G networks and also the upcoming 5G network. These networks are usually available within range of commercial cell phone towers. High speed network wireless LANs are inexpensive but have very limited range.

- Security standards: When working mobile, one is dependent on public networks, requiring careful use of VPN. Security is a major concern while concerning the mobile computing standards on the fleet. One can easily attack the VPN through a huge number of networks interconnected through the line.

- Power consumption: When a power outlet or portable generator is not available, mobile computers must rely entirely on battery power. Combined with the compact size of many mobile devices, this often means unusually expensive batteries must be used to obtain the necessary battery life.

- Transmission interferences: Weather, terrain, and the range from the nearest signal point can all interfere with signal reception. Reception in tunnels, some buildings, and rural areas is often poor.

- Potential health hazards: People who use mobile devices while driving are often distracted from driving and are thus assumed more likely to be involved in traffic accidents. (While this may seem obvious, there is considerable discussion about whether banning mobile device use while driving reduces accidents or not.) Cell phones may interfere with sensitive medical devices. Questions concerning mobile phone radiatiom and health have been raised.

- Human interface with device: Screens and keyboards tend to be small, which may make them hard to use. Alternate input methods such as speech or handwriting recognition require training.

In-vehicle Computing and Fleet Computing

Many commercial and government field forces deploy a rugged portable computer with their fleet of vehicles. This requires the units to be anchored to the vehicle for driver safety, device security, and ergonomics. Rugged computers are rated for severe vibration associated with large service vehicles and off-road driving and the harsh environmental conditions of constant professional use such as in emergency medical services, fire, and public safety.

The Compaq Portable - Circa 1982 pre-laptop

Other elements affecting function in vehicle:

- Operating temperature: A vehicle cabin can often experience temperature swings from -20F to +140F. Computers typically must be able to withstand these temperatures while operating. Typical fan-based cooling has stated limits of 95F-100F of ambient temperature, and temperatures below freezing require localized heaters to bring components up to operating temperature (based on independent studies by the SRI Group and by Panasonic R&D).

- Vibration can decrease the life expectancy of computer components, notably rotational storage such as HDDs.

- Visibility of standard screens becomes an issue in bright sunlight.

- Touchscreen users easily interact with the units in the field without removing gloves.

- High-temperature battery settings: Lithium ion batteries are sensitive to high temperature conditions for charging. A computer designed for the mobile environment should be designed with a high-temperature charging function that limits the charge to 85% or less of capacity.

- External antenna connections go through the typical metal cabins of vehicles which would block wireless reception, and take advantage of much more capable external communication and navigation equipment.

Security Issues Involved in Mobile

Mobile security or mobile phone security has become increasingly important in mobile computing. It is of particular concern as it relates to the security of personal information now stored on the smartphone.

More and more users and businesses use smartphones as communication tools but also as a means of planning and organizing their work and private life. Within companies, these technologies are causing profound changes in the organization of information systems and therefore they have become the source of new risks. Indeed, smartphones collect and compile an increasing amount of sensitive information to which access must be controlled to protect the privacy of the user and the intellectual property of the company.

All smartphones, as computers, are preferred targets of attacks. These attacks exploit weaknesses related to smartphones that can come from means of communication like SMS, MMS, wifi networks, and GSM. There are also attacks that exploit software vulnerabilities from both the web browser and operating system. Finally, there are forms of malicious software that rely on the weak knowledge of average users.

Different security counter-measures are being developed and applied to smartphones, from security in different layers of software to the dissemination of information to end users. There are good practices to be observed at all levels, from design to use, through the development of operating systems, software layers, and downloadable apps.

Portable Computing Devices

Several categories of portable computing devices can run on batteries but are not usually classified as laptops: portable computers, PDAs, ultra mobile PCs (UMPCs), tablets and smartphones.

A Palm TX PDA

- A portable computer (discontinued) is a general-purpose computer that can be easily moved from place to place, but cannot be used while in transit, usually because it requires some "setting-up" and an AC power source. The most famous example is the Osborne 1. Portable computers are also called a "transportable" or a "luggable" PC.

- A personal digital assistant (PDA) (discontinued) is a small, usually pocket-sized, computer with limited functionality. It is intended to supplement and to synchronize with a desktop computer, giving access to contacts, address book, notes, e-mail and other features.

- An ultra mobile PC (discontinued) is a full-featured, PDA-sized computer running a general-purpose operating system.

- A tablet computer that lacks a keyboard (also known as a non-convertible tablet) is shaped like a slate or a paper notebook. Instead a physical keyboard it has a touchscreen with some combination of virtual keyboard, stylus and/or handwriting recognition software. Tablets may not be best suited for applications requiring a physical keyboard for typing, but are otherwise capable of carrying out most of the tasks of an ordinary laptop.

- A smartphone has a wide range of features and install-able applications.

- A carputer is installed in an automobile. It operates as a wireless computer, sound system, GPS, and DVD player. It also contains word processing software and is bluetooth compatible.

- A |Pentop (discontinued) is a computing device the size and shape of a pen. It functions as a writing utensil, MP3 player, language translator, digital storage device, and calculator.

- An application-specific computer is one that is tailored to a particular application. For example, Ferranti introduced a handheld application-specific mobile computer (the MRT-100) in the form of a clipboard for conducting opinion polls.

Boundaries that separate these categories are blurry at times. For example, the OQO UMPC is also a PDA-sized tablet PC; the Apple eMate had the clamshell form factor of a laptop, but ran PDA software. The HP Omnibook line of laptops included some devices small more enough to be called ultra mobile PCs. The hardware of the Nokia 770 internet tablet is essentially the same as that of a PDA such as the Zaurus 6000; the only reason it's not called a PDA is that it does not have PIM software. On the other hand, both the 770 and the Zaurus can run some desktop Linux software, usually with modifications.

Mobile Data Communication

Wireless data connections used in mobile computing take three general forms so. Cellular data service uses technologies such as GSM, CDMA or GPRS, 3G networks such as W-CDMA, EDGE or CDMA2000. and more recently 4G networks such as LTE, LTE-Advanced. These networks are usually available within range of commercial cell towers. Wi-Fi connections offer higher performance, may be either on a private business network or accessed through public hotspots, and have a typical range of 100 feet indoors and up to 1000 feet outdoors. Satellite Internet access covers areas where cellular and Wi-Fi are not available and may be set up anywhere the user has a line of sight to the satellite's location, which for satellites in geostationary orbit means having an unobstructed view of the southern sky. Some enterprise deployments combine networks from multiple cellular networks or use a mix of cellular, Wi-Fi and satellite. When using a mix of networks, a mobile virtual private network (mobile VPN) not only handles the security concerns, but also performs the multiple network logins automatically and keeps the application connections alive to prevent crashes or data loss during network transitions or coverage loss.

References

- Zimmermann, Andreas; Henze, Niels; Righetti, Xavier; Rukzio, Enrico (2009). "Mobile Interaction with the Real World". MobileHCI'09, Article No. 106. doi:10.1145/1613858.1613980. ISBN 978-1-60558-281-8.

- Kjeldskov, Jesper (2014). Mobile Interactions in Context: A Designerly Way Toward Digital Ecology. Morgan & Claypool. ISBN 9781627052269.

- Love, Steve (2005). Understanding Mobile Human-Computer Interaction. Butterworth-Heinemann. ISBN 9780750663526.

- Cooper, Alan; Reimann, Robert; Cronin, Dave (2007). About Face 3: The Essentials of Interaction Design. Indianapolis, Indiana: Wiley. p. 610. ISBN 978-0-470-08411-3.

- "Hands-on with the HP Sprout, an imaging powerhouse built into a touch-friendly PC". PCWorld. Retrieved 2016-04-25.

- Communications, Texas. "Human-Centered Systems | Research Areas | Research | Computer Science & Engineering | College of Engineering". engineering.tamu.edu. Retrieved 2015-04-17.

- "Human Centered Systems in the Perspective of Organizational and Social Informatics" (PDF). philfeldman.com. Retrieved 2015-04-17.

Permissions

Index